A DEEPER SENSE OF PLACE

A Deeper Sense of Place

STORIES AND JOURNEYS OF
INDIGENOUS-ACADEMIC COLLABORATION

Jay T. Johnson and Soren C. Larsen

FIRST PEOPLES
New Directions in Indigenous Studies

Oregon State University Press   Corvallis

Library of Congress Cataloging-in-Publication Data

A deeper sense of place : stories and journeys of indigenous-academic
   collaboration / Jay T. Johnson and Soren C. Larsen, editors.
      pages cm
   Includes bibliographical references and index.
   ISBN 978-0-87071-722-2 (alk. paper) -- ISBN 978-0-87071-723-9 (e-book)
   1. Geographical perception. 2. Place attachment. 3. Environmental psychology.
   4. Indigenous peoples--Folklore. 5. Ethnopsychology. 6. Communication in
   folklore. 7. Place-based education. I. Johnson, Jay T.
   G71.5.D44 2013
   304.2'3--dc23
                                                                          2013013093

Oregon State University Press
121 The Valley Library
Corvallis OR 97331-4501
541-737-3166 • fax 541-737-3170
www.osupress.oregonstate.edu

Contents

TELLING STORIES IN THE CLASSROOM

Introduction
A Deeper Sense of Place
JAY T. JOHNSON AND SOREN C. LARSEN

The relationship between academic research and Indigenous peoples is steeped in a long and lingering colonial history. Beginning with the so-called Age of Discovery in the early fifteenth century, a large part of European colonial activity involved intellectual expeditions into the "field"—those regions and communities that lay beyond the figurative and literal comprehension of the Western mind. Such forays generated knowledge that described Native people largely from within European visions of economic and cultural development, effectively objectifying non-Western communities within racial and economic hierarchies of human evolution (cf. Blaut 1993). Once marshaled into the discourses of colonial science, fieldwork's descriptions, interpretations, texts, and maps were readily employed to legitimize the expropriation of Native lands and the relocation, containment, or outright extermination of those communities. Amid the violence of colonial resettlement, much less noticeable is the fact that most fieldwork simply failed to produce accounts that understood or described Indigenous worldviews on their own social and epistemological terms. As the social-science disciplines expanded during the early twentieth century, fieldwork's practitioners grew critical of evolutionism and became more self-reflexive methodologically, but still the overall effort remained one of theorizing the Native "Other" within Western academic discourse (e.g., ethnology, structuralism, cultural ecology).

Today, however, research between academics and Indigenous peoples is pointing toward more ethical possibilities, which we describe here as a "deeper sense of place."[1] Contemporary research collaborations are progressively challenging the colonial division between the field researcher—that is, the "objective" and mostly disinterested Western academic intellectual—and the Indigenous Other (person, community, or land) as a stand-alone object of study. Instead, research collaboration today begins more often with an open negotiation between Indigenous people and academic practitioners over the inquiry's purpose, design, and dissemination of results (see Smith 1999). Projects often use hybridized research methods that blend Indigenous and Western praxis, as is the case, for instance, in Participatory Action Research (PAR) (Kindon, Pain, and Kesby 2009), research storytelling (Christensen 2012), and new forms of Environmental and Research Management (ERM) (Pahl-Wostl 2007).

And today some academics are themselves Indigenous people, which creates rich possibilities as well as complications for field research. As they work across the liminal space between outsider and insider, Indigenous academics are frequently caught in between their academic work and their collaborations with Indigenous communities (see Fermantez in this volume). Negotiating this "tricky ground" can lead to greater understanding, but the challenges cannot be underestimated. Working toward community-determined outcomes that further self-determination can set Indigenous academics against the institutions paying their salaries. Working solely toward objective research and top-tier publications can push Indigenous academics further away from their communities.

As for academics working in the humanities and social sciences, methodological discussion has increasingly focused on the importance of relationships, reciprocity, and trust in research practice while accepting that the indirect, circuitous, and sometimes downright chaotic nature of field research can *still* yield valuable insight and understanding (Bishop 1996; Goulet and Miller 2007; Cerwonka and Malkki 2007; Johnson 2008). Partly as a result of its engagement with Indigenous and non-Western philosophies, academic discourse is also in the process of acknowledging the critical and active role that *place* has in research and intellectual collaboration. Place speaks to the holistic totality of human and nonhuman relations situated in a particular locale or region. Practitioners are recognizing that if field research is to be equitable, beneficial, and empowering, it must engage the complex realities and actors of place in a truly collaborative fashion. In this way, Indigenous communities and academic field practitioners are collectively working toward deeper senses of place at the dawn of the twenty-first century. The contributions to this volume are testament to this development.

Prospects for Self-Determination in the Relationships of Research

The trend toward more meaningful research collaboration was inspired in large part by two parallel developments over roughly the past half century (1960–2010): the emergence of Indigenous research paradigms from within and beyond the academy, and the elaboration of critical social theory in Western departments and centers for humanities and social sciences (see Denzin, Lincoln, and Smith 2008). This wave of paradigm change has, to date, touched every discipline to a degree, but it should be noted that some within anthropology took up this challenge several decades before geography and began to grapple with the concept of decolonizing their discipline as well as increasing collaboration with Indigenous peoples in their research (see Stavenhagen 1971; Nash 1975; Stull and Schensul 1987). Although anthropology may have initiated this push, we now see within every discipline in the social sciences a similar move toward collaboration with Indigenous communities.

As summarized by the Māori scholar Linda Tuhiwai Smith (1999), Indigenous approaches to research seek to decolonize intellectual practice not only by expanding what counts as legitimate knowledge and method, but also by enhancing the roles of relationship building and reciprocity in the process of using inquiry to enhance prospects for self-determination. As Smith (1999, 128) states, Indigenous research processes "are expected to be respectful to enable people, to heal and to educate. They are expected to lead one small step further towards self-determination." Importantly, what counts as "beneficial" research need not necessarily yield quantifiable outcomes or palpable "deliverables," but rather is envisioned as a long-term activity that over time empowers the historically marginalized. It also challenges non-Native practitioners to step outside of their intellectual and methodological conventions into a world in which knowledge-making is an ethical act of facilitating self-determination (Bishop 2005).

At roughly the same time, the so-called postmodern turn in literary criticism and later the social sciences fostered theories and methods that privileged marginalized viewpoints and subjects while documenting how colonial practice had distorted, suppressed, and even eradicated these worldviews. Such work criticized conventional academic practice as part of a broader colonial-capitalist enterprise underwritten by social inequality, oppression, and alienation from the lived worlds of everyday experience. The proliferation of "posts" in academic discourse (e.g., poststructuralism, postcolonialism, posthumanism) shows the philosophical-methodological effort to move beyond the strictures of modernist thought and allow entry to a whole host of human and nonhuman "others"—the marginalized, Indigenous, subaltern, hybrid, animal—into the global intellectual field of discussion and debate (see Panelli 2010). And as more individuals from Indigenous communities came to study and work professionally in Western institutions of higher education, the colonized have begun not only to speak but also to "counter-map" and "write back" against dominant intellectual discourse. Notable in cartography, for instance, is a trend of Indigenous atlas projects including *Denaina: A Sto:lo Coast Salish Historical Atlas*; *"Haa Léelk'w Has Aaní Saax'ú" / Our Grandparents' Names on the Land*; and *Čáw Pawá Láakni / They Are Not Forgotten: Sahaptian Place Names Atlas of the Cayuse, Umatilla, and Walla Walla*, in addition to atlas projects in Latin America, most notably among Maya and Mayangna groups (Wainwright and Bryan 2009). In the process, these intellectuals and their non-Native allies have created hybridized spaces of intellectual collaboration (e.g., the traditional territory, tribal offices, workshops, research forests, academic departments and courses) in which to imagine anew the practice and significance of field-based research.

Place as Active Participant in Collaboration

Although Indigenous research and critical scholarship are by no means identical (neither between nor within!), both tend to emphasize context, situatedness, and perspective—in short, *place*—in the intellectual process. This insistence on context runs counter to the modernist obsession with an objective and abstract space in which it is distinctly impossible to actually *dwell* (Ingold 2009). For Indigenous communities, knowledge without context, that is, *universal* or *abstract* knowledge, is typically seen as lifeless, limited, probably impossible, and possibly dangerous—all precisely because it has been divorced from its proper locale of origin. Indigenous ontologies structure worldly understanding instead through firsthand experience in *place*. These places of experience, however, range from what most Westerners would call the "real" world to include dreaming, memory, and spiritual journey. But in all instances, these places speak to a recognition that *context* is essential for knowledge. Knowledge comes in and through place: thinking and reflection invoke a set of relationships such that understanding quite literally "takes place." To say that Indigenous research is "placed" is simply to acknowledge the myriad and reciprocal relationships required for knowledge to be possible. When knowledge remains in its proper place, it cannot be transferred as the property of an individual, let alone a corporation or government. It is "intimate" (Raffles 2002), an active and ongoing collaboration among human and nonhuman beings in the lifeworld.

Research collaborations between Indigenous communities and academics not only "take place" in the home of the Indigenous but also depend on the participation of place. To collaborate with Indigenous communities is to engage with an ontological understanding that views their places as storyscapes. These landscapes are filled with histories memorialized through the toponyms that serve as placed mnemonics—not fixed, stagnant markers of history but living stories that re-create the ontological and epistemological foundations of the community through their retelling. By engaging in and with these places, researchers learn what it means to be a part of the community with whom they are collaborating.

Unfortunately, the mobility of research generally operates in one direction only and does not allow for the Indigenous community member to visit the university home of the academic. Increasingly this reciprocal travel is becoming a part of the development of an ongoing research relationship but it remains an all-too-rare occurrence. Despite this, critically engaged and reflexive researchers are aware that their places follow them into the field. We are marked by the landscapes we inhabit, and they inevitably follow us into our interactions with others.

Situated Knowledges and Self-Determination

Similarly, the critical scholarship of postphenomenological academics has elevated the primacy of place in contemporary Western (especially continental) philosophy (Ihde 1995; Casey 1997; Malpas 1999, 2006). No longer does the validity of knowledge rest on the reliability of the all-encompassing "view from nowhere" over an objective, Cartesian space—this epistemology has been deconstructed as ideological reification—but instead requires an ongoing sensitivity to ontological context, that is, the precise place(s) out of which specific knowledges emerge. From empirical histories that explore the actual laboratories where scientific experiments occurred (Livingstone 2003) to the ontological argument for situated knowledges (Haraway 1988), critical academic work has illustrated the dynamic and inextricable relationships between place and the production of knowledge. Specific environments (universities, classrooms, conference hotels, labs, the "field") reproduce scholarly subjectivities (student, professor, research scientist, administrator) and knowledges that range from the conventional ("Economics," "Sociology," "Political Science") to the contemporary ("Women's and Gender Studies," "Indigenous Studies"). Situated knowledges, in short, account for their geographies of production.

These intellectual developments unfolded in tandem with structural changes in higher education and the global political economy, and it is here that we can identify the nexus out of which contemporary Indigenous-academic research collaborations originated. Postwar identity politics and movements galvanized previously marginalized social categories (e.g., female, people of color, queer, Indigenous) and elevated their status within political spaces at the primary scales of administration (local, state, international). For activists operating under the broad label of "Indigenous rights," this political process met with fierce resistance but also forced some accommodations from state and international institutions.[2] These included recognition of Aboriginal Title (most notably in Australia, Canada, and New Zealand), land claims and Treaty litigation, compensation claims, state-sponsored development initiatives, and at the international level, the 1994 United Nations International Day of the World's Indigenous Peoples and the 2007 UN Declaration on the Rights of Indigenous Peoples. On university campuses, a host of "diversity initiatives" heightened the visibility of Indigenous and other marginalized people and issues by, for instance, helping these students acquire a college education, creating new ethnic studies courses and centers, and implementing review boards to ensure ethical research activities in Native and other historically marginalized communities. One commentator (Menand 2010), in fact, recently identified the expansion of ethnic diversity on college campuses during the 1980s and 1990s as the last in a series of "great expansions" in the student population attending conventional places of higher education (i.e., four-year colleges and universities).

This development unfolded rapidly in geography, which means that the intellectual landscape for Indigenous issues within the discipline was starkly different even a decade ago. At the dawn of the twenty-first century, more Aboriginal people were involved in geography than ever before, but the discipline seemed oblivious to the sea change under way even as it was embracing other marginalized positions such as feminine, subaltern, queer, and people of color. At the Association of American Geographers (AAG) annual meetings, attendance was chronically low at sessions sponsored by the Native American Specialty Group, and there was a pervasive feeling that Indigenous issues were peripheral to the organization's intellectual vibrancy (Shaw, Herman, and Dobbs 2006). This began to change, though, when in 2000 the new leadership within the group changed its name to the Indigenous Peoples Specialty Group (IPSG), a move intended to internationalize the group's purview and to match the increasingly comparative and international nature of Indigenous studies. In the standard peer-review outlets for geographical scholarship, little work was being published on Indigenous or Aboriginal issues; one rough count ranged from 1.67 percent to 3.5 percent of Indigenous/Aboriginal content in total geography articles from the period 1997–2004 (Shaw, Herman, and Dobbs 2006, 269). Beginning in 2003, the IPSG organized a series of sessions at successive AAG national meetings aimed at heightening the visibility of Indigenous research while working to "decolonize" the discipline. These sessions resulted four years later in a special issue of *Geografiska Annaler B* on the theme of *Encountering Indigeneity: Re-Imagining and Decolonizing Geography*. At roughly the same time, national geography organizations in other countries created Indigenous-centered specialty groups, including the Canadian Association of Geographers (Indigenous Peoples Working Group) and the Institute of Australian Geographers (Indigenous Issues Study Group). Government-funded research agencies such as the Social Science and Humanities Council of Canada developed new directives for Aboriginal research as demonstrated through their support of Canada Research Chairs on Aboriginal topics. Indicative of a new high-water mark in this increased academic visibility, the Indigenous Peoples' Knowledges and Rights Commission (IPKRC), a network for Native and non-Native practitioners, was formed within the International Geographical Union and held its first meeting in Brisbane, Australia, in 2006.

Broad and enduring support for Indigenous rights and scholarship remains frustratingly limited and elusive at all scales, however, and it is in relation to this problem that collaboration between Indigenous and academic partners offers a protective "nest" for envisioning a future in which nourishing and sustainable social and environmental relationships can be (re)fashioned through research activities. When these research relationships are productive and collaborative, they can become much like an extended family with all of the responsibilities associated with such interconnection. Indigenous researchers such as Russell Bishop (1996) encourage the formation of such long-standing relationships recognizing that "the ability . . . to build, maintain, and nurture relationships, and to strengthen connectivity are important research skills in the indigenous arena" (Smith 2005, 97). The creation of these research relationships, as described by a number of the chapters in this volume, is about nurturing and maintaining respectful, reciprocal connections among individuals, communities, and the nonhuman entities in the environment.

Although contemporary collaborations between Indigenous people and academics span the globe, readers will notice that the contributions to this volume come from the large immigrant-settler states of the world—Australia, Canada, New Zealand, and the United States. In these places, the British and later settler populations established robust university systems that early on supported large-scale field research as part of resettlement, nation building, and territorial expansion. Over the past half-century, though, Indigenous rights have transformed at least some parts of the research mission in these university systems to respond to Native concerns by, for instance, reinterpreting and teaching colonial history and by teaching about Indigenous societies from critical and insider perspectives, addressing land and Treaty claims, and promoting Indigenous cultural diversity and economic development on and off campus. As relationships developed between campus academics and Native people living in traditional lands, research collaborations have blossomed into sustained and innovative, albeit not always unproblematic, projects. The contributions in this volume explore the problems and possibilities of Indigenous-academic research collaboration against this backdrop of regional parallels and differences.

What Follows

As we survey these recent historical developments in Indigenous-academic collaboration, we are also looking forward to the future to envision what these research activities could, should, and will look like in years to come. To this end, we would like to highlight several prominent themes in the ongoing development of Indigenous-academic research collaborations that we believe will be significant in future developments. These themes speak to both the problems and possibilities of Indigenous-academic research collaboration by seeking to "move beyond" the invidious distinctions and delineations of colonized ways of knowing that continue to dominate academic discourse today. In lieu of a summary of this volume's contributions—we believe these speak well enough for themselves—we introduce and briefly discuss the themes that are engaged by and woven into the collection.

Themes
Methodological Hybrids/Hybridizing Methodologies

The common difficulties and challenges of collaboration we have discussed here constitute what Linda Tuhiwai Smith has termed "Tricky Ground" (Smith 2005). This tricky ground, the spaces between methodologies, ethics, researchers, and subjects, requires ongoing negotiation in order to build workable research relationships. Incorporating Indigenous research agendas with participatory methods will lead to reworking the field as a methodological site of agency. This is demonstrated in the chapters that follow as researchers and methodologies respond to the demands of open collaboration. The burgeoning cooperation between Indigenous academics and critical theorists is helping researchers find common ground amid the trickiness.

Research as Storytelling

There has been a recent significant resurgence in storytelling as a research tool, "wherein personal, experiential geographies are conveyed in narrative form" (Cameron 2012, 575). This method of narrating research experiences provides an expressive and affective tool that evokes emergent nonrepresentational and post-phenomenological geographies while empowering audiences toward new understandings and practice. Gibson-Graham (2006) elaborated on the political potential of storytelling to construct alternative subjectivities that challenge dominant discourses and enact social change. Stories express the symptoms of subjectification while serving as "productive, participatory, ontological interventions that might call into being alternative worlds" (Cameron 2012, 580). As Christensen (2012) has noted, this approach is particularly well suited to collaborative and participatory research with Indigenous communities because there are many synergies with Indigenous modes of making and sharing knowledge. Expressing one's research through narrative storytelling is not without challenges though. Questions remain: Who controls authorship? Should narration be in first person or third person? What are the implications of translating oral storytelling into text? The authors of this volume have struggled with these challenges but have chosen to engage the challenges of storytelling for the benefits afforded.

Place-based Learning

The importance of place as an active participant in collaboration cannot be underestimated. As a locale or situation where human and more-than-human others come together, the object of knowledge can be constructed, appreciated, and understood relative to its proper context and relationships. To effectively engage our research efforts with the struggles of Indigenous communities requires an approach that understands these struggles as place-based (Johnson 2012). To understand the community we must understand their place and how they have shaped and described it for themselves and to others.

Walking, Dwelling, and Knowing

The research discussed in this book is not conducted by reading the *Times* over a cup of coffee. This is research that is embodied and performative; it requires us to walk and dwell. This entails more than conventional participant observation, but rather an attunement to the embodied landscape as a primary way of coming to know ourselves in relation to others. We acknowledge, though, that walking affords an experience of embodied engagement only when we are "heading the same way, sharing the same vistas, and perhaps retreating from the same threats behind" (Ingold and Ingold 2006, 67). Walking and dwelling in collaboration constitute a sociable act. Walking and dwelling afford the opportunity to learn about the place-based struggles and storyscapes of our collaborators.

Prospects for Self-Determination

The publication in 1999 of Linda Tuhiwai Smith's book *Decolonizing Methodologies* marked a significant point in the decolonization project in research. The significance of this book to Indigenous academics cannot be overestimated, and perhaps not surprisingly the same can be said of its impact on critical theorists who see within its pages a call similar to their own for the social justice for oppressed groups. Since then, Indigenous academics and critical theorists have been building on the foundation Smith provided toward identifying and describing "the multiple layers of struggle across multiple sites" (Smith 2005, 28). Explicating sites of struggle together leads one step closer to a self-determination we can all share.

What follows are stories of engagement between academics (Indigenous and settler) and the Indigenous communities within which they work. Many of the stories are personal and describe how the academic has been changed by their somatic engagement with others, both human and more-than-human. We have divided the book into three parts. The first, "Poetics, Politics, and Practice" encompasses chapters that tell the stories of engagement and further explicate how such interaction is reshaping academics understanding of the storyscapes of Indigenous communities. The second part, "Reimagining Landscape, Environment, and Management," delves into how these research collaborations are affecting environmental geographies. The final chapter, in a part all its own, describes how places can be brought into the classroom to instruct and decolonize.

The work we celebrate in this volume was made possible by the efforts of a small but dedicated number of geographers who have arduously worked over the past couple of decades to criticize and deconstruct the discipline's long history of service to empire (cf. Godlewska and Smith 1994). They have made room for those who have followed to further articulate a discipline where Indigenous voices and struggles can be spoken and hopefully even heard. This volume is only one small contribution within the recent work toward equitable collaboration between academics and Indigenous communities. It is our hope that through this work we can promote the transformation of relationships between Indigenous and set-tler communities, thereby leading to a common, autochthonous commitment to being-together-in-place.

Notes

1. It almost goes without saying that colonial practices and expectations are embedded still within both the process of doing fieldwork and more broadly, the academy itself. We celebrate the increasingly collaborative nature of Indigenous-academic research despite the persistence of this colonial present.

2. It should be pointed out that some critics have argued that such accommodations actually diffuse real and substantive change to the system of states (see Žižek 1997).

References

Bishop, R. 1996. *Collaborative Research Stories = Whakawhanaungatanga*. Palmerston North, NZ: Dunmore Press.

———. 2005. "Freeing Ourselves from Neocolonial Domination in Research: A Kaupapa Māori Approach to Creating Knolwedge." In *The SAGE Handbook of Qualitative Research*, edited by N. K. Denzin and Y. S. Lincoln, 109–38. Thousand Oaks, CA: Sage Publications.

Blaut, J. M. 1993. *The Colonizer's Model of The World: Geographical Diffusionism and Eurocentric History*. New York: Guilford Press.

Cameron, E. 2012. "New Geographies of Story and Storytelling." *Progress in Human Geography* 36 (5): 573–92.

Casey, E. S. 1997. *The Fate of Place*. Berkeley: University of California Press.

Cerwonka, A., and L. H. Malkki. 2007. *Improvising Theory: Process and Temporality in Ethnographic Fieldwork*. Chicago: University of Chicago Press.

Christensen, J. 2012. "Telling Stories: Exploring Research Storytelling as a Meaningful Approach to Knowledge Mobilization with Indigenous Research Collaborators and Diverse Audiences in Community-Based Participatory Research." *Canadian Geographer / Le Géographe canadien* 56 (2): 231–42.

Denzin, N. K., Y. S. Lincoln, and L. T. Smith. 2008. *Handbook of Critical and Indigenous Methodologies*. Los Angeles: Sage.

Gibson-Graham, J. K. 2006. *A Postcapitalist Politics*. Minneapolis: University of Minnesota Press.

Godlewska, A., and N. Smith. 1994. *Geography and Empire*. Oxford, UK; Cambridge, MA: Blackwell.

Goulet, J.-G., and B. G. Miller. 2007. *Extraordinary Anthropology: Transformations in the Field*. Lincoln: University of Nebraska Press.

Haraway, D. 1988. "Situated Knowledges: The Science Question in Feminism and the Privliege of Partial Perspective." *Feminist Studies* 14 (3): 575–99.

Ihde D. 1995. *Postphenomenology: Essays in the Postmodern Context*. Evanston, IL: Northwestern University Press.

Ingold, T. 2009. "Against Space: Place, Movement, Knowledge." In *Boundless Worlds: An Anthropological Approach to Movement*, edited by P. W. Kirby, 29–43. New York: Berghahn Books.

Ingold, J. L., and T. Ingold. 2006. "Fieldwork on Foot: Perceiving, Routing, Socializing." In *Locating the Field: Space, Place and Context in Anthropology*, edited by S. Coleman and P. Collins, 67–85. Oxford; New York: Berg.

Johnson, J. T. 2008. "Kitchen Table Discourse: Negotiating the 'Tricky Ground' of Indigenous Research." *American Indian Cultural and Research Journal* 32 (3): 127–37.

——. 2012. "Place–Based Learning and Knowing: Critical Pedagogies Grounded in Indigeneity." *GeoJournal* 77 (6): 829–36.

Kindon, S., R. Pain, and M. Kesby. 2009. "Participatory Action Research." In *International Encyclopedia of Human Geography*, edited by Rob Nigel and T. Nigel, editors in chief, 90–95. Oxford: Elsevier.

Livingstone, D. N. 2003. *Putting Science in its Place : Geographies of Scientific Knowledge*. Chicago: University of Chicago Press.

Malpas, J. 1999. *Place and Experience: A Philosophical Topography*. Cambridge: Cambridge University Press.

——. 2006. *Heidegger's Topology: Being, Place, World*. Cambridge, MA: MIT Press.

Menand, L. 2010. *The Marketplace of Ideas*. 1st ed. New York: W. W. Norton.

Nash, J. 1975. "Nationalism and Fieldwork." *Annual Review of Anthropology* 4:225–45.

Pahl–Wostl, C. 2007. "The Implications of Complexity for Integrated Resources Management." *Environmental Modelling and Software* 22 (5): 561–69.

Pain, R. 2004. "Social Geography: Participatory Research." *Progress in Human Geography* 28 (5): 652–63.

Panelli, R. 2010. "More–Than–Human Social Geographies: Posthuman and Other Possibilities." *Progress in Human Geography* 34 (1): 79–87.

Raffles, H. 2002. "Intimate Knowledge." *International Social Science Journal* 54 (173): 325–35.

Shaw W. S., RDK Herman, and R. Dobbs. 2006. "Encountering Indigeneity: Re–Imagining and Decolonizing Geography." *Geografiska Annaler: Ser B, Human Geography* 88 (3): 267–76.

Smith, L. T. 1999. *Decolonizing Methodologies: Research and Indigenous Peoples*. New York: Zed Books.

——. 2005. "On Tricky Ground: Researching the Native in the Age of Uncertainty." In *The SAGE Handbook of Qualitative Research*, edited by N. K. Denzin and Y. S. Lincoln, 85–108. Thousand Oaks, CA: Sage Publications.

Stavenhagen, R. 1971. "Decolonizing Applied Anthropology." *Human Organization* 30 (4): 333–43.

Stull, D. D., and J. J. Schensul. 1987. *Collaborative Research and Social Change: Applied Anthropology in Action.* Boulder, CO: Westview.

Wainwright, J., and J. Bryan. 2009. "Cartography, Territory, Property: Postcolonial Reflections on Indigenous Counter-Mapping In Nicaragua and Belize." *Cultural Geographies* 16 (2): 153–78.

Žižek, S. 1997. "Multiculturalism, or, the Cultural Logic of Multination Capitalism." *New Left Review,* no. 225, 8–51.

POETICS, POLITICS, PRACTICE

Footprints across the Beach
Beyond Researcher-Centered Methodologies

SANDIE SUCHET-PEARSON, SARAH WRIGHT, KATE LLOYD,
LAKLAK BURARRWANGA, AND PAUL HODGE

Fig. 1

Laklak: When Ngapaki (non-Indigenous people) come, they wear shoes to look after their feet. But they take them off when they walk on the beach—that's where they start learning. When they're walking on the beach, they're learning the land.

Laklak: Our footprints in the sand, as we walk back and forth between houses, is the knowledge flowing back and forth from one end of the beach to the other.

Laklak: We can share. We teach them unity. We belong to this land. We are the Yolngu

Fig. 2

people. I want to talk about good things for reconciliation, unity, peace and coming together. We have to create together.

Fig. 3

The beach at Bawaka is at the heart of our research collaboration. Laklak and her daughter Djawundil's house is on one side of the beach, and when Kate, Sarah, and Sandie stay at Bawaka, they usually stay in Djawa's house on the other side of the beach. The majority of our time spent together has been under the trees in front of the houses on one or other side of the beach. It is across this beach that Laklak hollers to let Sandie, Kate, and Sarah know they should walk over to sit down and talk. It is across this beach that Laklak, Djawundil, and their grandchildren Nanukala and Shyrell walk to sit down and share their knowledge with Sandie, Kate, and Sarah. It is in the sand of the beach that our children and grandchildren delight in play. And it is across the beach that each new day sees new layers of footprints— dingo, crab, cane toad, seagull, crocodile, child, adult—tracking the interplay of knowledges and lives.

This is a story of lives entwined and of new places of being and belonging. It is also a collaborative narrative of unexpected transformations. The "interplay of knowledges" described above challenges many of the rigors and certainties required by and guiding academic conventions. The co-created narratives enabled by the Indigenous-academic collaboration tell a story of new places to belong as the three female academic researchers "take off their shoes," walk on the beach, and learn. It is also a story where the Indigenous Yolngu researchers and their families find a place to belong in the South East of Australia, in transdisciplinary spaces within the academy and in the homes and lives of the academics.

But it is more than that, too. In this chapter we aim to deepen current understandings of collaboration in geography. We challenge the researcher-centeredness of much collaborative literature by discussing two further methodological sites of agency: the families of all researchers involved in the collaboration and Bawaka country itself as it actively creates and is created by our collaboration. As with the beach at Bawaka and the inscription of knowledges back and forth, so too the long path between Bawaka and the South East marks the flow of knowledges to and fro. As we each find new places to belong both in and out of place, we transform ourselves, our families, and our geographies. In turn, our geographies, families, and places transform us. This collaborative process embodies new conceptual and methodological landscapes that challenge and transform traditional ways of imagining and enacting geography.

We begin the chapter with a discussion of the features of collaborative research in human geography and how they have emerged. We explore the main attributes that characterize a shift in methodological traditions and highlight participatory action research and the development of Indigenous methodologies. We emphasize several examples of Indigenous-academic collaborations to show the recent surfacing of transdisciplinary spaces within the discipline, which are representative of the kinds of transformed geographies that characterize our collaboration. Having introduced the contextual terrain, we embark on our own stories of entwined lives and transformation. To give voice to these personalized accounts, we speak in the first person to capture the highly situated meanings that each of us attaches to our cultural and context-specific practices. These shared stories are presented under three descriptive headings. The first frames the background and introduces the initial connections and hard work involved in the sheer logistics of conducting family accompanied fieldwork. Here we focus on the role of the researchers and the need for trust, respect, reciprocity, and flexibility in research collaborations. The following sections describe the methodological sites of agency that make up the rest of the chapter: families and nonhuman elements in Indigenous-academic collaborative research. Guiding these two sections is a brief synopsis of the literature on these emerging themes, which challenge existing conceptual and methodological understandings of what constitutes collaboration in geography.

On Collaboration: Who Are the Researchers?

Collaboration involves mutually inspired endeavor. It entails, among other things, developing connections, nurturing relationships, plans gone "wrong," co-learning and transformation, building trust and reciprocity, and linking efforts. In the humanities and social sciences, participatory action research (PAR), Indigenous methodologies, and Indigenous-academic collaboration have emerged beginning in the 1990s, significantly challenging and enhancing what it means to collaborate in research. In human geography, these collaborations are often inspired by the work of cultural and feminist social scientists in the late 1970s and '80s that sought to challenge the positivism of Anglocentric epistemologies. From this work, which also incorporated poststructural and postcolonial insights, came the idea that "objective" scientific knowledge was inherently exclusionary, partial, and highly racialized (see Clifford and Marcus 1986; Harding 1987; Haraway 1988; Said 1978; Stanley and Wise 1993; Thiong'o 1986). For many geographers, issues of positionality, reflexivity, representation and voice, and the politics of research and ethics became key considerations throughout the 1990s (*Professional Geographer* 1994; Gibson-Graham

1994; Hay 1998; Katz 1992; McDowell 1992, 1997; Proctor 1998; Rose 1997; D. M. Smith 1997). Significantly, it was the experiences and aspirations of the participants themselves, those who made research possible, that became the priority.

PAR and other versions of participatory research methods emerged as traditional academic methods were increasingly coming into question. As a collaborative research endeavor, PAR's emphasis on transformative social change and participant engagement marked a substantial shift from geographical traditions in which the researcher entered "the field," undertook data "collection," and then withdrew, leaving "the field" unchanged (Kindon, Pain, and Kesby, 2007). Consultation, cooperation, co-learning, and collective action between researchers and research participants feature strongly in PAR, as priorities are community-defined and set in motion along an iterative cycle of action-reflection (Kindon 2005; Parkes and Panelli 2001). Embedded within many PAR approaches is an explicit political agenda that often promotes participant empowerment (Cameron and Gibson 2005; Howitt and Stevens 2005; Monk, Manning, and Denman 2003), along with an acute awareness of and sensitivity to the often inequitable power relations inherent in any act of research (Kesby, Kindon, and Pain 2004; Kindon, Pain, and Kesby 2007).

The development of Indigenous methodologies within geography has brought another challenge to traditional academic methodologies and power relationships. In this case, authors have been at pains to highlight the colonizing nature of much academic research and have been keen to promote alternatives that both challenge the inherent power relationships and engage directly and respectfully with Indigenous knowledges (Howitt and Stevens 2005; Louis 2007; L. T. Smith 1999). Louis argues for research on Indigenous issues that is "more sympathetic, respectful, and ethically correct . . . from an Indigenous perspective" (2007, 133). This (post) colonial challenge to the academy has seen many geographers rethink the concept and practices of research through a range of Indigenous-academic collaborations.

These collaborations highlight a range of methodological considerations, including susceptibility to extended time frames, communicative variants, and cross-cultural matters (Carter 2008; Carter and Hill 2007; Coombes 2007; Hodge and Lester 2006; Mayo Komla, and Empowerment Research Team 2009; Schuler, Aberdeen, and Dyer 1999; Tipa, Panelli, and Moeraki Stream Team 2009; Wright et al. 2007). Schuler, Aberdeen, and Dyer's (1999) work with the Djabugay Indigenous community located in the rainforest region northwest of Cairns, Australia, for example, highlights the importance of extended preparatory activities and cultural awareness in tourism research design. The authors demonstrate the significance of engaging an "ethic of responsibility" to community concerns throughout the research process. This is particularly crucial in building initial relations during "the extensive preparation stage" (1999, 69), which, for academics, meant substantial time in the field. One of the conclusions of Schuler, Aberdeen, and Dyer (1999), alongside this prolonged planning phase, is that success might hinge on one's "responsiveness to contingency" throughout the project. This methodological necessity was evident, for example, when differing interpretations and expectations were negotiated between Djabugay community members and local Aboriginal Associations regarding aspects of the plan. Carter (2008) describes the steps of engagement involved in a collaborative research project assessing trepang (sea cucumber) stocks in the Maningrida and Cobourg areas in the Northern Territory, Australia. Emphasizing the same cultural sensitivities proposed by Schuler, Aberdeen, and Dyer (1999) in terms of time and contingency, Carter (2008) makes a case for an adaptive and mediated approach to collaborative work, which embraces place-based protocols and synthesized cumulative outcomes.

Tipa, Panelli, and the Moeraki Stream Team (2009) take these recommendations a step further in their collaborative research on the cultural and biological health of catchments and streams in Aotearoa / New Zealand. Negotiations between academics and the Māori Moeraki Stream Team (which is a subgroup of Te Runanga o Moeraki, Moeraki) included formalizing the relationship through a Statement of Research Collaboration aimed to provide "a practical foundation for conducting relevant and appropriate research" (2009, 99). Tipa, Panelli, and the Moeraki Stream Team (2009) noted the two-way knowledge exchange that flowed between members of the collaboration. For example, while the Stream Team gained a variety of research skills during the many interactions, academics benefited from unique learning opportunities of place-based histories and cultural practices. The kinds of sensibilities and communicative attentiveness that enabled the "responsible geographies" noted by Tipa, Panelli, and the Moeraki Stream Team (2009) also figure strongly in the collaborative work of Mayo, Komla, and the Empowerment Research Team (2009) on Indigenous Men's Support Groups conducted at Yarrabah in northern Queensland, Australia. The study, which reflects on the form and quality of the university-community collaboration involved in social health and empowerment programs, describes how the relationship was interpreted and enacted as a "research dance" between academics and staff members of Gurriny Yealamucka health service. The local men's dance group, Yaba Bimbie, performed the dance, which involved the collaborative team in a number of poses representing pain, response, and renewal. The performance referenced a traditional healing pool called Yealamucka, which the participants passed through, fulfilling a sense of trust and reciprocity. Communities, drawing on the example at Yarrabah, "may not only choose the type of research conducted, but have their own expressions to depict its value, process and rewards" (Mayo, Komla, and the Empowerment Research Team 2009, 140). Mayo, Komla, and the Empowerment Research Team. (2009) identify the way the Yarrabah collaboration was deemed "successful" via the interpretation of the research endeavor through dance.

Reflecting on research by Indigenous researchers at Charles Darwin University in northern Australia, Christie (2006) argues that Indigenous methodologies challenge the academy to go beyond interdisciplinarity by opening up spaces for transdisciplinary research. Wickson, Carew, and Russell compare interdisciplinarity with transdisciplinarity and emphazise that interdisciplinary research involves a development of the common framework within distinct epistemological approaches that are used, whereas the transdisciplinary approach requires a "development of methodology that involves an interpenetration or integration of different methodologies and, ideally, epistemologies" (Wickson, Carew, and Russell 2006). This transdisciplinarity not only recognizes the coexistence of different knowledge systems and practices but acknowledges the often incommensurate nature of these systems. Christie (2006) nonetheless urges the need for transdisciplinary spaces "within the academy where claims of alternative knowledge traditions and their collaborations can be addressed" (2006, 79). The epistemological inclusivity of transdisciplinary research authorizes the kinds of shared understandings that Laklak's affirmation—"we have to create together"—encapsulates. And of course this co-creation cannot be done in or through the university alone. Transdisciplinarity also calls for expansive recognition of knowledges produced in places *beyond* the university. In other words, Indigenous-academic collaboration occurs both *within* and *without* the university as participants, in this case the three female academics from South East Australia and a group of Indigenous Yolngu women from Bawaka, North East Arnhem Land, Australia, weave together their stories of entwined lives and transformation on the beach at Bawaka.

A Footprint in a Rock, the Fulfillment of a Vision, Hard Work

The issues of trust, respect, reciprocity, and flexibility identified above have all been key to the formation of our collaborative relationship at Bawaka. Here, we reflect on the formation of our relationship and how as a collaborative team we try to work toward mutual benefits.

Sandie: When I think about how fortunate and privileged we are to have met and gotten on so well with the Bawaka mob, I often think back to what first sparked our interest in Bawaka Cultural Experiences (BCE), the tourism business the Burarrwanga family own and run. Kate, Sarah, and I were working on developing a northern borderlands research area looking for creative synergies between Sarah and Kate's work in Asia and my work in Indigenous Australia. Sarah and I were at a Stepping Stones for Tourism presentation (which aims to guide Indigenous people through the key steps for developing and managing tourism), which a government employee did south of Darwin where she showed an image of the footprint in the rock of the Indonesian princess Bayini, who came ashore at Bawaka. Our ears immediately pricked up at this link between northern Australia and South East Asia, and we organized a meeting with the relevant government staff to talk through ideas about us getting in touch with BCE. What I really like about the image of the footprint in the rock is that it took three years and eight research trips for me to see the actual footprint and Kate and Sarah still haven't seen it. This is because our research directions were rethought once we met the Bawaka mob and worked together to see how our work could support their visions.

Laklak: Running the tourist business was my husband's dream or vision. He was a smart man, thinking of the future for his children—we are the first Yolngu people to start such a business. The business is about Bawaka people sharing knowledge with the world. It's how Bawaka people are, sharing knowledge with the world, learning from each other, Indigenous and non-Indigenous. This is the way of our future. The knowledge is from the land, we tell this to the tourists. They hear this, and they cry and cry. In other places there's fighting—we're for unity and peace. We do it for the children.

We teach people about how non-Indigenous law is changing every year. But our kids don't have to go to a school with teachers to learn our law. We have the teachers. My grandchildren come here; they learn how to get fish [guya] using a spear thrower [galpu], they learn how to put gara [spear] and the galpu and get guya. For the future I see two worlds. I have been doing lots of book writing, teaching, kids going through college, starting the business. Lots of non-Indigenous people are coming and learning our knowledge, our law. That's what I see, the boy standing with the spear. That is the bush university, the real life, the land and nature. The other side of the world that I see is the boy sitting on a rock at Bawaka playing with a computer. This kid can see a wider world, learning through a computer. That's the new generation, mixing the knowledges together. Then the boys can change over, boy with spear can play with computer and vice versa.

Now I work with Sarah, Kate, and Sandie. Three lecturers, doctors, who come and write, nice English, beautiful hearts. Every year they come here to help me with my family so we can understand each other and make a unity—Indigenous and non-Indigenous to make a unity and friendship for the future.

Kate: We are so lucky that through our research collaboration we can assist BCE with their vision, particularly through the coauthorship of our two books, one published on weaving and culture (see Burarrwanga et al. 2008) and one we are currently writing to reveal some of the many patterns, connections, and rhythms that underpin Yolngu relationships with each other and with country at Bawaka (see Burarrwanga et al. 2013). And this coauthorship is right in the zone of our collaborative aim of mutual benefits as Sandie, Sarah, and I, as academics, benefit hugely from the publication of the books as well as associated conference papers, journal articles, book chapters (such as this one), and teaching materials. We each have our personal visions too, about building personal connections with Indigenous people and enriching and expanding our personal lives and family life. Although we frame our collaboration in terms of mutual benefits, I think it is fair to say that Laklak's family's vision underlies and enables all our work together.

As with the Indigenous-academic collaborations discussed above, collaboration for us has fundamentally been about relationships. From our first time together, we respected each other and our work, got on and enjoyed the stresses and rewards of being in each other's company. We wanted to further build on our friendships, and the creative vision of Laklak together with the flexibility of the academics' research agendas meant we are able to harness academic research to support the aspirations of BCE. Christie's "transdisciplinary" spaces are constantly engaged, probed, and prodded as we acknowledge our misunderstandings, find common ground, keep relating. Engaging with knowledge produced in places beyond the university has required the building of new language skills, the opening of new ways of relating, and thinking beyond the human/nonhuman binary to challenge the ways we shape our shared moments into new knowledge. It also means acknowledging the often incommensurate nature of these alternative knowledge traditions and the constraints of university and government bureaucracies, which often fail to acknowledge or engage with the new ways of doing. We've found that this process is sometimes hard but always rewarding as we work through the angst, difficulties, and tensions so that we deepen our collaboration and relationships.

Sarah: We absolutely love the work and get so much out of it, but it can be challenging too. I suppose that is part of why we learn so much—we get taken out of our comfort zone. With our families it can be hard work organizing everything to get there. For Sandie and Kate it has always been difficult organizing the logistics of being away from at least part of the family, arranging babysitting and so forth. Plus I know there's the emotional challenge—hoping the kids will be OK. For me, with the last trip, I took my baby, not yet three months old. Before we left I'd occasionally have a flash thought—"Am I absolutely crazy??" It's also often nerve-wracking when we're there, ensuring we say and do the right things, that the children will be healthy and safe, that we bring the right food and communicate effectively about payments. When we have babies or children with us, they certainly make us less lonely and are fun to have around, but they can make it hard to be a "researcher." It's not easy listening, concentrating, and taking notes with a baby climbing all over you and trying to grab your pen. That's where working with Kate and Sandie has been so great: there's at least one of them around to help take down those wonderful words of Laklak even if I can't (and vice versa!). I do feel more at ease with each trip, though; the whole family really puts us at ease and makes us feel at home.

Laklak: It's not always easy for us either. I was very shy when we first met. We also worry a lot about how to get you to Bawaka, how to transport you. Even when Timmy's not here, he's worried too, nervous and worried about how to transport you. And when you're here, the whole idea of asking questions and responding is different and difficult for us. We're used to telling and being told. Listening to your questions and feeling like we have to answer has taken us a while to get used to.

The story of our collaboration does not end with an analysis of our researcher relationships. Although from a traditional academic perspective (authorship of texts, chief investigators on grant applications) it seems that our collaboration centers on the key researchers and authors of this chapter, we find that the agency of many who are invisible, ignored, or marginalized in the research processes in fact enable and enrich our collaboration. This broadens existing definitions of collaboration. In the rest of this chapter we look at two aspects of collaborative work that became significant mediating elements, or "co-creators," in our collaboration. First, we reflect on the role played by our own families in our research processes. Second, we discuss the way nonhuman agencies—weather, protective spirits, country—contribute to and shape the collaboration. These insights complement the cultural groundedness evident in the reflections on collaboration of Mayo Komla, and the Empowerment Research Team (2009), Tipa, Panelli, and the Moeraki Stream Team (2009), and Christie (2006), and yet expand on and add depth to these works.

Embedding Families in Research Endeavors

Although research has never been a solely individual task, only more recently has academia begun to address the way that family and friends affect research endeavors and are productive in these endeavors (Cupples and Kindon 2003; Price 2001; Raddon 2002; Reich 2003; Stack 2004; Starrs et al. 2001). This "challenge to the solitary fieldworker model" (Cupples and Kindon 2003, 213) also means that "the field" loses its "boundedness" and professional and personal roles become increasingly entwined (Amit 2000; see also Katz 1994; and Staeheli and Lawson 1994).

However, work that looks specifically at these aspects of co-production of research endeavors in collaborative fieldwork contexts is limited.

Some work focuses specifically on motherhood and the academy and the way the latter presents significant challenges in terms of juggling competing discourses on simultaneously being a "successful academic" and a "good mother" (Raddon 2002; Stack 2004). Others highlight the logistical aspects of being accompanied by partners and children on sabbatical. Commenting on "the nature of fieldwork-with-entourage" Starrs et al. (2001, 75), for example, note the differences between the actions of the lone researcher and that undertaken when accompanied by family. Reflecting on fieldwork in Spain, Starrs et al. (2001) stress the uncertainties around responsibilities that sometimes hindered research activities. Reich (2003) provides a different slant on the meaning of "accompanied work," reflecting on the way her pregnancy, while undertaking fieldwork, facilitated access and provided a level of credibility and relational commonality for participants.

The question of access and commonality also figures in work by Cupples and Kindon (2003) and Price (2001), which highlights how motherhood facilitates participant relations and enhances rapport. Price (2001), for instance, recounts fieldwork with her husband and children in Latin America, suggesting that her accompaniment provided a kind of safety in motherhood. Price (2001) contrasts her experience and the network of relationships that her motherhood (and marital status) provided with that of a young, single, foreign woman who might be viewed as a threat and in pursuit of things other than just data. The common concerns of motherhood, in this case, alleviated potential barriers and reduced suspicions.

Cupples reflects on the benefits and networks that motherhood enabled during her accompanied fieldwork (Cupples and Kindon 2003). She refers to how having children with her in Nicaragua went some way in achieving more egalitarian relationships with participants. Her children's presence led to participants observing her interactions and exhibition of cultural norms. It also allowed opportunities to express common roles and experiences and led to openings for elaboration on issues surrounding motherhood in Nicaragua. Cupples also states how her children were of particular interest to those they encountered in the country, and reflected on this in terms of facilitating rapport and general familiarity, a level of which would almost certainly not have been gained if unaccompanied (Cupples and Kindon 2003).

First Steps, Long Distances, Lives Entwined

Being women with children and families also plays a substantial role in our research collaboration. Be it in the north or in the south, our partners, children, and grandchildren do not just fit in and around our work; in contrast, they enable and enhance it. As the research becomes our family and we become family, we find new places of belonging and being.

Kate: As our relationships have developed, Sandie, Sarah, and I, along with our children and partners, have slowly been adopted into Laklak's family and given names and places to belong. Sometimes, it's taken a few attempts to make sure the names given were appropriate, showing the thought, joy, and laughter put into being adopted into the family and the intricate relationships involved. Coming to Bawaka and being welcomed and accepted means also being cared for and looked after, and that's how I always feel, particularly with the kids, that it's not just us looking out for them but a whole family, country, nurturing, teaching.

Laklak: Giving names and adopting you into our family is a way of saying thank you for writing the book and helping; it's a way of giving back. It's very special—you will always be part of our family, you and your family, your children and your parents, will always belong here. You will always know how you fit in. When you're old, you can always visit your family in Arnhem Land. And when I go away from Bawaka, I bring my grandchildren with too. Bringing the kids to Sydney for the book launches, exhibition, and workshops was important. Nanukala made lots of friends playing and exchanging culture (see figure 1). Sometimes when you leave, sometimes, I cry, I miss you. I think about you when you are gone. In Yirrkala, we talk about you. With the weaving book, we're always thinking about you and your family.

Sarah: When the Bawaka mob visited down south, there was quite a bit of talk about Nanukala and perhaps other kids coming down and going to university here. All the kids (from north and south) could grow up together and perhaps go to university together—look after each other. I really loved having the family come to visit Sydney and Newcastle, and particularly come over to my house for dinner. Finally, I had a chance to invite them into my home too. Matt did all the cooking too, as we were so busy with the launch itself, and he took it in his stride and really enjoyed it. They liked him too, and we both got names. I have a lovely memory of all the kids playing in my sister's little boy's room—getting out the toys and having such a lovely time.

Sandie: I wonder if I could do research at all if "my family" (or at least some parts of it—my breastfeeding babies for a start) couldn't come with me. And it was so clear that the babies and pregnancies did—and continue to—provide an ice-breaker, common zone, distraction—they ease the relationships so much. And enhance them as they move our research in certain directions. Is it a coincidence that we did a book about weaving and women's business and having babies and babies growing up while we had the two babes there . . . and is it a coincidence that we're now doing a book about Yolngu hidden mathematics and how and where everything belongs as we grapple with becoming a part of the belonging?

Limiting consideration of research collaborations to the role played by each individual researcher does an injustice to the relational network of beings that each individual is embedded within. As illustrated above, our various loved ones actively and constantly shape the type of research we want to do and the type of research we can do. In various ways they facilitate, block, deepen, and enrich our research collaboration, ensuring that not only are the researchers decentered but also that the research itself is embedded in considerations that stretch beyond academic demands.

In this way Sandie, Sarah, and Kate continue to challenge the academic "solitary fieldworker model" (Cupples and Kindon 2003) through a vision of collaborative research, or what we have referred to elsewhere as an interwoven learning exchange (Wright et al. 2007), that ensures that at least two of us are in the field at Bawaka if the other has family or other work responsibilities. We see this as a process of recognizing and reconfiguring power relationships as we, together with our co-researchers, reconsider the mutuality and reciprocity of academic processes and outputs. Laklak also draws on family support, for example recently sending her sister, daughter, and nephew to New Zealand for a geographers' conference and to work on a draft of our new book. The field is not necessarily in Bawaka; the researchers not isolated individuals; and the boundaries of our collaboration expand and shift as we make the most of opportunities while ensuring that communication and a shared vision are maintained.

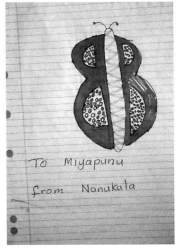

Fig. 4. The relationships with and between our children and grandchildren nurture, and are constantly nurtured by, our collaboration. This picture was drawn by Nanukala for Kate to give to her daughter Miyapunu.

Collaboration and Nonhuman Agency

Renee Louis in her discussion of Indigenous methodologies alludes to the expanded networks in which research is embedded and to which it should be accountable. She points to four unwavering principles in relation to Indigenous research agendas: relational accountability, respectful representation, reciprocal appropriation, and rights and regulation. Relational accountability "implies that all parts of the research process are related, from inspiration to expiration, and that the researcher is not just responsible for nurturing and maintaining this relationship but is also accountable to 'all your relations'" (Louis 2007, 133). These relations include not only human relations but limitless "nonhuman" entities, what are usually described in Western contexts as the elements, animals, trees, landscapes, and so on. In Yolngu cosmology, these relations are characterized by "dense webs of connection," with all cosmological elements embedded within the webs (Keen 1994; Wright et al. 2009). This precludes the possibility of separating human relations from any other relations and embeds humans, nonhuman animals, tides, moons, elements, trees, plants, landscapes, and places in the same relational frame.

A Yolngu relational worldview hence contrasts markedly with the exclusionary and racialized characteristics of positivist scientific knowledge based on a formidable Cartesian division between man and nature (Kenny 1968). A number of geographers have described how imperialist expansion and colonial exploration led to the scientific ordering of nature into a distinct hierarchy with the European viewing subject as the preeminent disembodied and distanced observer (Braun and Castree 1998; Castree and Braun 2001; Gregory 1994; Johnson and Murton 2007). This distinction marked the "Native" as Europe's necessary "other," and it also obliterated, until only recently, Indigenous ontologies and human-nature interconnectedness from Western understandings. In direct opposition to the Cartesian division, Cajete (2000) describes the holistic foundational context that underpins Native American perspectives where participation with the universe "illustrates the primacy of space and place in Native cosmology" (Cajete 2000, 20).

Geographers such as Castree (2000) and Whatmore (2002) have argued for the reengagement of society with nature, noting both the productive capacities of natural entities and, as Whatmore (2002) states, the tendency in geography to set up disciplinary divisions of labor between human and physical geography. The emergence of Indigenous geographies with its human-nature interdependence and "highly alternative pathways of (Indigenous) knowledge production" (Shaw, Herman, and Dobbs 2006, 274) has much to add in this regard. As Johnson and Murton (2007) assert, the reclamation of Native science represents a chance to reacquaint our (European) selves with the lived environment: to see afresh our intimate and creative participation with the natural world. Johnson and Murton (2007) see collaboration between Indigenous and "Western" academics as one way to re/write the Enlightenment metanarrative separating society from nature.

Protective Eyes, Female Presences, Country Caring

Our research collaboration and relationships of belonging are not just human relationships. Nonhuman beings actively contribute to and shape our collaboration. Indeed, the interrelated beings that are Bawaka country, formed and watched over by the protective spirit of Bayini and the Djan'kawu sisters, determine if and what form our research can and will take. They become important partners in the exchange and play a central role in creating and molding it.

Laklak: The animals and birds—they care for us. The moon, me, and the tides—we are always telling each other things and I then tell the people. When tourists and Ngapaki get to Bawaka, we have a smoking ceremony, which is very important to Yolngu people. We use a special tree, *jirka,* for the cleansing ceremony. It gets the spirit out, takes it away and replaces it with the Bawaka spirit. So the land and the sea and Bayini will recognize you and will look after you. Bayini has millions of eyes to see everything you do; she sees the bad and the good things. Bayini will protect the people and the land. The land will recognize you, look after you, protect you from snakes, spiders, etc. Bayini is always there.

Sarah: It was Bayini's footprint in a rock that first drew us to Bawaka, and the Indonesian princess who escaped off her boat to become the protective spirit of Bawaka has shaped our experiences in many ways—and in ways beyond our comprehension. She protects us and our family members when we visit; so, in a basic way, she allows our collaboration to proceed. She has also shaped the country that we inhabit when we get there—in terms of its physical characteristics such as the rock that marks her anchor in the bay and in terms of the social and spiritual world. She has visited us there on a couple of occasions, and I wonder whether her visit had anything to do with our being welcomed and accepted into the family (I don't know, but I wonder). One time, we saw her walking past Laklak's house when we were all down at Djawa's at the other end of the beach. One time we heard her laughing when we were out at Bayini Beach. There are other things too—I'm told I shouldn't wear my hair out loose when I'm there as she might get jealous and do something bad. Bayini has long beautiful hair (which I am sure is much nicer than mine!). Bayini has also perhaps helped create our families as she can help with women conceiving.

There was one time I put down Laklak's knife when we were out by ourselves collecting pandanus (leaves for making baskets). We walked away, and I suddenly realized I had left it. I couldn't believe it and thought, *Oh no, now I'm in trouble.* Feeling very incompetent, I sent a silent prayer to Bayini and walked back to the general area I thought I'd left it—we'd been wandering through the pandanus swamp, and I couldn't be sure of my sense of direction at all—and there it was, right at my feet!! Thanks, Bayini.

Kate: Bayini was key in making us welcome at Bawaka. As Laklak says, "Her eyes are everywhere," and therefore she sees everything that we do, good or bad. In the beginning this was quite daunting as we dealt with the angst over how to build the relationships with Laklak and her family, knowing that acceptance was instrumental in gaining respect and confidence from the Bawaka mob. Even the mistakes we made in the beginning, the ones I'm sure we still make, were seen by Bayini but seemingly accepted. I now feel much more comfortable with her presence, and she has cared for our children too; last visit she helped to heal Galpu when he had a fever for quite a few days at Bawaka.

Sandie: Bawaka is such a powerful women's place, and I definitely feel as if that has shaped our collaboration as women. Not only does Bayini shape the country of Bawaka and hence how we belong, but other female presences like the Djan'kawu sisters are creating, underlying, and overseeing everything we do and how we do it. They are in the sand dunes we drive through to get to Bawaka; they are the island that is right there as you meet the water of Port Bradshaw—and their power and strength runs through everything we do.

At Bawaka, nonhumans—landscapes, seascapes, animals, wind, sun, moon, tides, and spirits such as Bayini—constantly shape and influence our research collaboration. This collaboration and the way we make knowledge together are situated on, through, and with place. The Australian Aboriginal concept of country adds new dimensions to our research understandings, as country refers not only to a territorial place but contains multiple connotations that go beyond "place." As D. Rose (1996, 7) states:

> People talk about country in the same way that they would talk about a person: they speak to country, sing to country, visit country, worry about country, feel sorry for country, and long for country. People say that country knows, hears, smells, takes notice, takes care, is sorry or happy . . . country is a living entity with a yesterday, today and tomorrow, with a consciousness, and a will toward life.

Recognizing nonhuman agencies as part of our human relational sphere, as sapient and purposeful contributors to our research collaborations, opens spaces for more meaningful engagements with "place." In the context of our collaboration, it enables engagement with country so that the nonhuman agencies that constitute country—animals, plants, moon, sun, rain, wind, creator spirits, protective spirits—all interrelate to sanction our work, mediate what can be done, and inspire research directions (see Wright et al. 2012).

So not only do our walks back and forth across the beach at Bawaka nurture our collaboration, but the sand and beach, an integral part of Bawaka country, actively sustain our relationships. The beach is all around us, and it keeps on going. For Yolngu, this sustenance and nourishment is the same as Gurrutu—the Yolngu kinship system of relationships and responsibilities. As Sandie, Kate, Sarah, and their families are now embedded within the Yolngu "webs of connection," they clearly have a place to belong—not "just" in the family—but in a family that encompasses nonhuman family, that encompasses the country of Bawaka.

Laklak: Land is your family too. Place is your family too. You always come from the land. This place, Bawaka, is mother land to me. I am caretaker, the public officer. This is the Yothu Yindi relationship. You always have to think about the land, without it you have no matha—language, identity, culture, kinship.

New Places of Being and Belonging: An Ethics of Relational Collaboration (Beyond-the-Lone-Human-Researcher)

In this story of our collaboration, it is clear that researcher relationships built on trust, respect, reciprocity, and contingency are foundational. As we "co-create," exchange, and work toward mutual benefits, we draw inspiration from the work of other academic-Indigenous collaborations that also embrace the principles of Christie's (2006) transdisciplinary research.

While these ideas necessarily underpin appropriate research, we've shown that limiting consideration of our collaboration to the researcher relationships alone risks doing damage to the more extensive agents that all play important roles in it. As Louis (2007) argued, these agents— family members, loved ones, animals, spirits, seasons, country itself—are often not recognized in considerations of academic research. Place, even where it is recognized as rich, socially constituted, and dynamic, is more often seen as a backdrop than an active participant in collaboration. Ignoring the contributions that agents beyond the researcher play not only diminishes the collaboration but also limits the research processes and outcomes.

Engaging with extended networks of collaboration calls forth an ethics of collaboration. An ethics in which relationships, responsibilities, and accountabilities are no longer contained within the researcher-researched, or even researcher-researcher dynamic, but draw in a range of other nonresearcher agencies. In our case, our human and nonhuman families—Bawaka. There is little room for complacency here. Violent histories must not be compounded by academic ontological disrespect and violence to not only Indigenous peoples but also their nonhuman relations. Our research efforts must attend to an expanded sphere of collaborators and respond constructively to the new understandings, relationships, demands, and aspirations they engender.

Note

This essay and our research collaboration could not take place without our families from both up north and down south and without Bawaka itself. We are grateful to the people and country of Bawaka for permission to write about our research and wish to thank Bawaka Cultural Experiences, Macquarie University, and Newcastle University for financial and in-kind support that has enabled us to develop our research relationship.

References

Amit, V. 2000. Introduction to *Constructing the Field: Ethnographic Fieldwork in the Contemporary World*, edited by V. Amit, 1–18. London: Routledge.

Burarrwanga, L., D. Maymuru, R. Ganambarr, B. Ganambarr, S. Wright, S. Suchet–Pearson, and K. Lloyd. 2008. *Weaving Lives Together at Bawaka, North East Arnhem Land.* University of Newcastle, Newcastle: Centre for Urban and Regional Studies.

Burarrwanga, L., D. Maymuru, R. Ganambarr, D. Ganambarr, B. Ganambarr, S. Wright, S. Suchet–Pearson, and K. Lloyd. 2013. *Welcome to My Country*. Melbourne: Allen & Unwin.

Braun, B., and N. Castre. 1998. *Remaking Reality: Nature at the Millennium.* London: Routledge.

Cajete, G. 2000. *Native Science: Natural Laws of Interdependence*. Santa Fe: Clear Light Publishers.

Cameron, J., and K. Gibson. 2005. "Participatory Action Research in a Poststructuralist Vein." *Geoforum* 36 (3): 315–31.

Carter, J. L. 2008. "Thinking Outside the Framework: Equitable Research Partnerships for Environmental Research in Australia." *Geographical Journal* 174 (1): 63–75.

Carter, J., and G. Hill. 2007. "Critiquing Environmental Management in Indigenous Australia: Two Case Studies." *Area* 39 (1): 43–54.

Castree, N. 2000. "Nature." In *The Dictionary of Human Geography,* 4th ed., edited by R. J. Johnston, 537–40. Malden, MA: Oxford.

Castree, N., and B. Braun. 2001 *Social Nature: Theory, Practice, and Politics.* Malden, MA: Blackwell.

Christie, M. 2006. "Transdisciplinary Research and Aboriginal Knowledge." *Australian Journal of Indigenous Education* 35:78–89.

Clifford, J., and G. E. Marcus. 1986. *Writing Culture: The Poetics and Politics of Ethnography.* Berkeley: University of California Press.

Coombes, B. 2007. "Defending Community? Indigeneity, Self-Determination, and Institutional Ambivalence in the Restoration of Lake Whakaki." *Geoforum* 38 (1): 60–72.

Cupples, J., and S. Kindon. 2003 "Far from Being 'Home Alone': The Dynamics of Accompanied Fieldwork." *Singapore Journal of Tropical Geography* 24 (2): 211–28.

Gibson-Graham, J. K. 1994. "'Stuffed If I Know!' Reflections on Post-Modern Feminist Social Research." *Gender, Place and Culture* 1 (2): 205–24.

Gregory, D. 1994. *Geographical Imaginations.* Malden, MA: Blackwell.

Haraway, D. 1988. "Situated Knowledges: The Science Question in Feminism and the Privilege of Partial Perspective." *Feminist Studies* 14 (3): 575–97.

Harding, S. 1987. "Conclusion: Epistemological Questions. In *Feminism and Methodology: Social Science Issues,* edited by S. Harding, 180–90. Milton Keynes, UK: Open University Press.

Hay, I. 1998. "Making Moral Imaginations: Research Ethics, Pedagogy, and Professional Human Geography." *Ethics, Place and Environment* 1 (1): 55–75.

Hodge, P., and J. Lester. 2006. "Indigenous Research: Whose Priority? Journeys and Possibilities of Cross-Cultural Research in Geography." *Geographical Research* 44 (1): 41–51.

Howitt, R., and S. Stevens. 2005. "Cross-cultural Research: Ethics, Methods, and Relationships." In *Qualitative Research Methods in Human Geography,* 2nd ed., edited by I. Hay, 30–50. Melbourne: Oxford University Press.

Johnson, J. T., and B. Murton. 2007. "Re/placing Native Science: Indigenous Voices in Contemporary Constructions of Nature." *Geographical Research* 45 (2): 121–29.

Katz, C. 1994. "Playing the Field: Questions of Fieldwork In Geography." *Professional Geographer* 46 (1): 67–72.

Keen, I. 1994. *Knowlege and Secrecy in an Aboriginal Religion.* Melbourne: Oxford University Press.

Kenny, A. 1968. *Descartes: A Study of His Philosophy.* New York: Random House.

Kesby, M., S. Kindon, and R. Pain. 2004. "'Participatory' Diagramming and Approaches." In *Methods in Human Geography,* 2nd ed., edited by R. Flowerdew and D. Martin, 144–65. London: Pearson.

Kindon, S. 2005. "Participatory Action Research." In *Qualitative Research Methods in Human Geography,* 2nd ed., edited by I. Hay, 207–20. Melbourne: Oxford University Press.

Kindon, S., R. Pain, and M. Kesby. 2007. *Connecting People, Participation and Place: Participatory Action Research Approaches and Methods.* London: Routledge.

Louis, R. P. 2007. "Can You Hear Us Now? Voices from the Margin: Using Indigenous Methodologies in Geographic Research." *Geographical Research* 45 (2): 130–39.

Mayo, K., T. Komla, and the Empowerment Research Team. 2009. "The Research Dance: University and Community Research Collaboration at Yarrabah, North Queensland, Australia." *Health and Social Care in the Community* 17 (2): 133–40.

McDowell, L. 1992. "Doing Gender: Feminism, Feminists and Research Methods In Human Geography." *Transactions of the Institute of British Geographers* 17 (4): 399–416.

———. 1997. "Women / Gender / Feminists: Doing Feminist Geography." *Journal of Geography in Higher Education* 21:381–400.

Monk, J., P. Manning, and C. Denman. 2003. "Working Together: Feminist Perspectives on Collaborative Research and Action." *ACME: An International E-Journal for Critical Human Geographies* 2 (1): 91–106.

Parks, M., and R. Panelli. 2001. "Integrating Catchment Ecosystems and Community Health: The Value of Participatory Action Research." *Ecosystem Health* 7 (2): 85–106.

Price, M. 2001. "The Kindness of Strangers." *Geographical Review* 91 (1–2): 143–50.

Proctor, J. D. 1998. "Ethics in Geography: Giving Moral Form to the Geographical Imagination." *Area* 30 (1): 8–18.

Professional Geographer. 1994. Special Issue: "Women in the Field." *Professional Geographer* 46 (1).

Raddon, A. 2002. "Mothers in the Academy: Positioned and Positioning within Discourses of the 'Successful Academic' and the 'Good Mother.'" *Studies in Higher Education* 27 (4): 387–403.

Reich, J. A. 2003. "Pregnant with Possibilities: Reflections on Embodiment, Access, and Inclusion in Field Research." *Qualitative Sociology* 26 (3): 351–67.

Rose, D. 1996. *Nourishing Terrains: Australian Aboriginal Views of Landscape and Wilderness*. Canberra: Australian Heritage Commission.

Rose, G. 1997. "Situated Knowledges: Positionality, Reflexivity and Other Tactics." *Progress in Human Geography* 21 (3): 305–20.

Said, E. 1978. *Orientalism*. London: Penguin.

Schuler, S., L. Aberdeen, and P. Dyer. 1999. "Sensitivity to Cultural Difference in Tourism Research: Contingency in Research Design." *Tourism Management* 20 (1): 59–70.

Shaw, W. S., RDK Herman, and G. R. Dobbs. 2006. "Encountering Indigeneity: Re-Imagining and Decolonizing Geography." *Geografiska Annale* 88B: 267–76.

Smith, D. M. 1997. "Geography and Ethics: A Moral Turn?" *Progress in Human Geography* 21 (4): 583–90.

Smith, L. T. 1999. *Decolonizing Methodologies: Research and Indigenous Peoples*. London: Zed Books.

Stack, S. 2004. "Gender, Children and Research Productivity." *Research in Higher Education* 45 (8): 891–920.

Staeheli, P. F., and V. A. Lawson. 1994. "A Discussion of 'Women in the Field': The Politics of Feminist Fieldwork." *Professional Geographer* 46 (1): 96–102.

Stanley, L., and S. Wise. 1993. *Breaking Out Again: Feminist Ontology and Epistemology*. 2nd ed. London: Routledge.

Starrs, P. F., C. F. Starrs, G. I. Starrs, and L. Huntersinger. 2001. "Fieldwork . . . with Family." *Geographical Review* 91 (1–2): 74–87.

Thiong'o, N. 1986. *Decolonising the Mind*. London: James Currey.

Tipa, G., R. Panelli, and the Moeraki Stream Team. 2009. "Beyond 'Someone Else's Agenda': An Example of Indigenous/Academic Research Collaboration." *New Zealand Geographer* 65 (2): 95–106.

Whatmore, S. 2002. *Hybrid Geographies: Natures, Cultures, Spaces*. London: Sage.

Wickson, Fern, Anna L. Carew, and A. Wendy Russell. 2006. "Transdisciplinary Research: Characteristics, Quandaries and Quality." *Futures* 38 (9): 1046–59.

Wright, S., S. Suchet-Pearson, K. Lloyd, L. Burarrwanga, and D. Burarrwanga. 2009. "'That Means the Fish Are Fat': Sharing Experiences of Animals through Indigenous-Owned Tourism." *Current Issues in Tourism* 12 (5): 505–27.

Wright, S., S. Suchet-Pearson, and K. Lloyd. 2007. "An Interwoven Learning Exchange: Transforming Research-Teaching Relationships in the Top End, Northern Australia." *Geographical Research* 45 (2): 150–57.

Wright, S., K. Lloyd, S. Suchet-Pearson, L. Burarrwanga, M. Tofa, and Bawaka Country. 2012. "Telling Stories in, through and with Country: Engaging with Indigenous and More-Than-Human Methodologies at Bawaka, NE Australia." Special Issue: "In Between Worlds: Place, Experience, and Research in Indigenous Geography." *Journal of Cultural Geography* 29 (1): 39–60.

Singing the Coast
Writing Place and Identity in Australia
MARGARET SOMERVILLE

In the beginning was the mother place.

I am parked at the estuary at Moonee Beach looking through the curved branch of a eucalypt tree. It is a blue sunny day, low tide, with strands of blue-green water winding across the wide stretch of sandy estuary. All is rounded here. The rounded knoll of a shady reserve with tents and cabins is bordered by a sweeping curve of golden sand and curved channels of water. Beyond is a small, protected beach flanked by two close headlands. A sprawling grassy dome guards the southern end of the beach, and to the north, low dark bushes mark its reach. Past the curve of sand, hazy in the distant blue sea, are the two curves of an island split in two.

I feel a sort of pressure to find a special meaning in this place, the place of creation. And yet I find most meaning in the everyday, in reading the intimate details of the marks on the vast sandy expanse of estuary. Everywhere are patterns of tiny balls of sand and thumb-sized crab holes, worm trails, and three-pronged bird prints crowded around the channels. Last night's shower has left dimples of rain all over and the tide leaves its ripples as it washes over the sand. Along the edges, around the broad curve of the estuary, are patterns of driftwood and debris left from the tide's reach. This morning there have already been plenty of people making new marks after high tide's clean wash. There are patterns of human foot-prints, of bare feet, feet with shoes, children's and dog's footprints, round and round, running, playing. I read it as a place of play, rich with life.

Walking back, I see a young woman with a baby tucked close to her in a sling talking to another young mother with a baby in her belly. Their kids run round and play in the safety of the shallow waters. Aah, a deep breath of recognition. This is enough for today, I think; for the time being the place has given me all that I need. I leave for my meeting with Tony who has sent me here to this place.

Place/Time and Writing

This chapter is a reflection on the construction and meaning of *Singing the Coast* based on a ten-year collaboration with Gumbaynggirr people on the mid-north coast of New South Wales (Somerville and Perkins 2010).

I begin the chapter at the same beginning place as I began the book because it is a story about place, time, creation, and the written word. At the end of the writing, after ten years of collaborative research and engagement, I traveled from my new location in southern Victoria to meet with Tony Perkins, the coauthor, to talk about the book. I had many new questions about the mother place, because I had chosen to begin the substantive chapters with the story of the Women Who Made the Sea. This story is about two sisters who traveled the perimeter of Australia making the sea and sand that shapes our island continent. It seemed to be an important story that might offer a way to enter a different sort of understanding of place and identity in Australia. The two sisters ended their work by crossing their digging sticks at Split Solitary Island just off the coast of Moonee Beach.

I had many unanswered questions. Where did this story fit into the landscape? What were the places of its beginning and ending? How did it connect with the multitudes of other stories about the creation of the landscape and all of its creatures? These are complex questions that are part of a larger context that has taken me ten years to begin to unravel. Tony's response was to send me to the place. So I go to a place I have been to before, a taken-for-granted beach place, like all other beach places in Australia. On the one hand, I have a deep sense of the significance of this place, the intensity of the storylines that intersect there, but on the other hand, it is just a normal beach place with a caravan park and estuary, headlands, beach, and sea. How do I reconcile these things? What sense can I make of the intersection of these meanings? In a sense these questions are the quintessential questions about writing *Singing the Coast.*

So the beginning point of *Singing the Coast* is not time but place. It is a particular place in the landscape, but it is also all places. It is the place of creation. And in a sense the particular place is unknowable to me as an outsider, but there is also a sense in which I can know it through my experience as a woman, as a mother, as a sensing body, as a collaborator, and as a writer of its stories. So the beginning of this writing, this act of creation, is a stance, a way of entering the unknown where time exists only in layered folds of place.

The beginning point of a book of writing typically establishes a sense of chronology, based on a Western understanding of the forward movement of time. A book is numbered from page 1 sequentially to the end. Reading is directed from the left to the right and top to bottom through each page sequentially throughout the text in an ordered linear progression. A narrative has a structure of a beginning, a middle, and an end, and then it is over. The place/time of creation is not like this. The place/time of creation in this story is cyclical. There is no beginning or ending because each time the story is told, the place and all its creatures come into being. Each time I hear the story, or parts of it, I learn a little more, in layers over time. So in writing this book the beginning point is the end point as well, completing the circle/cycle.

Gumbaynggirr Identity

They always told me first
up here is your mother
it's like a spirit mother
of the Gumbaynggirr people.
Up this way people would say
that's your mother, your mother's from here
it's important area to you
that's where your spirit mother
she come from there.

Gumbaynggirr identity is inseparable from place. Even when Tony was interviewed about his sense of regional knowledge by a young Gumbaynggirr researcher well known to him, he began with a statement of his own identity-in-place. He performed his initial response as a form of address, a formal protocol of introduction:

Tony Perkins, the name. I am a local person from the northern area of the Gumbaynggirr. All my relatives come from this area, but I got associated with other Elders' groups within Gumbaynggirr through different types of marriage in the clan groups. The things that I say are things that have been passed on, like knowledge passed on to me from Old People that is now deceased. Mainly all the things that are knowledge that I will be saying has been told to me from the Elders in the Red Rock–Corindi area.

In introducing himself in this way Tony summarized the intertwining of self, people, and place in personal identity. He described himself as a "local person" identified with a particular area of Gumbaynggirr country. Identity in country is organized according to particular local areas, or clan groups, which he describes as being like the children, all deriving their origin from the mother place. Through marriage across clan groups he is connected to the wider Gumbaynggirr territory, to "other Elders' groups." His authority to speak is related to knowledge of country that was passed down orally by the Old People and by Elders who are recognized as having authority in the Red Rock–Corindi area.

Tony began his learning from his grandfather, Clarrie Skinner, through the things they did together in their daily lives—collecting and catching food from sea and bush, building shelters, and telling the spirit stories of their places. Later, he learned the stories of initiation through which the deeper knowledge of country was transmitted, and he was partially initiated himself. When he was about ten or eleven, the time when a boy would begin the learning involved in making the transition into manhood, his grandfather began teaching him the rules of living in this country. This sort of knowledge is learned in country, and Tony remembers the exact spot where his grandfather began to teach him this deeper knowledge. His grandfather, like many of the Old People, was an initiated man and had learned his knowledge of country through the cycles of initiation.

> But my grandfather he would—I remember him showin' me the initia-
> tion marks on him, on his chest, an' that sort of thing I seen. He ex-
> plained you know, what that was for, what it was about. An' I saw Bing
> and Bruce's father, 'cos my grandfather and Bing and Bruce's father
> they were stepbrothers, sort of like brothers. They were brothers. An'
> I saw both of them. They both showed me and explained the marks
> and things on the body from initiation.

The marks of initiation on the bodies of these men represented the deep knowl-edge of country that was passed on during initiation. The scars hold the knowledge of these men in bridging the time before and the time after white settlement. They are evidence of these men's authority in country and the means through which Tony gains his authority to tell this story in place, and of places. They are also symbolic for Tony of the whole process of translation in telling this story, of the movement from transmission through ceremony in country to recording oral stories.

For Gumbaynggirr people a sense of identity in country is constructed from the inside, from the center of one's being. A sense of boundaries is important because they signify identity and knowledge in country. Local clan boundaries are linked to story knowledge that was "passed down . . . when the Old People were around." They heard so many stories of their places of belonging and identity that they became familiar with their home territory. The sense of the boundaries of their clan country was also related to familiarity with the places where they habitually traveled and camped. "We can put lots of dots on a piece of paper within a certain area, but outside that area you might find only a coupla dots, but they're more ceremonial type camping areas when you're travelin' from one area to another."

The boundaries of local territories were learned from the inside in an experiential way and through listening to stories. Tony said the new way of putting lines on a map to represent boundaries and identity in country causes many problems. Lines on a map, he said, "hem people in" because they are contrary to a sense of local country defined from within and expanding outward through relationships and connections. These lines on a map do not conform to country as it is understood through the delicate negotiations with others involved in boundary work.

Lines on a map are a construct of a Western culture of writing. To understand a relationship to country that is not defined by print literacy is to understand country through other knowledges: through walking and camping, eating from a place, oral stories, spiritual intensities, relationships, connections, and negotiations.

Learning Country: An Ontology of Unknowing

Coming to know the landscapes and stories of coastal Gumbaynggirr country was a matter of crossing many boundaries for me. My home of twenty years was in the town of Armidale on the northern tablelands of New South Wales at the western edge of Gumbaynggirr country. Although I grew up in Sydney, I was birthed into the landscapes of New England, on the northern tablelands of New South Wales, through my work with Aboriginal people there (see Cohen and Somerville 1990).

To go to Yarrawarra I moved from the sparse, dry landscapes of the New England tablelands down through the wild gorge country to the flat warmth of the coastal plains.

When I arrived at that place for the first time, the meanings of these landscapes were largely opaque to me. I began to learn the place by walking from Woolgoolga to Corindi Lake to feel the measure of its beaches. The Old People measured out their country by the distance of their daily walk, half a dozen beaches, headlands, estuaries. They called the strip of coastline between Red Rock and Woolgoolga "McDougalls' Run." Herbie and Abraham McDougall were two of the Old People, brothers and initiated men, who came to settle in the area around Corindi Lake. The story goes that one of them camped on Red Rock headland and the other on Woolgoolga headland. When they visited each other they walked up and down the coastline between Woolgoolga and Red Rock, defining the extent of their local country in terms of the walking distance between the two places. In doing this walk they were also carrying out their responsibility to protect the places and the people, talking to the coastline as they walked.

I remember one morning walking McDougalls' Run as if it were today. All is movement and sound. Birds are calling all around, sound of waves breaking on the beaches, movement of walking along beach and over headland. This morning the tide is coming in and waves are breaking toward the top of the beach on soft dry sand. I walk along one beach and climb up over the headland, then down onto the next, legs aching as feet sink into sand, trying to work out the rhythm of tides to see if I can walk to Corindi next week. Even when the waves go back, my feet sink into the freshly wet sand, not like the firm sand at low tide. On some beaches patches of grey pebbles make a shaly sound, swish swish swish. The pebbles are cold and smooth, moving in layers each time a wave washes over. I have to hurry now because if the tide is really high, I won't make it over the estuary at Arrawarra where the people stopped and camped. I wade across the estuary knee deep, along the beach and over another headland, until I enter the hidden opening where Corindi Lake meets the sea. At Yarrawarra everyone wants to catch up on the beach gossip—weather, fishing, tides, estuary. We talk, and I learn. As I walk the beaches, I learn these places in a different way.

As a non-Aboriginal Australian, I need to open myself to the materiality of the places of the Aboriginal people, as well as their stories. In my journal writing I trace my place learning and my growing responsiveness to place. I had to learn a new way of seeing, and a new way of writing, to move outside of the academic writing genre to embody place in my work. I learned that I am required to put myself bodily in the places of these stories. This learning demands an attentiveness to place from the whole body: "The body, and not only the ear, is a trembling flame, a vibrating surface, ruffled water. The body does not photograph the world, but filters it across permeable membranes" (Carter 1992, 129).

The weather, wind, rain, storms, sunshine, the beaches, sand and water, and the rhythm of tides and cycles of seasons are all part of this attentiveness to place. It is place learning that derives from a deep, embodied intimacy. This place learning gives rise to a different sense of self, an understanding of self-becoming-other in the space between the self and a natural world composed of human and nonhuman others, animate and inanimate, animals and plants, weather, rocks, and trees.

An Epistemology of the Space in Between

Tony established Yarrawarra Aboriginal Corporation and initiated the collaborative research with the University of New England because he felt that the unique culture of the northern Gumbaynggirr people was not recognized: "We can't continue to be a hidden race of people, and we've come to terms with the fact that there is only one way to get this message out." Their culture was the lake, beach, and sea where they led their daily lives, and there was much pressure on their landscapes from coastal development. Tony believed there was an imperative to get the message out so that others could learn how to know and protect their country. He felt that in the local club he was only one voice among a racist and uninterested crowd. By combining with university researchers he believed they could use research as a new "weapon" to establish their rights to the land.

They formed the Garby Elders, named after gaabi, the swamp wallaby, who inhabited the coastal bushlands with them. Together they made the difficult decision to pass on the stories and knowledge of these coastal landscapes in a different way. In the space of just over a generation, they had moved from transmitting cultural knowledge about country through initiation cycles and ceremonies to recording oral stories and places using modern technological equipment.

> I spent so much time with my grandfather and grandmother, and I think what I am trying to do is carry that role, that message that times are changing so fast and we have to speak out now. A long time ago we'd keep it all in our heads and we'd pass something on that way. Now we're better off researching everything, recording everything, getting it all down. I noticed it's a new way of doing it, putting it down on the tapes or the video and keeping it like that. It's very sad, but we can't wait around for the right person to pass things on to. It's been a hard decision for us to make because our Old People couldn't see what we're doing today—the video camera and computers. They wouldn't know we had to make up our mind to go that way.

In all of our work together Tony recorded his remarkable knowledge through oral storytelling. We recorded the whole body of work that underpins the book in stories and conversations with each other. Tony chooses to remain essentially oral. He can read and write but has never wanted to become a writer or a reader of written words. When I was seeking feedback on his stories as transcribed written text, I read them to him and recorded his oral responses. Both Tony and I are acutely aware of the politics of representation. We are aware that writing from the space in-between Aboriginal and non-Aboriginal voices and identities is a risky business.

This positioning of me as writer and Tony as the holder of oral knowledge, is something to be worked with, to interrogate. It is the political site of the contact zone. We did ten years of research work together in a collaboration that was generated by Tony, and throughout this time he continually positioned me as writer and himself as storyteller and commentator. This positioning between white writer and black storyteller is assumed to be a position between the powerful (writer) and the nonpowerful (speaker). In this popular stereotype Tony is positioned as the powerless, marginalized, place-based Indigenous person whose knowledge is about to be stolen and used for the purposes of promoting the ambitions of the colonizer/writer. And yet this was never our experience of the collaboration. My task, my responsibility, was to collect, compile, make sense of, and assemble a written text that could get the message out to serve Tony's purposes.

In many ways the structure of *Singing the Coast* is determined by the voices of the oral stories. These stories were recorded and transcribed and then clustered and reclustered according to standard ethnographic practice. The departure from this practice was in the assembling of the book itself. The chapters and sections within chapters, and the sequences of the overall narrative, originated in the oral stories themselves. Through the process of clustering and reclustering the transcripts, new understandings emerged about the meaning of Gumbaynggirr places at both a material local level, and at a metalevel of meaning. At the material local level the transcript clusters revealed the nature of local place knowledge and at the metalevel, a story about creation, about generating knowledge from the space in-between, emerged.

The way that oral stories were represented in the written text was essential to communicating the understandings of the processes of translation between place, story, and writing. Some stories were included as conversational, explanatory accounts within the text. Some stories appeared as distinct storytelling events, separated out from the flow of writing by indentation and ascription of ownership. Other stories were chosen as representative of a collective idea and these were scanned in lines according to the rhythm of the spoken word. The inclusion of stories in this format left white space for silences, absences, and other possibilities that might lie unspoken on the blank page.

Local Place Meanings

There are three substantive chapters in *Singing the Coast* that develop an understanding of local place knowledge. They are about the material translations of No Man's Land, the food ecologies of eating from place, and the experience of spirits in places. I briefly summarize them below in order to illustrate the relationship between place, story, and the written text.

No Man's Land

Them times
you find a lot of camps
along the back of the beaches
or headland
along the edge
of a creek or lake
'cause they all jumped over

the other side
of the fence
No man's land
that's what they call it.

In *No Man's Land*, we follow the material translations that took place when this group of northern Gumbaynggirr people came to live outside the fences of the encroaching white settlement at Corindi Beach. In the narrow coastal strip they called No Man's Land, Gumbaynggirr people negotiated the terms of their engagement with white culture. Here, on the other side of the fences, they believed they were free of government and church intervention. They built shelters, improvised all of the necessary household objects and artifacts, made new music and sang new songs. It was through these material improvisations within the liminal space of No Man's Land that their old cultural practices made new stories. This is also a process of cultural translation through which cultural knowledge of local places, including language and story, is changed to incorporate the radically different context of their relationship to place.

Eating Place

Just along the beach
beautiful blue beach in there
mullet come in the mouth of the lake
a terrible lot of them
mostly big sea mullet,
along the beach for pipis[1] and things,
we ate lilly pillies, wild cherries, raspberries,
five corners, they're nice,
and just along the beach
you get them little white berries
we used to eat those,
geebungs, another one,
rolypolies, gooseberries,
you're never short of things
to eat.

Stories of gathering, preparing, and cooking food from their local places were by far the most common stories told by northern Gumbaynggirr people. When these seemingly diverse stories were clustered to explore what they meant in terms of a relationship to local places, a surprising finding emerged. It became clear that they fell into natural groupings according to the different places, and therefore ecosystems, where these foods came from. Yarrawarra people lived on prawns, crabs, and fish from the estuary; turtles, swamp hens, and eels from the swamp; pipis, gugumbals, and abalone from the intertidal zone; mullet, tailor, jewfish, and so on, from the sea; kangaroos, possum, and porcupine from the surrounding bush-lands; and turtles, ducks, and cobra from the river. In between all of these places, they ate native fruits such as lilli pillis, wild cherries, nyum nyums. and pigface as they walked through the dunes and coastal heathlands. When people tell stories about eating all of these foods, they talk about them in terms of the places where they come from, their local food ecologies. This intimate, embodied knowledge of particular local places through eating food is the fundamental economic basis of knowledge of country and of caring for country through ceremony.

Spirits in Places

There's different times through the year
you could be peggin' out clothes
or just walk out on the front verandah
there's a breeze blowing
you just feel real close
this is when I really miss the Old People,
specially all the grand aunts and mum,
it must be just the change of season
or something.

I had not intended to write about spirits, but the spirit presences that inhabit these places and their stories were insistent. I had never specifically asked about spirits in places, but when I looked at the body of stories, there was a profusion of stories about spirit presences. Of primary importance in this concept are the Old People, the actual people who lived through the time before white settlement and the time after, bridging two eras of place history. The spirits of the Old People inhabit the landscape through place memories, through their stories and place practices, and through the ways they translated their spiritual practices in response to white settlement and loss of land. The land also has its own spirits in the special places remembered and visited through the stories of the Old People.

The writing about spirits in places, more than any other aspect of the work, began from a place of unknowing. This is an ontological stance, where knowledge unfolds through my engagement with the stories. I have a conversation with them in which I try to understand. Sometimes this conversation is mimicry; that is the first way one learns, by repeating what one hears. This is how I had to learn to interview language speaker and cultural knowledge holder Bing Laurie, because his words and language were so foreign even though he was mostly speaking in English. I had to repeat each small narrative section of his stories to know that I was following the sense of them. In an oral culture this cultural learning is circular, repetitive and iterative. It builds up from listening and being there for a long time, hearing the same stories over and over. I wanted to parallel this experience of learning in the text.

It was challenging to write about this partial and incomplete knowledge of spirits in places. It was hard to write the sense of the missing bits, the importance of silence and respecting what cannot be said. It was important to tell these partial stories in a way that they are experienced not only as absence but as a fertile potential. I drew on my sense that the spirits had always been there, immanent in my place writing. I am the writer of these places; that is the work I bring to this text. Whenever I am in these places with soft vision, I am surrounded by the spirits of the Old People in all the stories I know. I have been introduced to them from the beginning, intentionally, as part of my learning. So, from the space between Tony's stories and my learning, I needed to be able to give a sense of the profound meanings of this spirit world. I wanted to explore the absences and presences of spirits in places, and the remarkable translations that these stories of spirits in places perform.

Connecting the Dots

We're parked at Sou' West Rocks overlooking the mountains, I don't know what they call 'em in English, but the Gumbaynggirr people call them Marrgaan,[2] the place of the rock wallaby. And Margaret's got out to take a photo as usual, thank you very much.

Gula points in Gumbaynggirr territory to all the mountain peaks. Hills all have a storyline attached to them that interconnects each and every one of 'em. Just like its people, oh just like your story Margaret, you know, your connecting the dots story. Gumbaynggirr people done it thousands a years before you even thought of it. Whadya think of that. Tralaala. (Ken Walker)

After three years of researching local place knowledge, in the second project, "Connecting the dots," we asked: How do Gumbaynggirr people move from local to regional knowledge without losing the specificity and materiality of the local? In the conversation above, recorded as part of a journey around his country, Muurrbay

Elder and cultural knowledge holder Ken Walker makes his prior claim to the concept of "connecting the dots." He lays the ground for the connections between peoples, and between places, in the storylines that connect up every aspect of his landscape.

In the "Connecting the dots" project we mapped some of the major storylines onto the landscape in a process of deep mapping whereby the events in the creation stories were reconnected to country. Gumbaynggirr people, in common with most other language groups in Australia, had been forbidden to speak their language and only in isolated pockets such as Yarrawarra in northern Gumbaynggirr country had any language speaking remained. Even there, the Elders only spoke language when they were drunk, a residual effect of punishment and resistance. Tiger Buchanan, described as the last of the storymen from Nambucca Heads in the south, had recorded many language words and creation stories with linguists in the 1960s. He was acutely conscious, as most Aboriginal people were, that their language held their relationship to their landscapes and needed to be preserved. In the 1990s Muurrbay Aboriginal Language and Culture Centre was established "to bring the language home."

Deep mapping involved recording the oral stories onto a road map, marking each of the places of storytelling events. The road maps were scanned onto the computer and using Photoshop, roads, towns, and other artifacts of white settlement were removed. Photos and story text were then superimposed onto the now blank canvas in a reversal of the tabula rasa whereby the Australian continent was assumed to be an empty space. Detailed language work by Muurrbay was required to translate storylines and link creation stories onto specific places.

The storylines that link the events of the creation ancestors are primarily walking trails that link local places to each other across country. To understand how they work it is important to experience them as actual tracks along which one might travel from place to place. As part of our work with Muurrbay we mapped Uncle Martin Ballangarry's memories of walking from Bowraville Mission to the Island, recording his story as we marked the places of his journey on the map. To do this is to enter this world of knowing country through walking.

The linking trails, then, are the actual walking tracks that people followed when they traveled back and forth through country. They are the walking trails of the ancestral beings as they moved through the landscape. In deep mapping the storylines of the hero ancestor, Birrugan, and the Women Who Made the Sea, we were following the process of reconnecting story to country in the language work that Tiger Buchanan began and Muurrbay continues.

The first part of the Women Who Made the Sea begins in southern Gumbaynggirr country at Scott's Head in "the time when we all began." The two sisters, angry that

Table 1. From "The Making of the Sea"

Bawngangagay ngilinadu gawnggandu; wurraangagay. "Ngaarruwa" yirraang; ngaarruwayagay buwaangagay gala wajaarr; "giduurra!"— giduurray. Jalayayagay yarraang gawngganba. Gala yarraang wanggaan Yaarrigay galagala bawngangagay, yarraangagay. Ngiling jawagarr biiwayay.	When the women dug into the ground and pulled out their yamsticks calling, "Turn into water!" it did just that; and when they struck the ground, calling, "Turn into sand!" it did just that. The two young women then kept going; one North, and the other one South, each digging as they went. And that's where the story finishes.

Source: Gumbaynggirr Language and Culture Group 1992, 72.

they had been left behind and pursued by an unwelcome lover, decided to make the waters rise and cause their errant tribe to be stranded out at sea. They began their journey to make the coastline of what we now know as Australia, at Moonee Beach,[3] the place of the mother. One went north and the other went south, and they met up again at Moonee Beach at the end of their journey.

> After they completed their circle of Australia as we call it now, making the sea and the sand, they met again at Moonee Beach and they swam out to the ocean and they crossed their yam sticks. And the place where they crossed them is called Split Solitary Island. If you look from a certain angle you'll see it like crossed yam sticks. And from there, the sisters went up into the sky, up into a star cluster we call Janagan. You'll know it better as the Seven Sisters or the Pleiades. And that's where the story ends.

The storylines that follow these trails link the many smaller stories of particular events that happened along the way as the ancestral beings created the forms and all the living creatures of the landscape. A storyline is the plot or narrative outline of the story, and this becomes a songline once again when language, story, people, and place are reconnected. This happens when the intimate details of local places are known and cared for. Each of the story places where events happened is a special place, or mirlarl, a place of ceremony. In ceremony the place and all its creatures are created anew. So too in telling the stories. Deep mapping is the process whereby the larger narratives are reconnected to country, reclaiming their original status as songlines. Ongoing language work and storytelling in country keeps the local connections strong and helps people care for country.

Notes

1. "Pipis" are shellfish. "Lilly pillies" (variously spelled), geebungs, and rolypolies are fruit of native plants.
2. Wallaby:

    black ~ gaabi

    grey ~ buliin

    female greyface ~ jirriwarr

    male scrub ~ girrbaam

    rock ~ maarrgaan

3. Moonee Beach, Moony-Moony Munim-Munim Wirriiga (Wirriiga [The two Wirriiga women who made the sea went across there to become Split Solitary Island. Moonee Beach (yam-stick place on) Ganaygal.

References

Carter, P. 1992. *The Sound In-Between: Voice, Space, Performance*. Sydney: University of New South Wales Press.

Cohen, P., and M. Somerville, M. 1990. *Ingelba and the Five Black Matriarchs*. Sydney: Allen and Unwin.

Gumbaynggirr Language and Culture Group. 1992. *Gumbaynggirr Yuludarla (Gumbaynggirr Dreamings: The Stories of Uncle Harry Buchanan)*. Nambucca Heads, NSW: Gumbaynggirr Language and Culture Group.

Somerville, M., and T. Perkins. 2010. *Singing the Coast*. Canberra: Aboriginal Studies Press.

In the Canoe
Intersections in Space, Time, and Becoming
RDK HERMAN

On a cool clear morning in Kawaihae, Hawai'i, I sat with a gathering of Hawaiian men atop Pu'u Kohola heiau, the temple built in 1791 by Kamehameha I to unite the islands. We rose before dawn, bathed in the sea, donned something approximating traditional garb, and entered with ceremony this temple of state. It was a seemingly random set of circumstances that brought me here. I had met with Mel Kalahiki, a Hawaiian elder, regarding an Indigenous geography project I wanted to do on Nu'uanu valley, inland from Honolulu. Within five minutes of meeting him, I was invited to come to the Big Island in August for this ceremony. I continued to attend this ceremony for five years, until my elder and chief, Mel Kalahiki, stepped down and passed the mantle to his son. Then, it seemed, my time was done.

I have since written about Pu'u Kohola as a symbolic landscape (Herman 2008a). For that study, I conceptualized the relationship between time and space using the oceanic metaphor of the canoe. On an oceanic voyage, the passengers remain in the same location the entire time: *in the canoe.* The canoe stays in one place. Between departure and arrival, the people have always been in the canoe, but during that time, the space underneath the canoe has moved, bringing the destination to them. I then applied this to Pu'u Kohola as a place moving through time like a canoe on the ocean. It is also a journey of meaning, and it has different passengers along the way.

My coming to participate in this ceremony tells another story of the intersection of place, time, and people, a story that substantially changed my interaction with the community I was working with and which continues to pose questions for me regarding who I am in relation to these people, this place, and the work I have been doing. In this essay, I want to take the canoe metaphor in a different direction, one that focuses on the journeys that are involved with place-based fieldwork in Indigenous settings and the deeper sense of place that these experiences can provoke.

My intent is to conceptualize the research project itself as the canoe. It is the vehicle that brings together you the researcher, the community members with whom you are working, and the place itself for a period of time, possibly a lifetime. All of these have their individual trajectories before, after, and even during the project and are not necessarily in the same place at the same time. But in fact they are all the paddlers that move the canoe forward. I see in this metaphor a means for theorizing Indigenous geography fieldwork in a way that enables us practitioners to be more effective both as scholars and as human beings.

Each of us approaches our work with our own distinct maps and tools, derived from who we are and the choices we have made. These inform us both epistemologically and theoretically for the work we do. To the extent that "research is me-search," these are maps of *being* and *becoming*. They are maps of our expanding understanding of our world and our place in it, should we choose to recognize them as such. Such recognition is my point here.

Maps of Being

In my own case, the maps I gained extend the notion of "more than white"—which has been used to craft this present volume into a broader cross-cultural and cross-epistemological milieu. Although I was raised in the Judeo-Christian tradition (my father a Jew, my mother a Christian), I early on took a keen interest in world religions and majored in comparative religion as an undergraduate. Here, I focused particularly on Buddhism, Taoism, and Hinduism.

These traditions share some common principles and differ markedly from the Judeo-Christian tradition in their epistemological starting points. For me, the basic principles may be summarized as follows:

- The manifest world arises from the unmanifest, and returns to it
- This world that we understand as multitudinous and diverse has a fundamental, underlying unitary nature
- There is a pretty straightforward formula for human action that can move us toward greater understanding of, and ultimately unity with, this divine nature.
- The path for each individual is different, depending on our personal makeup and experiences (karma), but has some basic characteristics of
  focusing the mind,
  dismantling the ego, and
  letting go of attachments
- Finally, Hinduism and Buddhism share a notion of karma as defining our manifestation, and our connections with people, places, and so on. Karma (or cause and effect) accumulates over eons of death and rebirth.

On the whole, these principles are not uncommon to Indigenous understandings, though they are articulated differently in each case. In all cultures, we find recipes for how to become more fully human, and one can find these same principles in the Christian gospels. But in contemporary US culture, we seem to have lost the central principle that this is our real mission in this life. We can reach back to blame the Catholic Church, the Scientific Revolution, and the Protestant Reformation (Herman 2008b), or turn to more recent forces, including industrial capitalism, large corporations, television, and so on, all of which I think are culprits. Current Western science and much of popular culture are hostile to serious discussion of the unmanifest and the true business of being human.

At the same time, there are some more recent Western maps that have tried to clue us in. Two that I found useful are those developed by the psychoanalysts Carl Jung and Stanislav Grof. Jung's mapping of the unconscious is very much in accord with Eastern religions, albeit in a different code. Jung focused on the unconscious as the interface between manifest and unmanifest aspects of the psyche, and of the relationships of the self to the world. He wrote that "the unconscious undergoes or produces change." And once he had familiarized himself with alchemy, he went on to state that "the unconscious is a *process*, and . . . the psyche is transformed or developed by the relationship of the ego to the contents of the unconscious. . . . In collective life [that transformation] has left its deposit principally in the various religious systems and their changing symbols" (Jung 1961, 209).

For Jung, psychology was a field where biology and spirituality met. To use current terminology, we might phrase this by saying that humans are biological organisms with certain *hardwired* programming and simultaneously spiritual beings with *software* that drives us toward a state of greater wholeness he called individuation. Individuation may be a more mundane goal than the enlightenment sought by mystics, but it is nonetheless the outcome of the same general process. Jung remarked on the lack of boundary between manifest and unmanifest realities, pointing out particularly in his discussion of synchronicity that states of mind and external occurrences can appear causally linked without any apparent connection. Jung concluded, "Since psyche and matter are contained in one and the same world, and moreover are in continuous contact with one another and ultimately rest on irrepresentable, transcendental factors, it is not only possible but fairly probably, even, that psyche and matter are two different aspects of one and the same thing" (Jung 1954, 215).

Synchronicity was also noted by psychedelic researcher Stanislav Grof who drew on three decades of clinical research with LSD. Grof elaborated a new model of consciousness based on what he called the most challenging element resulting from psychedelic research: the transpersonal experience. "The common denominator of this rich and ramified group of unusual experiences is the individual's feeling that his or her consciousness has expanded beyond the ego boundaries and has transcended the limitations of time and space" (Grof 1985, 41).

A significant aspect of some transpersonal experiences is their interconnection or interwovenness with the fabric of the material world, where occurring events in people's lives mirrored stages of their psychic journeys. This is a minor phenomenon reflective of a much broader model of reality that Grof proposed.

Drawing on the physicist David Bohm's theory of the structure of the universe and voluminous data from his own psychedelic research, Grof argues that the phenomenal, perceived world represents only a fragment of reality, the *unfolded* or *explicate order* that is contained within and emerging from the *enfolded* or *implicate order* that is its source and generating matrix (Grof 1985, 83). This model was the only way to explain the phenomena he had encountered and the data he had amassed. Grof was drawn—as I and many others had been—to Capra's discussion in *The Tao of Physics* (1975) regarding the dual wave/particle nature of electrons and subatomic particles: "Particles are merely local condensations of the field; concentrations of energy which come and go, thereby losing their individual character and dissolving into the underlying field" (Capra 1975, 196–97).

Capra also turned to Eastern mysticism as portraying this more fluid sense of the world in which we are less like fixed entities and more like fluctuating pools of energy that interact with other patterns of energy around us. I sometimes follow Jung in referring to this as an "energic" model of the world and sometimes simply call it the "spiritual" approach, because here is where the manifest and unmanifest worlds can be better comprehended and worked with together. The general principles of this model include:

- There is no clear boundary between consciousness and the world;
- States of mind and worldly interaction are mutually constitutive;
- Where we are at in our Being affects what encounters we actually have in the world, and how those encounters play out;
- There is an organic, preprogrammed tendency or drive in human beings toward a state of higher integration of the self and between the self and the world;
- There is, however, an alternative tendency to pursue mundane self-satisfaction and go deeper into selfishness, attachments, and confusion. This has its own allure—we might call it the Dark Side—hence our religions warn against it.

If we wanted to map a general understanding of systems that might precariously be lumped together under the heading "Eastern mysticism," it might look like a mandala (figure 5). The mandala suggests a tiered mountain, with enlightenment

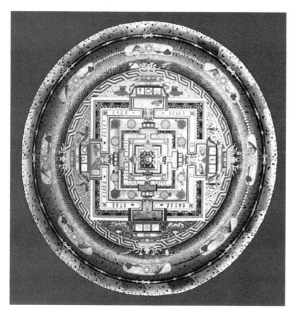

Fig. 5. The Kalachakra Mandala

in the very center. One approaches it from one of the four directions, and all the symbolism and imagery in here represent the kinds of obstacles and encounters one might have en route. It is a figurative map of the journey to enlightenment.

Practice

These maps are all very exciting, but maps are one thing and making the journey is another. Joseph Campbell (1988) pointed out that each religion is like a distinct software program: if you truly use it, it will take you to fulfillment (enlightenment, freedom, individuation, call it what you will). But, the key is that you have to actually follow the program. Knowing how the program works and having the disk in your drawer still doesn't accomplish anything. Moreover, doing the program takes real work and effort. I didn't understand this as an undergraduate religion major. But then in 1982 I took advantage of my college's rotating quarter system to spend two months in residence at the City of Ten Thousand Buddhas, an orthodox Ch'an (Chinese Zen) monastery in Northern California. Master Hsuan Hua, Ninth Patriarch of the Wei Yang Sect, transplanted this Chinese tradition virtually unchanged onto American soil. The schedule was quite rigorous. Days started at 3:30 A.M. Here I learned the meaning of spiritual practice: that what you know or believe in is a very small part of religion. The real business is what you actually do in your everyday life. If you are walking the path to enlightenment, then every thought, word, action, and encounter is a moment for you to practice, to *be conscious* and act consciously. Belief and faith are means—they keep your eye on

Table 2. The Buddha's Eightfold Path.

Right View	
	Wisdom & Knowledge
Right Intention	
Right Speech	
Right Action	External Conduct
Right Livelihood	
Right Effort	
Right Mindfulness	Internal Conduct
Right Concentration	

Note: The division into the three fields of Wisdom & Knowledge, External Conduct, and Internal Conduct are mine. Of course, all three are interrelated in their functioning.

the goal—but are not ends in themselves. Texts show the way, but one still has to make the trip.

The Buddha himself summed this up in his recipe known as the Eightfold Path. These are the things you need to do, he said, that will enable you to release your attachments. That is, they are another recipe for becoming fully human. I organize these eight guidelines into three groups: Wisdom and Knowledge, External Conduct, and Internal Conduct:

In reality, Buddhist practice is much more complex than this, involving many vows for monks and nuns—and some for serious lay people—to help us regulate our behavior. The monks and nuns then engage in that rigorous schedule of hard work, meditation, and other practices. And this is true also for Yogis and other true mystical seekers. The work is hard and the dedication must be 100 percent. But on a more mundane level for us as average mortals, the principles are the same: orient your life—as much as you can—in a way that aligns you toward the goal of liberation and enlightenment.

The word "Right" generally used to translate these Buddhist concepts for me aligns with the Hawaiian term *pono*. *Pono* means "right," "things as they should be," and always conveys to me a larger sense of "cosmically right." I compare it to the old Chinese notion of things being in accord with the will of heaven: that there is an order and balance to the universe, and when you act in accord with this, things prosper and thrive. But if you run contrary to this, disharmony ensues and trouble results. To NOT be *pono* creates an imbalance within the self, the community, and up to much larger scales. We are part of the machinery of the universe, so being "right" in our conduct has implications beyond ourselves. Hence, this term conveys to me a sense of responsibility beyond myself.

Walking the path is not easy, regardless of which map one uses. Buddhism offers the Six Paramitas ("Perfections") as strategic approaches to being *pono* in the face of internal and external obstacles (table 3).

I find notable here the juxtaposition of inner-focused and outer-focused principles, such as meditative effort (inner) with generosity (outer), wisdom (inner) and patience (outer). Clearly, all of these have both internal and external resonance.

The Six Paramitas are comparable to the Seven Grandfather teachings found in Anishinaabe tradition. As told by Anishinaabe elders,[1] in this story a village youth named Little Boy goes in search of knowledge to help his people. Along his journey, seven grandfathers in animal form teach him the important lessons for being fully human: love, honesty, respect, truth, bravery, humility, and wisdom. Like the Eight-fold Path and the Six Paramitas, this list demonstrates a mix of external effort, internal effort, and letting go of ego. By the time Little Boy returns to his village, he is an old man. Thus the story imparts the message that it takes a lifetime to learn these lessons but also that we won't learn these if we don't go looking in the first place.

Table 3. Buddhism's Six Paramitas and the Anishinaabe Seven Teachings

Buddhism	Anishinaabe
The Six Paramitas	The Seven Grandfathers' Teachings
Generosity	Love
Ethics	Honesty
Patience	Respect
Effort	Truth
Meditative Concentration	Bravery
Wisdom	Humility
	Wisdom

So it is important both to have good maps and to have a good practice or vehicle to enable one's journey on the path. Here again a chance encounter in Hawai'i led me to adopt a method that was taught by a traditional healing *kahuna*, Morrnah Simeona. Simeona had a personal revelation that she used to reformulate the traditional Hawaiian practice of conflict resolution, *ho'oponopono*, into a powerful tool for taking responsibility and clearing up negative energy and karmic obstacles. *Ho'oponopono* again uses this word "*pono*" and means "the act of making right," of setting things in order. Often simply called "cleansing" by its practitioners, it is an active meditative practice that restores balance within the various aspects of the self by clearing away karmic obstacles. As a daily practice, it includes clearing obstacles in advance with people and places we work with.

The map for this practice draws quite openly on Buddhist/Hindu notions of karma (cause and effect, accumulated energies and ties) and samsara (cycles of death and rebirth) and combines them with a uniquely Hawaiian map of the body-mind. Working with the unconscious as the interface between the physical, mental, and spiritual realms, it enables one to work with the relationship between manifest and unmanifest realities more directly. By cleaning up the mess on the unmanifest side through releasing negative energies and karmic ties, our actions and encounters in the manifest world move forward more smoothly and productively. Here "forward" and "productive" mean not just the obvious, get-the-job-done aspects of life, but the business of *becoming*, the forward motion toward becoming fully human, and acting in accordance with the will of heaven.

Again, if we see the living world as vibrant pools of energy that are constantly interacting and interpenetrating in ways that take concrete form in the manifest world, then this system makes sense. Deal with it before it becomes manifest. And if you have to deal with the manifest on the spot, work on the energy behind the situation to enable you to act freely and appropriately. An example I often use for this is the common experience of encountering someone for the first time and hating them (or being hated by them) immediately. That's karma: you've encountered each other before, and the negative energies are piled up from past lives. Clean it up and you can get along better, perhaps even become friends or allies. Don't, and you may continue to lock horns for reasons you cannot fathom. This has important relevance for doing ethnographic fieldwork in other places, especially Indigenous settings where engaging the unmanifest is still culturally relevant.

Thus far, I have outlined epistemological and (for lack of a better word) *spiritual* tools that are certainly "more than white." But for me the "white" part, Western geography, is the hermeneutic anchor to all of this. Here is a discipline that elaborates a great many things about how the world works. Like de Blij (1981), I see geography as the hub of the wheel of academic disciplines, providing spatial context

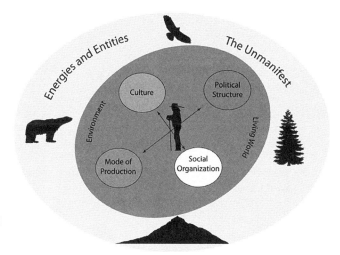

Figure 6. A way of conceiving Indigenous geography as materialist geography contextualized by a relationship to the unmanifest.

and understanding to economic, social, and cultural life. If one is to act effectively in the world—on issues such as social justice, hunger, poverty, and the like, then geography offers a very powerful set of tools and models. This is all the more true for contemporary g informed by critical theory, elaborating and identifying relations of power. Critical theory provides maps of how NOT to engage in practices that create unequal or exploitative relations of power, a problem for geography and ethnography since at least the nineteenth century. Especially in working with Indigenous peoples, we are always contending with the matter of decolonization and the role we play as scholars in regard to self-determination. Smith's (1999) work on this topic is often pointed to. I would add that the decolonizing of research methodologies is an important aspect of being *pono*. Combining critical geography with the spiritual tools and models I have outlined above greatly enhances both. At the same time, I emphasize that the standard tools of geography fieldwork are still valid and potent, and form an important part of my toolbox. Critical geography merely ensures that I use these tools more wisely and respectfully.

This is the portfolio of maps and tools I have in place before actually doing fieldwork in Indigenous settings in the year 2000. It has since been useful for me to draw on a Marxian model to how Indigenous geography differs from the contemporary Western framework (figure 6). I start with Marx's four categories of mode of production, social organization, political structure, and culture, placed in the environmental context and organized in such a way as to emphasize that these are part of an interconnected system in which changes in one can affect the other three. We know now that changes in culture can affect mode of production (e.g., the growing desire for organic foods affecting agricultural practices), and that two cultures can have the same mode of production but organize very differently (e.g., socialist versus individualist) to produce very different political structures and cultures. The environment is the setting in which all of this takes place, offering certain limits and possibilities, and the cultural landscape is the product that reflects how the system manifests. This alone is a useful teaching model for introductory geography classes.

But for Indigenous geography, there is an additional factor that needs to be added. Where the basic Marxian model focuses exclusively on the manifest world (physical and mental), Indigenous understandings include the unmanifest world as well, whether it be the creator or any messengers therefrom, or a more general sense of the creative force manifesting in various ways, as well as animal spirits and a whole spirit world, and indeed perhaps the whole of creation as alive, aware, and consciously interacting. For Indigenous peoples, this is a normal and accepted aspect of reality that guides our actions in the present, particularly toward the environment and its many nations of beings, and toward each other.

This model codifies what I have come to realize over the course of my work in Indigenous communities. But in addition to this static model, there are dynamic aspects of actually doing the work that merit attention. In the following sections, I present four themes drawing on the experiences I have had and the lessons I have learned from my work in Indigenous settings during the last decade, including a Hopi community in Arizona, three land divisions (*ahupua'a*) in the Hawaiian Islands, and four communities in western Micronesia.

Positionality

Both in terms of approaching fieldwork in Indigenous communities and in terms of striving toward being more fully human and acting appropriately in the world, the matter of first importance from the outset is, Where do I stand in relation to this work, this place, and these people? From what position *within myself* am I moving forward into this project? Is this project *pono*, and am I going about it in a way that is *pono*?

I began my project, *Pacific Worlds*, while an assistant professor at Towson University in Baltimore. *Pacific Worlds*[2] was based on the *Indigenous Geography* project I had helped design for the Smithsonian's National Museum of the American Indian in 1999. It involves producing profiles of Native communities using ethnographic fieldwork as well as bibliographic research on those communities. The text predominantly derives from interviews with community members, so that they themselves are explaining their communities to the reader. This is a mediated form of ethnographic representation, what Kurin (1997) calls "culture brokering." As the geographer, with a clear map of what categories of information I want to present, I work with the community members who actually provide the content.

From the outset, this involves the task of convincing reluctant Indigenous participants to grant me interviews that I would edit and post on the internet for the world to see. Although appropriate methodologies of informed consent, review and editing, and final approval worked to assure the empowerment of the community in determining the content, there is still that potential reaction of *Who the hell are you that we should share this with you and with the world*? One thing I knew for certain was that this work demanded an extraordinarily high level of integrity from me. In approaching these communities, I had to demonstrate honesty and integrity in my very *being*. Everything about me, my methodology, and the project's design and purpose had to be *pono*, or this was not going to work. Consequently, the project can be understand by what Wilson (2008) would call "research as ceremony." It's not just about my doing, but about my Being.

Hence as I undertake my work, I am doing my *ho'oponopono* practice in advance to clean up with the people and places with whom I am working. And, I am opening myself to the uncertainty of the journey, putting myself in a space where I may be mindful enough and guided to do what is *pono* and away from what is not *pono*, all the time bearing in mind that I am a catalyst that may produce unexpected consequences. Once one is in this frame of mind and positioned in this manner to do fieldwork, actually going into the field and doing this kind of work in Indigenous settings still isn't easy, but the process leads to deep and profound experiences of place.

Walking the Land

The great adventure of any field-based cross-cultural study is having one's framework of the world expanded, challenged, and reshaped by the encounter. The first and most explicit encounter with an Indigenous geography is the grasping of a spatial-cultural system very different from one's own. It's straightforward cultural geography work in the best tradition of the discipline, combining the drive to understand more deeply and to grasp in a more personal, physical way, what this landscape means and how it works. Again, each cultural system involves a different mode of production, set of social relations, structure of power, and cultural understanding. However paved over by colonization, this basic geography is a starting point for Indigenous-geography research. If we as cultural geographers are going to "get it," we have to engage with this as best we can. Although we are outsiders whose understanding will always be partial at best, we need to engage empathetically and viscerally. We're not going to grasp any of it if we don't get our feet on the ground.

So, I have found in every case that a first step—and many steps thereafter—is to *walk the land*. This usually involves both an initial reconnaissance shortly after my arrival, as well as ongoing sojourns during the course of the research. In the first case, this involves a semi-methodical field reconnaissance—on foot and by car as necessary—to familiarize myself with the layout of the place, the cultural landscape, the natural environment, the commercial activities, and whatever is there. It invokes both our skills as trained geographers to begin interpreting the cultural landscape, spatial organization, and physical environment of the place—the external side of place-based understanding—and our phenomenological skills to feel the place, to let the land (and sea and air) speak to us, and have our own existential relationship with the place unfiltered or distracted by the input of other people. This is just groundwork, and many things will be meaningless to me until my guides explain them, but at least I have an initial sense of place and am already asking myself questions that may be useful in the interviews to come.

From there, the process becomes informed by the ethnographic information and personal interaction with the community members, going to the various places mentioned by the participants or found in the bibliographic research. There are the places of which you are told and not taken to but which you have to explore on your own, or places to which you are taken but make a return trip on your own to explore in greater depth. Many of these are easy and obvious, but some of them involve real adventure to locate. Caves, ruins, legendary sites, and storied places—these can involve difficult and even dangerous exploration, invariably done on my own. And the medium is the message: the trouble it takes to get to these places, or to locate places long forgotten, brings us closer to the land, and closer to the experience of the people who once used these sites. Next to the interviews with elders, I find this is the most meaningful part of the fieldwork.

I place "walking the land" in distinction from the requisite site visits with local informants. Walking with a guide is certainly a major part of the fieldwork, and most of the important sites are within close access to the village being studied. Those interactions with people and place where you are asking questions of your guide as you go can be rewarding for the guide as well, as often she or he takes for granted things in the landscape that are reawakened as meaningful when you point them out and ask about them. In one such case neighbors came out and all started sharing their childhood stories about the object in question. The researcher can serve as a catalyst for reawakening interest, discussion, and new awareness of cultural sites.

But there is something critically experiential about walking the land alone using all six senses[3] to grasp a sense of place unmediated by others; to come to one's own relationship with the locale. Of course, walking the land must be done mindfully. On Saipan, my community contact warned me repeatedly not to go walking across people's properties, and I later learned that the danger was quite real. But, I had always intended to stick to the roads anyway.

Place as Message

Long before I read Keith Basso's (1996) work, "Wisdom Sits in Places," my Hawaiian colleague Carlos Andrade had elaborated to me how Hawai'i's storied places "provide lessons, examples, through the words and through the eyes of the stories and of our ancestors" (Andrade 2001). He pointed out that "place-names themselves are messages from the ancestors that contain warnings, or urgings to look at something important there. They're stories about how to live" (*Pacific Worlds* 2001). He was pointing to the example of Keʻe ("avoidance") Beach at Haʻena, Kauaʻi, that had once been sacred and *kapu* ("taboo"), as an example where the name prompted you to a course of action for your own safety.

In an earlier work (Herman 1999), I examined Hawaiian place-names and how they differ qualitatively from the more recent overlay of American, Anglophone place-names that took hold particularly during the Territorial period (1900–1959) when the islands were a US colony. I have seen this also on Guam (Herman 2008c). Compared to the United States, where place-names are so often commemorative, Indigenous place-names tend to reflect greater sensitivity to the environment and greater influence of cultural meanings and practices.

Gilgillan (1886), a missionary who lived among the Ojibway in Minnesota, wrote that "the Ojibway Indian is a very close observer, a name either of a person, or a place with him always *means something*, and is never a mere arbitrary designation as with us, but expresses the *real essence of the thing*, or its dominating idea as it appears to him." Other writers either deplored the allegedly "prosaic character" of American Indian place-names (Read 1934) or alternatively overromanticized Indian connections with nature (Pearce 1951; Vogel 1963); nonetheless, the characteristics of Native place-naming practices show a more acute attention to the particular and eschew commemoration of people (see Waterman 1922).

Thornton (1997) points out that place-names intersect language, thought, and environment: they provide valuable insights into cultural understanding of the world and how the landscape is used to communicate those understandings. Studying this intersection of language, culture, and landscape was most prominently pioneered by Waterman (1922) and Boaz (1934), though linguists of varying competencies have explored American Indian place-names since Schoolcraft (1845) and Trumbull ([1881] 1974). Place-names are the first, but by no means the last, area of indigenous-geography research where language is important.

Much of what makes an Indigenous geography unique is encoded in the language: geographic schema, terminology, classifications, and categories that map out a very different but very pragmatic and coherent notion of places, their uses, and the responsibilities of people in and to these places and to each other. Language is the key to understanding the cultural messages of places. In Hawaiian language, winds and rains of different valleys have distinct personal names—there are twelve named winds in the little valley of Ha'ena alone, each with different characteristics and each expressing meaning. The use of place-names in Hawaiian poetry and chant is powerful and has been aptly discussed by Luomala (1964), Pukui, Elbert, and Mo'okini (1974), Handy and Handy (1972), Kimura (1983), and Pi'ianai'a (n.d.).

Also, in language are the words to designate different kinds of places, different use areas, and all the categories and taxonomies of places that make up the cultural landscape in the terminology of the community itself. This includes terms of direction, as well as rich cultural understandings of the directions that are particularly characteristic in American Indian traditions. Without access to the language, one misses some of these messages and this richness of expression about place. So it behooves us, as researchers, to gain as much of the Native language as we can, or at least to investigate areas of geographic terminology and taxonomy.

Place and Experience

The phrase "the power of place" is a cliché for the importance of geography in everyday life. But, places have power, and visiting places affects us. Places evoke feelings. Granted, "feeling" is a mediated experience, filtered by one's thoughts and experiences, so sense of place can be highly subjective. Other times, the energy of a place is so clear and overwhelming that it is hard to dispute. Here too it is up to us to be informed by the culture we are researching, to listen to their understanding of the world and the relationships with animals, plants, and spirits. Part of this is found in the two layers of knowledge and language discussed in the previous sections. But moving beyond these, places speak to us directly.

Indigenous cultures worldwide have identified sites of particular energy, or places where the boundary between the manifest and unmanifest worlds seems less rigid: sacred places, places magical to varying degrees, places to go for wisdom and guidance. Generally, we find such places in the wilderness. For wilderness itself— the absence of human society and its formations—opens to us the myriad societies of beings with whom we share the planet and the various forces of nature within which they operate. So, it is here that we go to learn from the earth itself: How does this place speak to you?

For me, no matter how many maps I have of the universe as a fluid place, I don't normally live in a society for which that is an actual ontology. In Hawai'i, for the Hawaiians I work with, it very much is a lived reality. I can't experience that the way they do, but I can listen and learn, and adapt my own ontology. My own experience becomes informed by Hawaiians and Hawaiian culture. But it's up to me to do the work.

Elsewhere I have elaborated the relationship between the unmanifest world

(*Po*), and the manifest world (*Ao*) in Hawaiian cosmology (Herman 1999). Energies and entities are understood as flowing back and forth between these two realms. Gods manifest as plants, animals, and phenomena. Deceased family members can be deified and in turn can manifest as sharks, owls, and other forms, and this appearance of the spiritual in the material is not abnormal. Modern Hawaiians often tell me stories of experiences they have had that one might call "supernatural" but to them reflect a coherent and reasonable worldview. Understanding nature and the spirit world as alive, aware, and interactive with humanity makes for a different relationship to the world; it invokes more care, more respect, and the responsibility to tread more consciously.

This brings us back to walking the land. The solo journeys to remote places, informed by the host culture, give us that opportunity to have our own experiences of place: to stand there and listen, and feel, and to try to imagine ourselves in the place of the old ones who once were there and grasp at how they might have experienced this place.

For my project on Nuʻuanu Valley, I had thorough documentation of the sites in the valley from previous researchers (Sterling and Summers 1978) who culled through the historical documents and interviews with elders. But the landscape had changed considerably in the fifty to one hundred years since most of those statements were made, and painstaking research on the ground was required. In the end, I located most of the sites, including legendary spots and important sacred places that disappeared off maps a century ago and are probably known to very few people today. It is easy to revel, Indiana Jones–like, in the thrill of "discovery." But these were opportunities to respect these sites and the spirits that may dwell there, to feel the *mana* (power, energy) of these places, and to experience them as part of a landscape still present yet invisible.

Across these different aspects of the field experience, there is the "deeper sense of place" that comes from weaving together an Indigenous geography. It is a story of how layers of Indigenous cultural landscape work together and transform one's sense of place and of being in those places. In any historic place, we have the opportunity to extend our senses, our imagination, our experience of *being* into a level deeper than the contemporary landscape affords. In places of Indigenous legendary importance, we can not only reflect on the meaning of the stories of these places and what they teach us, but open ourselves to the power of place that is undoubtedly why the people of old pointed these sites out to begin with. Place is the crucible of our deeper understanding, in which we are transformed through an alchemy involving Indigenous knowledge. Our obligation to do right by the community informs that. We may go alone, but we do so in the context of our relationships and responsibilities.

Project as Voyage

These various experiences and engagements with place lie within the context of the much larger voyage that is the research project itself: the experience of working with the community and the challenges of ethnographic fieldwork generally. There are culture gaps to be negotiated. There are temporal gaps between the "traditional" culture we may have studied and the contemporary amalgam—with all its mixed values, tensions, and struggles—in which we are working; and there is the reconciling of what we are doing with the needs and aspirations of the community such that we are helping to dismember—rather than perpetuate—a colonial legacy.

In the course of this kind of project, we are working with Native peoples and historical texts to tell their stories of these places. Our experience of the work and the product we create—the story we tell—are intertwined: they are facets of the same journey. Understanding them as taking place within a web of responsibilities and impacts should hone our sense of responsibility: the role of *being* for all involved. And with knowledge comes responsibility to share knowledge when it is called for by members of the community, and not to share certain information with others.

We need to be mindful that our research produces a product—whether a journal article, a website, or whatever—and that product also travels through space and time. And other people's paths intersect with it by reading it, and sometimes then they intersect with our own paths by contacting us for further information. Our work has ongoing impacts of which we have no control. So there is a responsibility not only in the knowledge we gain, but in what we produce with it. That responsibility is even greater when we work with Indigenous peoples, the need to be *pono* more acute.

In these undertakings, we are "in the canoe," steering a project through the time/space/people milieu. Working in concert with the participants, we are both mediating and producing information, interpretation, and representation of this place and these people. For its duration at least, we are all intersected by the project, traveling together for a time until the project comes to its conclusion. As project director, one takes the role of the navigator whose paramount responsibilities are not just for the project and its results, but also for managing the relations and participation of everyone and everything involved and seeing the journey safely and productively to a close. One doesn't know, when setting off, which way the winds will blow, or how hard. One doesn't know all the reefs, currents, and shoals to be navigated, and one will have to act in the moment. But when you place yourself in the manner of being *pono*, then those "chance" encounters become meaningful, even powerful.

The research project is a subjourney within one's life voyage. It is a highly dynamic experience that, whether or not we work with it as such, will enhance our being in powerful ways. This *is* the spiritual path. If we recognize that and work with it, then we are engaging in our own *becoming* through the act of fieldwork. The more we engage with this process consciously, the more we experience *becoming* during the course of our research. And we walk away from it changed. I am changed, they are changed, and the understanding of the place has been augmented. The place has spoken to me, taught me lessons. The participants have shared the lessons they have learned and perhaps come to see things in a new way through their encounter with me and my project. It may have them asking new questions of themselves or of this place, inasmuch as it has made me ask new questions of myself.

This is a lesson I have learned from my research with Indigenous peoples. But I would go further to say that in any endeavor, we are in the canoe. We participants come into it from our different trajectories; we are crewmates together to accomplish the goal, and then we move on—sometimes together, sometimes not. But it is how we are *Being*, as we do what we do, that is the most important matter of all. It may take a lifetime to become fully human, so best to work at it in every opportunity.

Notes

1. This version of the story is derived from the Anishinaabe section of the "Our Universes" exhibit at the Smithsonian National Museum of the American Indian, and originates in consultation with Anishinaabe elders.

2. The site is online at www.pacificworlds.com. All aspects of it are free and noncommercial.

3. In Buddhism, the mind is the sixth sense, and its sense-objects are thoughts.

References

Andrade, Carlos. 2001. *Pacific Worlds Haʻena website: Footprints.* http://www.pacific-worlds.com/haena/stories/stories.cfm.

Basso, Keith H. 1996. "Wisdom Sits in Places: Notes on a Western Apache Landscape." In *Senses of Place,* edited by Steven Feld and Keith H. Basso, 53–90. Santa Fe, NM: School of American Research Press.

Boas, Franz. 1934. *Geographical Names of the Kwakiutl Indians.* New York: Columbia University Press.

Campbell, Joseph, with Bill Moyers. 1988. *The Power of Myth.* New York: Doubleday.

Capra, Fritjof. 1975. *The Tao of Physics.* Boston: Shambhala.

De Blij, Harm. 1981. *Geography: Regions and Concepts.* Hoboken, NJ: John Wiley and Sons.

Gilfillan, Rev. Joseph A. 1886. "Minnesota Geographical Names Derived from the Ojibway Language." *Geological and Natural History Survey of Minnesota, 15th Annual Report*, 451–77.

Grof, Stanislav. 1985. *Beyond the Brain: Birth, Death, and Transcendence in Psychotherapy.* Albany: State University of New York Press.

Handy, E. S. C., and E. G. Handy. 1972. *Native Planters in Old Hawaiʻi: Their Life, Lore, and Environment.* Bernice P. Bishop Museum Bulletin 233. Honolulu: Bishop Museum Press.

Herman, RDK. 1999. "The Aloha State: Place Names and the Anti-Conquest of Hawaiʻi." *Annals, Association of American Geographers* 89 (1): 76–92.

———. 2008a. "Pu'u Kohola: Spatial Genealogy of a Hawaiian Symbolic Landscape." In *Symbolic Landscapes,* edited by Gary Backhaus and John Murungi, 91–108. New York: Springer.

———. 2008b. "Reflections on the Importance of Indigenous Geography." *American Indian Culture and Research Journal* 32 (3): 73–88.

———. 2008c. "Inscribing Empire: Guam and the War in the Pacific National Historical Park." *Political Geography* 27 (6): 630–51.

Jung, Carl. 1954. "On the Nature of the Psyche." In *Collected Works,* 2nd ed., 8:159–236. Princeton, NJ: Princeton University Press.

———. 1961. *Memories, Dreams, Reflections.* New York: Vintage Books.

Kimura, L. L. 1983. "The Hawaiian Language." In *Native Hawaiian Study Commission: Report on the Culture, Needs, and Concerns of Native Hawaiians,* 173–203. Washington: Native Hawaiian Study Commission.

Kurin, Richard. 1997. *Reflections of a Culture Broker: A View from the Smithsonian.* Washington, DC: Smithsonian Institution Press.

Luomala, K. 1964. "Creative Processes in Hawaiian Use of Place Names in Chants." In "Lectures and Reports 4th International Congress for Folk-Narrative Research, in Athens." *Laographia* 22:34–37.

Pacific Worlds. 2000. "Hawai'i—Ha'ena." http://www.pacificworlds.com/haena/index.cfm.

———. 2001. "Hawai'i—Nu'uanu." http://www.pacificworlds.com/nuuanu/index.cfm.

Pearce, T. M. 1951. "Some Indian Place Names of New Mexico." *Western Folklore* 10 (3): 245–47.

Pi'ianai'a, I. A. n.d. "The Expression of Place in Hawaiian Folk Songs." Manuscript, University of Hawai'i.

Pukui, M. K., S. H. Elbert, and E. Mo'okini. 1974. *Place Names of Hawai'i.* 2nd ed. Honolulu: University of Hawai'i Press.

Read, William Alexander. 1934. *Florida Place-Names of Indian Origin and Seminole Personal Names.* Baton Rouge: Louisiana State University Press.

Robertson, Iain, and Penny Richards, eds. 2003. Introduction to *Studying Cultural Landscapes,* 1–18. London: Arnold.

Schoolcraft, Henry R. 1845. *Report of the Aboriginal Names and Geographical Territory of the State of New York.* Part I. *Valley of the Hudson.* New York: Printed for the author.

Smith, Linda Tuhiwai. 1999. *Decolonizing Methodologies: Research and Indigenous Peoples.* London: Zed Books.

Sterling, Elspeth P., and Catherine C. Summers. 1978. *Sites of Oahu.* Honolulu: Bishop Museum Press.

Thornton, Thomas F. 1997. "Anthropological Studies of Native American Place Naming." *American Indian Quarterly* 21 (2): 209–28.

Trumbull, J. Hammond. [1881] 1974. *Indian Names of Places etc., in and on the Borders of Connecticut: With Interpretations of Some of Them.* Facsimile ed. Hamden, CT: Archon Books.

Vogel, Virgil J. 1963. *Indian Place Names in Illinois.* Pamphlet Series no. 4. Springfield: Illinois State Historical Society.

Waterman, T. T. 1922. "The Geographical Names Used by the Indians of the Pacific Coast." *Geographical Review* 12 (2): 175–94.

Wilson, Shawn. 2008. *Research Is Ceremony: Indigenous Research Methods.* Black Point, NS: Fernwood.

Anagyuk (Partner)
Personal Relationships and the Exploration of Sugpiaq Fishing Geographies in Old Harbor, Alaska
LAURIE RICHMOND

> Places, we realize, are as much a part of us as we are
> part of them, and senses of place—yours, mine, and
> everyone else's—partake complexly of both.
> —Keith Basso, *Wisdom Sits in Places*

When I traveled to Old Harbor, a remote Alaska Native fishing community of 230 on Kodiak Island, Keith Basso's *Wisdom Sits in Places* is the only book that I brought with me (Basso 1996). Its dog-eared pages followed me on skiff rides, camping trips, and to the various houses of generous community members who took me in. My research in Old Harbor dealt with the impact of fisheries management strategies on Alaska Native fishermen. I planned to explore the way that fisheries and wildlife management policies impacted and interacted with local relationships to place. In this regard, Basso and others who endeavored to explore the ineffable concept of "sense of place" served as my guides (e.g. Basso 1996; Feld and Basso 1996; Erdrich 1988; Chatwin 1988; Brody 1981). After years of coming back to Old Harbor each summer as well as one fall and winter, I began to realize that the bulk of my understanding of sense of place in Old Harbor did not derive from my more academic-minded surveys, interviews, or community-based mapping projects, but rather from the deep, complicated, and eternally treasured friendships that emerged when my scholarly guard was down. In his work with the Western Apache, Basso describes how senses of place persist both on the community and individual level. In Old Harbor, I discovered a scale of relating to place that was somewhere between the two. Through the movements, experiences, and yes friction (!) shared by two friends, places can become co-inhabited, co-created, and co-sensed.

During my stay in Old Harbor I spent some time working at the village's only general store. I worked there as a favor to a friend who owned the store and needed to leave town for a long stretch. Most days I didn't mind too much because it afforded me the opportunity to strike up conversations with the various community members and fishermen who stopped in. But, I hated working at the store when it was a calm sunny day. On the wind- and rain-battered island of Kodiak, nice days are a rarity to be pounced upon by any number of outdoor activities—all beginning with the step of rubber boots into a skiff.

On such a nice day, Laurence, an elder with whom I have developed a friendship, comes into the store, and I ask him what he's up to. He says, "Nothin'—notta thing." We both agree that it would be a great day to go out. Finally, I look at him and say, "Well, let's do it. Let's get the hell outta here and head to the cabin for a night." I leave a handwritten sign on the store indicating that it will be closed for two days. Next, we go through a rapid process of packing for a night at the cabin. I grab some things: sleeping bag, rain gear, extra clothes, a warm jacket, books, notebooks, sunscreen, water, and stuff them into a dry bag. Then at his house, we gather some auxiliary food: pilot bread crackers, candy bars, rice, canned beans, and spices. We will catch fish to eat. We grab guns, fishing rods, a chain saw, a wheel barrow for hauling, extra life jackets, and a bunch of other stuff. I sit down at the skiff and start piling the monstrous amount of stuff that we bring for only one night's stay. It is kind of incredible considering how little Laurence actually owns. He goes back for one more thing. When he returns, I say, "I think that you forgot something." He looks up and says, "What?" I say, "You forgot the kitchen sink." He scoffs and pushes us off. We are on our way. The sun beats on our faces; the wind blows. As he steers the skiff, Laurence smiles widely and says to me, "This is the best kind of partner—one that will leave at a moment's notice."

The word he uses—partner—is a loose translation of a Sugstun[1] word *anagyuk*. It does not refer to the romantic couple kind of partner, but to a deep friendship—to the relationship between two people who go hunting, adventuring, and merry-pranking together. The relationship between anagyuk is also very geographical. It is rooted in experiences that happen in the landscape: in movement throughout the island, adventures in the ocean, beaches, land, and mountains. It is rooted in places: cabins, camping spots, fishing holes, and secret hunting spots that only the two share. Under somewhat unlikely circumstances, Laurence and I became anagyuk—and for the record, this is the name he gave our relationship. Over the course of several years, I hung out with Laurence and traveled in his skiff around the island. These times are where I, a fisheries researcher concerned with growth trends and scientific plots, with policy language and regulatory areas, began to learn about a new, fuzzier and hauntingly beautiful personal way of knowing and being connected with place.

Laurence is something of a recluse. He lives alone in a house that is separated from the village by a beach road that is flooded out during high tide. That house is in addition to the cabin he has on a lagoon many miles by sea from the village. He has no electricity or running water. He collects his water from a neighboring stream, which in the summer nearly dries up, leaving sketchy dirt-flaked water to which he pays no mind. He lives in a small one-room cabin with furniture and dishes that are well worn with age, and a line that holds rows of drying, dirt-encrusted cotton socks. In the winter he leaves the window cracked opened so that cold birds can rest and sleep under his drying laundry. He has a small generator that he uses each night to watch an hour or two of TV. His favorite show is *Cheers*. He still tells the story about when he visited one of his sons who has moved to Maine. He flew into Boston and on their way up to Maine he asked his daughter-in-law if they could stop at the Cheers pub to have a beer and take a picture. She said no because they were in a hurry and she had to get to Maine. He still fumes over this when he thinks about it. It just would have taken a couple of minutes. He has told me the story at least three times. These are the kinds of things that make him upset.

He talks about his respect for animals and recounts in detail the community of animals (deer, bears, birds, foxes) that he has watched pass by his cabin, then reminisces about the days when he was a young hunter shooting baby cubs for fun to watch how angry their mothers would get: always simultaneously confirming and contradicting any expectation that one might have of the "true native." Sometimes he can come across as unrelentingly ornery, mean, and unsentimental. Other times his eyes relax and you can see the underpinnings of true compassion and sorrow. He has such nostalgia for the way that life used to be, sometimes it is painful to even hear him talk about it. He says: "That was a good life. Never going to come back. Never."

Although every generation is nostalgic about the past, it is hard not to see some truth in Laurence's yearnings. Life in the village is vastly different from the way that he grew up. Increased regulations on hunting and fishing have eroded many of the outdoor freedoms that he enjoyed growing up. Laurence lived a life working hard and living free. He hunted, fished, worked in canneries; he worked as a bear guide leading outsiders on hunts; he hunted foxes and sold their pelts. He would seasonally roam the island with his friends—boating, hiking, fishing, hunting, and eating whatever animal or fish crossed their path along the way. He played pranks, lived with different families in different villages, slept in cabins and *barabras* (traditional Sugpiaq structures dug into the ground).

The word *anagyuk* has history for Laurence. His previous and real anagyuk, a man nicknamed Lobaki, has long since passed away, and I get the sense that when this man died, so did a piece of Laurence. He talks about him wistfully, almost as someone reminisces of a past lover. Laurence grew up in the village of Kaguyak, which is a bit southwest of Old Harbor. Laurence always moved about the island from job to job and adventure to adventure. One day he ended up in Old Harbor and met Lobaki. As many have recounted, it was love at first sight. From the minute they met they were joined at the hip. They were infamous rabble-rousers. There are countless stories of the kinds of pranks they would pull on fellow village members and the outsiders who would come to visit.

Laurence and Lobaki were bear guides, taking rich American hunters on trips to shoot large bears for display in their homes. For Laurence, this was the best life he ever had. He got to meet people from "all corners of the world. Most nice. Some assholes," but he didn't care, he would be rude right back to the assholes. They had near scares with bears and got to spend summers and falls in the woods and beaches. Laurence stopped being a guide when the guiding regulations and restrictions were put in place. These regulations created a bureaucracy that made it nearly impossible for Native hunters to become official guides. The last Native guide on the island passed away several years ago.

So how did Laurence become my anagyuk? Especially since he has sent many unsuspecting researchers and language recorders scurrying to the door. Laurence and I were introduced by a friend of mine who grew up in Old Harbor but has since moved out of the village. She and I worked together at Old Harbor's cultural camp. One day she suggested that we kayak over to his house for a visit. She said that she had always wanted to be closer to Laurence but never got the chance. She felt like he was an elder from whom she could have learned a lot. I am sure that without her I never would have had the stones to go over to his remote home. And for her gift in establishing this friendship, I will forever be grateful. When we met, he told me that I should come back some time, and I did, and we bullshitted. Then I visited again. Then we went out in the skiff. Then we planned to go out in the skiff again. See, being a partner isn't in the talking so much as in the doing.

Laurence and I spent three summers, one fall, and one winter, hanging out and hatching little adventures. When the weather wasn't nice we would bullshit, tease each other, listen to the radio, watch for wildlife, and play cards. On nice days when the tides were right we were outta there, riding hog-happy in the skiff throughout the seascape.

We went to Barling Bay for humpies (pink salmon), to Herring Lagoon to stay at his cabin, to Three Saints Bay to look at ruins of an old cannery, to the edge of Kaiugnak Bay to catch black bass, to Big Crick to cast for silver salmon, to Sitkalidik Island to gather salmonberries, to Port Hobron to walk through the wreckage of the abandoned whaling ship, to MacDonald's lagoon to catch a view of the open ocean, to Amee Bay to go beachcombing, and to Fang Point to tie driftwood logs to the back of the skiff and drag them home for firewood. All of this traveling in the open water exhausted me. Laurence used to tease me about my propensity for taking naps on the beach when we landed somewhere. He said,

"You're just asking to get attacked by a bear sleeping on the beach like that."

On one trip, Laurence took me to Refuge Rock, a place of a tragic history for the Sugpiaq people of Kodiak Island. To get there we drove down MacDonald's Lagoon, a long bay. At the end of it, we parked the skiff and had to hike over a tall berm. From the top of the hill we could see the open ocean and a view of a small rock island that one could only walk to during low tide. During the beginning of Russian rule, the Russians had planned to attack and subjugate the Sugpiaq people in the area. To escape, the people hid on this island which is now known as Refuge Rock. The Russians found them and attacked. Rather than be killed or taken captive, many people jumped off the cliffs of the island to their death. It is estimated that five hundred men, women, and children were killed during the attack. Months later, a woman from Old Harbor tells me that the Sugstun word for this place is *Awa'uq*[2] which translates to "we are numb."

As we are cutting through the reeds to get a view of the island, I ask Laurence about what happened to his ancestors here. Never one to get sentimental in even the most emotional of places, he says mockingly, "I don't know, I forgot to ask them." I ask another question, and he says, "Shut up, you." I am not fazed by this because incessant teasing is our way. It is the way of anagyuk. I ask him yet another question about the place and he says, "I forgot to look it up in the book," which is a joke, knowing that none of this stuff is in a book. To which I reply, "Which book is that: the book of assholes?" To which he counter-replies with a smirk, "Yeah, and you wrote it." After this banter we pause in silence for a long while, listening and watching as the waves crash against this historically marked geographical feature.

One day in the skiff we see a large gray carcass floating. We slow down next to it, and I say, "Wow, what is that?" He says confidently, "It is a dead seal." I am not so sure. I say, "Are you sure, it is so gray, it doesn't really look like a seal." He says, "Yeah, it's a seal. I wouldn't have said so if I weren't sure. If you fell into the ocean and floated for that long you would be gray like that too." But, I can see that the floating body has claspers (shark sexual organs), which I know from my fish biology classes at the university far away, is indicative of sharks. I smile and say, "I don't think it's a seal, go back and check." He groans loudly in such a convincing portrayal of anger that I have to ask him: "Are you really mad or just fake mad?" He laughs and pulls the skiff next to the carcass. When we get close, we realize that it is in fact a shark—probably killed as it was cut out of a tangled fishing net or line. He says, "Well, I'll be darned" and I laugh in triumph. Western outsider knowledge, perhaps just this once, trumping the old man.

When Laurence and I are out at his cabin this year, we go along the beach to cut up driftwood to store for future use in the woodstove. After about an hour of working with the wood, I look back toward the cabin and see a little brown dot emerging from the grass right in front of the cabin. A bear! A cute little bear who has just been sitting there watching us work I am totally amazed. I tell Laurence, and he looks back and says, "Oh yeah, that guy's always watching me." He asks, "Do you have your camera?" I say, "Darn it. No, I left it in the cabin." He says, "Too bad we could have gotten a really good picture." I say, "Shoot." We work for a while, and the bear continues to watch us. I am filled with joy, thinking about this amazing "Sugpiaq moment," in which we are working chopping wood for the stove and a bear is watching us. I couldn't be happier. Finally we are finished, and it is time to head back to the cabin. He says, "Do you see how the bear has moved down closer to the beach?" I say, "Yeah." As we approach the cabin and the bear, Laurence holds his gun, because you never know what a bear is going to do. He jokes that he'll shoot right at him. I tell him no. As we get closer to the bear, I am having more trouble making out its shape—the object does not seem to be turning into a bear form. Until finally I realize it is not a bear at all. It is a giant log that sticks up in the grass with a couple of points that look like ears. When I say, "Hey, it's not a bear, it's a log," Laurence starts laughing uncontrollably. He had of course known the entire time and played the whole the bear's moving, gun-toting scene for kicks.

One day, I bring small USGS maps of Kodiak Island with close-up views of the bays around Old Harbor. I show them to Laurence, and he casually picks up one of the maps and holds it out, moving it back and forth until it comes into focus. "Huh," he says, and I can see how in his mind he is doing the reverse of what I do with the maps. Instead of working from the map to the world, he's trying to get a bearing on how the entirety of the landscape that he has come to know through countless journeys and labors corresponds to the lines squiggled on this laminated page. After a moment it seems to click in place; he gets his bearings within the paper landscape and begins to look at the map as if he is reminiscing with an old friend. His thoughts seem to wander. He doesn't share much with me, letting out a few huh's, grunts, and sighs. He reads the English names that they have given for the various bays, lagoons, and rivers of the island, many of which he is seeing for the first time. He seems to delight in sounding out these new names, imagining what others who named the landscape might have encountered. He says, "'Deadman's Bay,' oh-wee, that's a good name for that one. I used to hate going fishing down in there. It is so deep. You could get lost at the end of that bay. Was always happy to be done fishing there."

In this moment, I see that these multiple ways of knowing and naming places might be able to coexist; they don't always have to be in tension. The landscape surrounding Kodiak certainly has been imbued with all kinds of relations of power. It contains unmistakable traces of colonial influence. Although this reality should be unpacked and revealed, we can take a moment to delight in the pure pleasure of

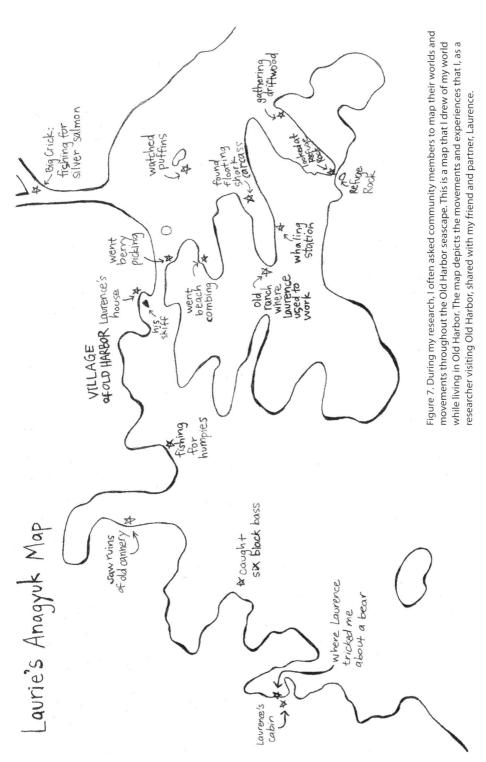

Figure 7. During my research, I often asked community members to map their worlds and movements throughout the Old Harbor seascape. This is a map that I drew of my world while living in Old Harbor. The map depicts the movements and experiences that I, as a researcher visiting Old Harbor, shared with my friend and partner, Laurence.

place—of the multiple, layered, and changing relationships between the landscape, the individuals, and their partners who are inextricably wrapped up in one another. Place-names, whether in English, Russian, Sugstun, or even the numbers and letters of fishing zones, speak to the wonder and possibility of locations experienced by people—by anagyuk.

I am reminded of the times that I have watched representatives of the Alutiiq (Sugpiaq) museum work with elders to record and write down the Sugstun names for the oceanic places throughout the island. We would sit with a few elders and a giant nautical map and painstakingly go through all of the bay names asking what each one was called in Sugstun. Without fail, each time we would end up reaching a point where the group could not recall the names of any more places. Either I or a museum representative would point to a bay and say, "What is the Sugstun name of that bay?" The group would look at each other and sigh, "Gosh, what is the name of that place? It's on the tip of my tongue." Then someone would say, "Hey, so-and-so would know the name of that, you should go ask him." Another would say, "Yeah, so-and-so used to fish there all the time; you should ask him the name of that bay." As a group, they try to remember who, among those that are still alive, most inhabited that place. The name of a place resides within the person who most sojourned there.

In my travels through the seascape with Laurence, a deeply personal connection to the landscape became clear. For Laurence, these places on the land or on the sea contain memories. They were places where loved ones were lost at sea, where times were spent with friends who have long since passed, where plans were hatched and lives were carried out. Some of the stories he told me; most he didn't. Landscape, so often generalized in the form of maps and charts, boundary lines and borders, exists too on the tiniest of scales—in the minute filaments connecting heartstrings to terrain.

This personal connection with the landscape can be tenuous, though. It can and has been interrupted by natural resource policies that act to shape and regulate the relationship individuals have with the places they have come to know. It's not that residents of Old Harbor are unconcerned about "conservation" or the well-being of the resources in the area (though this is not to say that they are perfect conservationists either). But from their perspective, these policies can only be seen as a troublesome and unending string of interventions into their relationship with this place. Bear-guiding restrictions work to prohibit community members like Laurence from maintaining a guiding career. Privatization of commercial fisheries limits fishing opportunities and the subsequent fishing journeys throughout the island. The delineation of regulatory areas in the local fisheries restricts the movement of Old Harbor fishermen through space. Seasonal, geographic, and take restrictions on the harvest of local resources such as the humpies, the silvers, the reds, the kings, the seals, the puffins, the oiuduks (clams), the deer, the bear, and even the driftwood and whale bones that line the beach, all serve to intervene in the seasonal round of resource use.

Laurence told me, "I laugh at them and each new thing that they think to regulate." Earnest regulators who are concerned with the status of a particular species might not fully comprehend the ways they also affect these personal maps of place. But, culture and the relationship with place are never static. These policies and regulations have a way of being incorporated into the process of people and place. This explains why on the opening day of deer season, Laurence smiles at me with a toothy grin and says, "Grocery store's open."

When I am not in Alaska, Laurence will sometimes call me for a quick conversation, never one to linger on. This means so much to me. One spring we discussed my visit the coming summer, and he said, "I sure am looking forward to having you out here." I tell him that I am looking forward to seeing him too. Laurence has become one of the most important people in my life. And I now know that he—our friendship and the things we have learned together—is the reason I came on this journey at all.

The house from which I write about this research is filled with maps of the island and pictures of places. One day a friend of mine looked at the maps and asked, "Are those hanging here for your research or just for you?" I paused for a second and said, "I don't even know how to answer that question—the two are so intertwined." I see that the maps on my wall are as much to reminisce as to write a research paper. They contain my memories as well as the ones of people I stayed with and interviewed. I started to think about my place in all this. I thought about how whenever one of us travels by the spot on the beach where he pointed to a log and told me it was a bear—either in real life or on a paper map—we will at least have a chuckle in our heads thinking: that is where Laurence so easily tricked Laurie into believing a piece of wood was a bear. I began to understand that on these skiff rides with Laurence, my anagyuk, my partner, I humbly, improbably even, had become a part of this landscape. And it—well—it had forever become a part of me.

Addendum: When I first mentioned (over the phone) to Laurence that I might want to write about him he said, "piss on you," and hung up fairly soon after. His reaction affected me deeply. I felt like I had betrayed him and our trust. I began to seriously question my role and purpose as an academic scholar in an indigenous setting. As a researcher was I basically a glorified spy? How could I do this job and honor my relationships? In the immediate future, I was prepared to give up on this writing project altogether.

The next time that Laurence called, I discussed our relationship and the writing process with him in a way that I never had before. In a way, this particular project sparked a new kind of openness and communication between us—both about what I was doing in Old Harbor and about what our relationship means to each other. I told him that I was looking at fisheries issues and that through him and other people in Old Harbor I had begun to learn that fishing regulations are more than mere policies or changes to protect fish—they also affect the lives of fishermen in deeply personal ways. I wanted to be able to convey this kind of personal story in my writing. I then told him that I would never write anything about him that he didn't want me to and would drop the idea completely. He told me that he was glad that I brought it up and that he had been thinking about it a lot. He said that he would think about it some more and get back to me.

A few days later he called me back and said that he had considered it and that he felt I was right about the fishing policies and that what happened in Old Harbor with the loss of fishing was really bad. He said that when I come to visit I should bring what I wrote and that he had a few other things that he wanted to tell me.

I traveled to Old Harbor that summer and brought with me the above piece of writing. As we sat together in his small cabin I began to nervously read what I had written aloud. He listened, occasionally letting out a laugh, seeming more embarrassed than anything. At the end he barely addressed the content. He told me it was okay to print it. He then said, "I bet those guys back in the university are sure going to get a kick out of some of those stories. Nice things you said about me. Now, let's get out of here."

Three days later we went out on another skiff ride together to pick berries and grab some driftwood. As we entered into a long bay, Laurence turned to me and said, "Have you been to this bay before?" I said, "No I don't think that I have, I think you only took me to MacDonald's lagoon which is one bay over." He smiled and said, "Think about it." In a minute I noticed the wreckage of the whaling station and said, "Oh yeah, we have been down here before." Laurence smiled and he said, "Yes, remember? This is the place where we found the floating shark body, the one from your story."

Notes

Of course, I thank Laurence Ashouwak, my friend and partner, who listened to this piece and came with me on this journey. I will forever be grateful for our friendship. I also thank my good friend La Verne Hutto for introducing us. I am very appreciative of Jay Johnson and Soren Larsen, the editors who put this exciting project together. In addition, I am grateful for Lena Amason's thoughtful comments on an earlier draft. Molly May, Naheed Aaftaab, and the University of Minnesota American Indian Studies work group also provided helpful guidance with the writing. I also thank the Old Harbor tribal council and community for working with me on this research project. Mary Haakanson and Phyllis Clough: thank you for putting up with me my during my visits to the community—your hospitality knows no bounds. I am also grateful to the Alutiiq Museum for allowing me to work with them on place-name projects and helping me learn more about the language and history of the region. My research was supported through the generous assistance of the National Science Foundation, the University of Minnesota Interdisciplinary Center for the Study of Global Change, and the University of Minnesota Consortium on Law and Values in Health, Environment, and the Life Sciences.

1. There is significant debate about what to call the Alaska Native people and related language group from the Kodiak Island, Alaska Peninsula, and parts of the Kenai Peninsula regions. At present, the most commonly used name is Alutiiq. However, these terms derive from the names that Russian settlers gave to the people from the region. Some Alaska Natives from the region have advocated using the terms that their ancestors and elders used to describe their people and language: Sugpiaq to describe the people (meaning "the real people") and Sugstun to describe the language.

2. Stella Krumery, pers. com.; Alutiiq Museum, pers. com.; Jeff Leer, pers. com. The Alutiiq museum staff provided the proper Alutiiq spelling for the word. Many of these place-names and spellings have been generated through the Alutiiq museum's collaboration with Jeff Leer from the Alaska Native Language Center, University of Alaska, Fairbanks.

References

Basso, Keith H. 1996. *Wisdom Sits in Places: Landscape and Language among the Western Apache*. Albuquerque: University of New Mexico Press.

Brody, Hugh. 1981. *Maps and Dreams*. Prospect Heights, IL: Waveland Press.

Chatwin, Bruce. 1988. *The Songlines*. New York: Penguin Books.

Erdrich, Louise. 1988. *Tracks*. New York: Henry Holt.

Feld, Steven, and Keith H. Basso. 1996. *Senses of Place*. Santa Fe, NM: School of American Research Press.

The Micropolitics of Storytelling in Collaborative Research

Reflections on a Mapping Project with the Cheslatta-Carrier Nation in British Columbia

SOREN C. LARSEN

In the summer of 1998 I was a twenty-two-year-old graduate student in anthropology from Kansas living with the Cheslatta band of the Dakelh (Carrier) First Nation in north-central British Columbia.[1] Although I did not know it at the time, interpersonal growth is a common experience for those engaged in long-term collaborative fieldwork (Coffey 1999; Fabian 1979; Young and Goulet 1994), and it is an explicit and fundamental part of inquiry in Indigenous research in particular (Denzin, Lincoln, and Smith 2008; Kovach 2009; Smith 1999). The goal of Indigenous research is not to comprehend the world as an object, but rather to move *through* the world as a way of knowing in a journey that transforms all those involved (Cajete 2000). These transformations, in turn, build relationships that enhance prospects for individual and collective forms of actualization. Interpersonal growth is therefore a central part of Indigenous efforts to achieve self-determination through intellectual and creative activity.

In the pages that follow, I reflect on my experience in a mapping project with the Cheslatta in 1998—the first of what would be six seasons of fieldwork with the community—to explore how the interpersonal dynamics at work in storytelling connect with Indigenous goals for self-determination in the context of collaborative research. Much Indigenous-academic collaboration has, of course, focused directly on storytelling as both a form of cultural expression and a means of cultural survival (Cruikshank 1990; Kovach 2009). Here, I describe what my Cheslatta collaborators taught me about the value of *informal* and *extemporaneous* storytelling in the collaboration process. For them, impromptu storytelling was a culturally appropriate way to build relationships and establish trust, engage and work through the historical legacies of colonialism, and create empathetic, relational understandings that could be shared with others, again through story, within and beyond the research team. I came to see how the Cheslatta were using our collaboration to create opportunities for tales to be told—routinely, spontaneously, as a matter of course—in a "micropolitics" of storytelling (cf. Christensen 2012; Gibson-Graham 2006) that contributes broadly to the interpersonal relationships needed for self-determination.

* * *

I began searching for a Master's thesis topic in anthropology during the fall of 1997, and while on the internet I came across a web page posted by the Cheslatta-Carrier First Nation. The band was asking for assistance in its protest against a hydroelectric dam that the Aluminum Company of Canada (Alcan) intended to build in the region. As an undergraduate, I had done a historical ethnography and mapping project with elderly farmers in Tennessee who had been relocated in the 1940s when the Tennessee Valley Authority (TVA) built the Kentucky Dam. The prospect for comparative research seemed both apparent and attractive. If the Cheslatta had a project they needed help with, I could volunteer my time in exchange for the opportunity to do my thesis work with the community. So I immediately called Mike Robertson, the band's senior policy adviser and the contact listed on the page, to ask if research assistance was needed for the following summer. He said the chief and council would have to vote on it, and that the vote might take some time. Six months later and after several anxiety-ridden followup calls from me (each one revealed that the council still had yet to vote on the matter), Mike called back with a decision: "We don't promise you anything with your research, and I can't guarantee anybody will talk to you. But you're welcome to come to Cheslatta Territory."[2] Undaunted by the caveat and exhilarated by the invitation, I made myself ready within the month and left for British Columbia in May.

Shortly after my arrival, discussions began with Chief Marvin Charlie, the Band Council, and Mike over the research design. I told them of my interests in ethnography and participatory mapping; they replied that the band needed a map of historic land "use and occupancy" for its treaty claim. A government agreement, I learned, started the Treaty Commission five years earlier to address outstanding issues regarding Aboriginal rights and contemporary Native claims to land, resources, and political sovereignty. Unlike in other parts of Canada, British Columbia's colonial governments did not sign treaties with most Native polities in the province, which means that the bulk of these claims are unresolved today. A number of twentieth-century developments—Indigenous activism, court cases and litigation, roadblocks and protest, the recognition of Aboriginal rights in section 35 of the 1982 Constitution Act—compelled contemporary governments to address the issue. The B.C. Claims Task Force was established in 1990, and settlement procedures were inaugurated when the first treaty commissioners were installed in 1993.

The treaty process requires Native groups to provide evidence of traditional territory, often described in the shorthand as "use and occupancy" of the land prior to European sovereignty, which in British Columbia is marked by the Oregon Treaty of 1846. Mapping use and occupancy has been one way to document territory, and this is precisely what the chief and council were asking me to do in the proposed project. The mapping would be complicated, however, because the Cheslatta had not been living in the territory for almost fifty years. In 1952, the federal government's Department of Indian Affairs (DIA) relocated the band from its homeland so that Alcan, the same company as above, could construct the Kenney Dam, Nechako Reservoir, and Skins Lake Spillway for hydroelectricity and aluminum-smelting operations in Kitimat. The spillway was Alcan's response to a request from the Department of Fisheries and Oceans, which was concerned that the drawdown of water in the Nechako River would threaten the salmon fishery in the Fraser watershed. The spillway took surface water from the reservoir, carried it through the Cheslatta River, and deposited it back in the Nechako for the salmon downstream. This diversion, however, converted the Cheslatta River, technically a creek with an average flow of only 100 cubic feet per second, into a drainage channel with flows that would far exceed that volume (Christensen 1995). Much of the band's reserve land would be flooded, so Alcan colluded with the DIA to relocate the community.

According to expert testimony in the band's 1990 court case against the Government of Canada, the DIA officials who arrived in the main Cheslatta village by helicopter on April 21, 1952, allegedly coerced the elders into signing the Surrender documents. At least some of these signatures, most simply lettered "X" on the line, were forged (Christensen 1995). The Cheslatta abandoned their homes, but only after the DIA informed them that the Royal Canadian Mounted Police (RCMP) would force them out if they did not leave voluntarily. The DIA then bulldozed and burned the village, including their Catholic church as well as most of the spirit houses located in the two cemeteries on the site. The band lived in a makeshift refugee camp near Grassy Plains, an Anglo-Canadian settlement some thirty miles to the north, for almost a year until the DIA provided eleven widely scattered parcels of farmland to replace the land lost in what the community came to know, apocalyptically, as "The Flood." Then, in punctuation of a tragedy no one thought could get any worse, Alcan's spillway malfunctioned in 1957, issuing forth a wall of water so colossal that it gouged a seventy-five-foot canyon out of what once was the creek bed and washed away the graves of seventeen ancestors laid to rest in the cemetery on Reserve Number Nine (Christensen 1995). Most of these remains have never been recovered.

This tragic history loomed as the elders and I began working together in the band office's feast hall to produce maps that would illustrate the community's patterns of occupation and resource use before The Flood. We used modified topographic maps showing the terrain prior to 1952 with most European toponyms removed and Indigenous historical references (e.g., the Cheslatta villages and trails) included. With colored pens, the elders depicted their family and group activities on transparent mylar film overlain on the maps. We tape-recorded the accompanying "interviews"—I had drafted a formal and rather lengthy protocol—but the activity turned almost immediately into storytelling. I tried my best to listen, remembering what Mike Robertson told me the day before the first mapping session: "With the elders, just make sure you stay quiet. Be patient; let them talk. The less you say, the better." Playing the microcassettes now over a decade later, I can hear myself listening, long periods of silence in the elders' stories as they map and remember, me wanting to ask so many questions—and I did ask more than a few—but always trying to hold off, cautious not to interrupt the next prospect in the narrative.

There were stories about life before The Flood. Well into her late eighties, Christine McIsak remembered these times vividly:

> Before The Flood, we were never hungry. Down at Cheslatta there was fishing. Oh boy, really good country out there. Big trout, nice and red and fat. My mom would smoke them, and there would be red fat running down. One summer, my dad got a mowing machine at Bella Coola and carried it on horseback all the way up and down the mountains to Cheslatta. When he got it back, all the white men wanted to use that mowing machine. They were jealous! And every winter when we had the big church feast at Christmastime, all the Uncha Lake people would come and all the Anahim people, too. We were all happy that time, gee really happy. Yeah, I miss that country.

There were stories about The Flood. Ann Troy grew up near Grassy Plains, not far from the refugee camp established in the aftermath of exodus:

> Things changed after the land was flooded and my family moved up to the place here at Grassy. They had to move quick because the water was already coming up, so they didn't take too many things, just a few belongings. They left the traps and everything they used to cut hay

with. Then the DIA burned the houses down, just to make sure they didn't come back! Can you believe that? When they got here, it was bad. People were dying. Nobody had anything. But we made it. My daddy bought some land here. He bought an old schoolhouse cheap from the white people, and he dragged it across the field to this land. And so that was our new home. That's where we had all our Masses, in the schoolhouse.

And there were stories about the perseverance of tradition in the wake of The Flood. Chief Marvin Charlie:

In the old days, when my father was teaching me how to hunt and trap, he never told me, "You gotta do this" or "You gotta do that." He was funny. He just does it, and I learn from that. One time, we were sitting by the campfire having supper after hunting all day, and I leaned my gun against a tree. You're not supposed to do that. So he got up, put his plate down, walked over, and hung my gun up on a limb. Then he came back, picked up his plate, sat back down, and said nothing.

We lost so much of our traditional ways when we left the territory. Those ways are coming back now. I'm talking about it. The rest of the elders are talking about it. I remember what I've been taught. The rest of the elders remember what they've been taught.

One day, I was with my son, fishing down at Cheslatta, where my dad used to take me. You always honor the fish you catch by putting the intestines back in the water. But my son doesn't know that. He just throws the fish on the ground. So I take the intestines out and carefully place them in the water. I say nothing. And so that's how he learns, too.

The storytelling almost always seemed more important than the mapping, or at least it took center stage. The Cheslatta tell these stories to keep their connection with territory alive amid the destructive forces set in train by relocation. The stories "re-member" this connection in narratives that evoke and sustain a way of being and knowing based on direct and ongoing interaction with the territory and the intergenerational journey through territorial space (Larsen 2006). The paths traced by these narratives connect the past with the present, bridge the generations, and orient the community toward the future. Storytelling is an essential way of coming to know one's place in the community and its relationship to the world beyond (cf. Cajete 2000; Kovach 2009; Smith 1999).

I was no exception to this storytelling practice, but it was inflected through the process of doing collaborative research. In other words, I gained an identity in the community as the places I inhabited and moved through were "storied" and connected together into a narrative shared by the group. This was my "path" through the community territory, and it was an integral part of the collaboration. It transformed me from an outside researcher into an active participant who was coming to know the community by finding his own place within it. Not just a social place or a metaphorical place, but in the beginning, quite literally a place where I could stay.

My original (and now of course in retrospect, hopelessly naïve) plan for lodging had been to camp out for the duration of the research, using the back of my truck when it rained and taking showers at provincial campgrounds. I simply did not have much money to make it through the summer. Mike let me stay at his ranch in the days immediately after my arrival, but soon he said the band had offered me "a gift," free lodging in a cabin on Reserve Number Eleven. It was an isolated locale. To get there required traveling several miles from Mike's ranch on Uncha Lake Road, then going off-road and directly across a meadow where the cabin sat against a dark emerald-green wall of forest.

The cabin was a two-room spruce-clapboard trapper's hut that hadn't been permanently occupied, or at least not in some long time. The interior revealed this to be the case. Rodent droppings were everywhere. Dirty tattered underwear sat crumpled up in a gross paper-mâché on the water-stained plywood floor (the roof leaked). Some animals had crafted nests out of old newspapers and trash. But I was grateful for the lodging, this gift. I had nothing else, and was amazed at the band's generosity despite not even knowing me. So I cleaned the place up a bit, and though there was no running water or electricity, the woodstove offered warmth when the night got cool, and a wind-up radio Mike lent me provided companionship in the form of CBC Radio. But I was perpetually leery. There were bears—during my time there I saw one crossing the meadow, leisurely and imposing—and also potential passers-by: Mike had warned me about some teenage boys who lived a few miles down the road and liked to cause trouble. Sleeping through the night was no small challenge given my fears and the myriad nocturnal noises stoking these apprehensions.

Then late one evening came a knock at the door. I panicked at first, but then thought it could be Mike. So I rose from my chair and turned the handle. Standing there at the threshold, a Native man. Tall and muscular with oil-black hair and dark eyes, his high cheekbones reflected the dull light of my table lantern. Upon closer inspection, he really was a teenager, probably about eighteen years old, had no car and obviously walked right up to the place. We stared at each other for a moment until he made a motion toward me, and I dodged it by backing off, which had the effect of me appearing to invite him in. So there we stood in the front room, the woodstove burning fiercely.

"You live here, eh?" he asked.

Yes, I said, the Cheslatta offered me this place to stay while I worked for them this summer. My words were shaky, weak. A lump in my throat made it difficult to speak.

"Oh . . ." his voice trailed off. He walked confidently into the back room, looked around like he owned the place. He turned around to face me. "I live down the road. Saw somebody moved in here."

I didn't know what to say. So I asked him if he wanted a cigarette. He grabbed up the offering from my outstretched hand, sat down on the cot and lit the thing. Now he smoked in silence, and it appeared the exchange had broken some of the tension, at least for him.

"Well, this is my grandfather's trapping cabin. Cheslatta says they own it, but they don't." He stared right at me. I explained that I knew nothing about this, that I thought it was Reserve land. "But they don't *own* it, eh?" He waited for me to say something. But I didn't.

He continued, "I lived here two summers ago. Built the chimney and put the woodstove in. Me and my brothers, we still use it for trapping in the winter, too." I said nothing again.

Finally, and matter of factly, he said, "My uncle was murdered in here couple years ago." He ashed his cigarette on the table. "Back there," he gestured to the second room. Now I was stunned, thoughts racing. I honestly did not know how to respond. So I uttered something like, Oh, I'm sorry . . . , but my voice tapered quickly into nothingness.

He put his cigarette out on the plywood floor, stood up, moved toward the door, and looked at me one last time. A little smile appeared on his face just then as he pointed to the ceiling and declared: "You should leave: your roof leaks."

I had had enough of this cabin. I didn't know if the visitor was serious, but I didn't want to test him, either. So the next day, I left the reserve for a provincial campground, and there I resided until the hosts informed me of a small rental house nearby. It had no running water but did offer electricity, undamaged roof, bunk bed, kitchenette, and an incredible view of the lake, all at a price far too cheap to pass on, especially after my parents offered to lend me the funds to pay for the rent. Promptly but delicately, I informed Mike and Chief Charlie of my new residence. To my great relief, both assented and said they understood. The whole thing seemed to be resolved.

Friday of that week, the band hosted what it billed a "Country & Western Dance" in the community hall at Grassy Plains. The women at the band office made sure I was going to come: "We want a dance with the Nedo [white guy]!" The dance turned out to be a wonderful affair. I had good conversations with the elders, danced with the office women, and met more than a few new people. After the dancing was done, a small group of us gathered around one of the tables where the women began feeding me little Dakelh phrases (*mussi cho* means "thank you"; *hadih* means "hello"), laughing heartily at my inchoate pronunciation. At some point in this conversation, Daryl Jack, maintenance man for the band, asked me in a voice loud enough for all to hear, "So, you still in that cabin on Number Eleven?"

Daryl's question stopped everyone from talking. All eyes were on me. Remembering that this had been a "gift," I sheepishly told everyone that no, I had moved out. I really needed electricity to work on my maps, and the new place had more space for laying them out on the table. Plus I could cook my own food there and not have to use the kitchenette in the band office. (I did not mention the leaky roof for fear of appearing more toffee-nosed than I already felt.) There was a pause following my explanation as the tinny steel guitars in Waylon Jennings's *Rainy Day Woman* echoed through the hall. *Now*, I thought to myself, that was the end of it. I'd explained my move to the community grapevine without offending anyone, or at least not apparently so.

But just at that moment, Daryl slapped his hand on the table and cried out: "We know! We all put bets on how long you was gonna stay in there! Hela!" At that whoop, the whole table erupted into laughter and plastic beer-cup toasts.

Someone yelled, "Who won the bet?"

"Not me! Not me!" came the response.

"Must have been the chief who won!" More laughter.

Daryl went on, "Jason said he went down there that night and scared you good!" And it was then that I saw him, the same young man who had come to visit me at the cabin and told me to leave. Sitting there just one table over, he gave me that same wry smile. Despite his best efforts to oust me at the right time, he obviously had not won the bet.

Late in the dance, after midnight when most everyone was gone, I fell into conversation with Gerry and Janet Whitford. Gerry asked if I was interested in taking an overnight ATV trip with him to Belhk'achek, which was the main Cheslatta village before relocation and the place from which the band departed the territory in 1952. The elders I had been mapping with talked about it constantly, and Gerry promised we would have a fantastic time. "No doubt about it," he said. Gerry needed not compel me: I was thrilled by the prospect, and within minutes he and I found a weekend that would work. Satisfied that plans were in place, he got up to visit with some friends who were about to leave.

So now it was just Janet and me. We sat together for a small time in the wake of Gerry's absence. Then she asked me, "So why did you come all the way here, to Cheslatta?"

Her question took me by surprise. I was well aware of my own motivations for making this trip, but it never occurred to me to share this with Janet, or any of my collaborators for that matter. So I told her about my grandfather Papa's cabin on the bluffs of the Tennessee River, where I did the historical ethnography with the farmers relocated by the TVA, my first "real" research project as a college student. The cabin occupies a singular place in my childhood memory. Even though my family and I visited only once or twice a year, I felt at home-in-the-world in that place. I told Janet about the tumbling hollows of oak and shagbark hickory, the tall tales Papa would tell around the dinner table, the view off the deck out over the river to the blue sky that seemed to roll on forever. Then, sometime in high school, I learned about the TVA, the relocation, and the dam that eventually paved the way for real-estate developments like the cabin I loved so much. (Papa bought the cabin from a developer-friend as a weekend retreat from his high-stress banking job in Memphis.) Having made this discovery, my childhood utopia vanished. It became the product of a difficult history, a place made possible by hydraulic control, social engineering, forced relocation, and the banking industry. The cabin's transformation in my memory sparked a research interest in how large-scale water development projects have affected, transformed, and in some cases destroyed our relationships with place. Here I am at Cheslatta, then. This is the path that brought me here.

"Oh, yeah," Janet said, acknowledging my story but saying nothing else. I could not make out her reaction. I chided myself for being melodramatic, having turned my grandfather's weekend retreat into some kind of white-kid vision quest. So I deflected attention away from my story by telling Janet how impressed I was by the resilience of *her* community, by its steadfast commitment to never give up. This community, I said, has somehow survived The Flood. Against all odds, it has resurrected itself from near-annihilation.

Janet reflected on my words for a moment. She replied, "This community still has big problems, you know? We have a long way to go." I nodded, now a little embarrassed by my optimism.

But Janet hadn't gotten to her point yet. "Sometimes I think our history is too painful to even talk about," she said. "But we need to talk about it. We need everybody to tell their story—you, me, everybody. That way, we know where we come from and who we are, and where we want to go."

* * *

The mapping project continued apace as the summer unfolded. The elders and I were making good progress producing mylar sheets marked up with colorful dots and lines indicating traplines and hunting trails, cabins, village sites, all the good places for bear and beaver and berries—solid evidence of the band's "use and occupancy" before The Flood. But the stories, as always, seemed more important than the mylar film.

Then the weekend came for my trip with Gerry to Belhk'achek. We loaded his ATVs in the back of his truck on a Friday afternoon and made the long trip from his house in Burns Lake to a camp at Targe Creek, where we stayed for the night. Early the next morning, we unloaded the ATVs and were off. Almost immediately, I noticed how Gerry seemed to relish the thrill of the precariously steep angle on a sidehill, gunning the machine for just enough speed to defy the gravity of the slope. I figured he knew what he was doing, but almost as soon as the thought crossed my mind his ATV spilled over sideways and rolled violently down before lodging tightly between two big black spruce. Fortunately, Gerry came up smiling, his tuft of white hair poking out from underneath his cap. He dusted himself off, inspected his bike perched in the trees, and said we should just ditch the ATVs, walk the rest of the way there. I deferred to his judgment—he knew this territory far better than I, and these were *his* ATVs after all (we did eventually get the ATV unstuck on the return trip)—but it took a whole day of traipsing through bushy, mosquito-ridden terrain, mostly because Gerry was wearing tight cowboy boots that made him walk bowlegged and slow. It was a miserable hike.

When we finally reached Belhk'achek at dusk, the atmosphere—and my mood—changed markedly. The place had a quiet intensity, like a thunderstorm you can see, but not hear, looming on the horizon. Moving through the flat open space of lodgepole pine, me behind the ambling Gerry, I was surprised to find the village still evident after this many years. There were remnants of house foundations and walking trails, collapsed snake-fence rows, the decaying skeleton of a traditional rack for smoking meat and fish. The place offered a strange feeling, as if someone or something still *lived* there. Evidence of recent use was clear—fire pits with half-burnt logs, makeshift tables for cleaning fish, a lean-to shelter. But life had stopped suddenly in this place, without warning, so the community itself still seemed to have a presence. It was like entering someone's house when they're not at home. The village remained charged with the emotions and memories of an entire people. It was waiting for its people to return.

I walked out of the pine forest into the meadow by the shore of the lake. The cemetery appeared, the white crosses of the spirit houses reflecting softly in the last of the day's light. The band painstakingly restored this cemetery and had it consecrated by the Catholic Church in 1993. The church, in fact, consecrated the entirety of Cheslatta Lake since the remains of ancestors from the cemetery at Reserve Number Nine are still buried somewhere beneath the water. Cemeteries haunt the collective memory of relocation: they were demolished, burned, washed away. As I approached the heavy jackleg fence bordering this sacred place, all the stories I'd heard about The Flood came cascading into my head, a chorus of voices telling of appalling coercion and cruelty, of the terrible pain of exodus and loss.

"We tried to talk to the DIA, but they just pushed the words back in our mouth. They never even listened to us."

"And the buildings, they *burned* all the buildings. They did that to push us out. They just washed us out."

"We thought this was a free country, but this is not freedom! If we did that to them, they'd put us in jail!"

Then I remembered Ann Troy, the woman I interviewed early in the summer, the one who told me how the Cheslatta used her home, the schoolhouse her dad bought, as their new church after the DIA burned the one that once was here, at Belhk'achek. Her voice emerged from the choir:

> When I was just a little one, at church time, all of the elders they used
> to come together to our house at Grassy and talk about The Flood.
> Like when they opened the dam and all the caskets of our ancestors
> floated away into the lake. I used to think it was just a story. But it was
> a real story. They used to sit there, and they used to cry. That was the
> big thing I remember.

I thought of the hush that fell upon us then, me and Ann, sitting on the wooden stairs leading to the front door of her home. I simply could not formulate a response. Any reply I could imagine putting into words seemed woefully inadequate, like the words themselves would fall apart just as soon as they came out of my mouth. How do you respond to the searing memory of a community's devastation? How do you respond to the knowledge that someone—people acting in the interests of money and power and the abstractions of modernity—willfully intended and delivered that destruction? How do you respond to a "real story" like that?

Standing there at the cemetery in Belhk'achek, the place that waits for its people to return, silence was all I could summon.

* * *

A few days before I was scheduled to leave, the band held a "potlatch luncheon" for me at the office. All of the elders I worked with attended, and they stood up in turn to speak about our research. No one said anything about "use and occupancy"; no one said anything about treaty or maps. Instead, they talked about how I left home to live with them, what their first impressions of me were, of my willingness to sit there and listen, and of the memorable events that punctuated our summer together. Our interactions had become stories—Reserve Number Eleven, the trip to Belhk'achek—these and other stories were told. I was given three gifts: a large clock depicting the band's four crest animals in beautiful primary colors, a pair of moosehide baby booties with decorative beading (Gerry saying, *It's time you started working on that family!*), and money to pay for gas on the way home.

I was overwhelmed. All of this was so unexpected. I hadn't realized the project had been this meaningful for them, at least not in this way. More to the point, I hadn't realized the project had been so meaningful for *me* in this way. Graduate school seemed to emphasize a set of research practices designed to ensure a quality product at the conclusion. Manage your time effectively, eliminate distractions, synergize your efforts, and focus on the end game: results, thesis, project deliverables. The research product validates the research experience. The elders were telling differently. The interpersonal dimensions of the research were just as significant as the tangible outcomes, and the storytelling was an integral part of our coming to know in this way.

The stories were not an ancillary or ephemeral part of the research. As Ann had said, stories are "real." But unlike The Flood, these stories told about how people from two vastly different backgrounds—the student from Kansas and the Native refugees from Cheslatta—collaborated in a research engagement that, at least in some small measure, contributed to the interpersonal growth required for the ongoing work of self-determination.

* * *

As Linda Tuhiwai Smith illustrated in her book *Decolonizing Methodologies*, Indigenous research is grounded in the pursuit of self-determination and is just as concerned with process and practice as with empirical results, theory, and conclusions. Indigenous research processes, she wrote, "are expected to be respectful, to enable people, to heal and to educate. They are expected to lead one small step further towards self-determination" (Smith 1999, 128). With respect to a qualitative method such as the interview, then, the "quality of interaction is more important than ticking boxes or answering closed questions" (136). Importantly, Indigenous research need not necessarily yield direct or immediate results, but rather it is envisioned as a set of diverse projects that over time empower the historically marginalized to reclaim self-determination as individuals and communities. Smith outlined a set of twenty-five projects that range from claiming, negotiating, and returning to revitalizing, celebrating, and, of course, storytelling.

Storytelling occupies a central place in Indigenous methodologies because narrative and knowledge are understood to be inseparable in epistemological, cultural, and political terms (Cajete 2000; Denzin, Lincoln, and Smith 2008; Kovach 2009). Storytelling contributes directly to the work of self-determination by facilitating cultural survival through the intergenerational transfer of knowledge (Cruikshank 1998; Smith 1999), helping people engage and overcome historical trauma[3] (Brave Heart and DeBruyn 1998) and the psychological legacies of colonialism[4] (Duran and Duran 1995; Jordan 2011), and promoting the development of postcolonial, relational identities grounded in empathy and interpersonal engagement (Coombes et al. 2011; Johnson 2008; McKnight, Hoban, and Nielson 2011; see also Stephens, Silbert, and Hasson 2010).

Indigenous communities are not alone in recognizing the power of story and its foundational role in knowledge-making and self-actualization. Storytelling is one of the main ways, if not *the* way, people have made sense of the human experience in all its richness, complexities, contradictions, and changes (Cruikshank 1998; Gold 2002; Johnson 1987; King 2005). To participate in story is to understand the world through encounters with fellow dwellers past and present, real and unreal, human and nonhuman. Stories preserve the dynamic moment of encounter as the basis for genuine meaning and knowledge. In this way, storied knowledge remains connected to its places and people of origin; this is partly what makes it "relational." By telling and listening to stories, we engage these relational ways of knowing to make connections despite stereotypes, essentialism, and (in)difference. We are connected by the stories we tell and by our shared human capacity for storytelling. As Tom King (2005, 2) so eloquently put it: "The truth about stories is that that's all we are."

The Cheslatta people I worked with were pointing to the prospect of an Indigenous "micropolitics" of impromptu storytelling (cf. Christensen 2012; Gibson-Graham 2006) in which collaborators improvise narrative as a way of building interpersonal relationships, trust, and relational knowledge grounded in the actual places of research—on the trapline, trail, and highway; and in the band office, elementary school, and home (see Basso 1996; Brody 1981; Cruikshank 1990, 1998; Thornton 2008; Watson and Huntington 2008). The improvisatory nature of this practice means that collaboration need not focus on storytelling for a storytelling politics to have currency. It enriches collaborative work of all kinds, from land-use mapping, resource management, archaeological and archival study to GIScience, curriculum development, and ecological research. Telling stories extemporaneously but consistently, collaborators pursue a double vision, with one eye on enhancing collaborative projects that address the colonial legacies confronted by Indigenous people in particular, and the other on trying to understand the legacies of dislocation that we all share in the wake of European modernity[5] (Garbutt 2006; see also Godlewska, this volume).

The micropolitics of impromptu storytelling do not end with the formal conclusion of the research project. By sharing our collaboration stories with others, we invite these audiences to take the same journey into cross-cultural experience, question the oppressive conventions of colonial discourse, and participate in the genuine discussions needed to move beyond colonized relationships. When told over and again, the stories will range far from the traditional territory, providing transformative ways of thinking about ourselves, our communities, and our relationships with place.

Interpersonal comportment is an essential element in any collaboration. In Indigenous-academic work that focuses directly on narrative, oral tradition, and life history, the research design provides a relationship structure in which stories can be told, interpreted, and appreciated (cf. Cruikshank 1990, 1998). In other collaborations, the space required for impromptu storytelling will depend more exclusively on constructive interpersonal behavior and awareness. The stories will be more haphazardly told and embedded within other activities. Occasionally, the pressures associated with the primary research agenda will dampen or even close off the opportunity altogether. And listening to each other's stories is not always easy or comfortable. So behaving in a way that encourages storytelling is essential (Denzin, Lincoln, and Smith 2008; Kovach 2009). This entails listening more than we normally do, and listening first as a precondition for speaking and relating. It means being patient and waiting for stories to arrive on their own accord, and making time for activities that appear tangential but just may lead to a good story. Non-Native researchers need to be willing to share their own stories, not only to express where we come from—our own "standing places"[6]—but also to make public our commitment to the narrative exchange (Fee and Russell 2007).

In the end, these micropolitics require that we let ourselves be vulnerable (cf. Behar 1997) to the crazy logic of storytelling, relaxing our concern for the objective research goals, procedures, and timelines to make room for empathic dialogue, unexpected developments, and interpersonal growth in the collaboration process. Impromptu storytelling therefore resonates not only with Indigenous methodologies but also with other forms of reflexive qualitative praxis, including reciprocal and feminist ethnography (Behar and Gordon 1995; Cerwonka and Malkki 2007; Lassiter 2001), participatory action research (Pain 2004), interactive interviewing (Ellis et al. 1997), research storytelling (Christensen 2012), and friendship methodology (Tillmann-Healy 2003), to name only a few. It also connects with a resurgence of geographical interest in story as a micropolitical force for change (Cameron 2012).

Broadly speaking, self-determination refers to the capacity for people to self-organize freely and decide how they want to live with one other in explicit commitment to mutual support and empowerment (Day 2005). The paradox of self-determination is that it is an intensely interpersonal affair, one that simultaneously engages and exceeds the boundaries of cultural difference. In other words, the empowerment of *self* depends on cultivating connections with others, within and beyond one's own cultural group. And here is where storytelling excels. I do not wish to overstate its power, nor do I intend to suggest that storytelling alone will transform the legacies and structures of colonialism. Legislation, litigation, protest, and structured research collaboration have created real opportunities for the pursuit of self-determination in British Columbia and elsewhere. The micropolitics of impromptu, everyday storytelling complement these formal and institutional approaches, but they operate a little differently. At once immediate and incremental, intimate and interpersonal, erratic and on target, these stories bind us together as culturally diverse human beings. So despite its unpredictable ways, extemporaneous storytelling practice is worth striving for in any and all collaboration. For if we allow adequate time and have enough patience, our collaboration stories will help generate the genuine relationships needed to realize the vision of a reciprocal, shared, and multifaceted self-determination.

Notes

I thank all the people at Cheslatta who taught me the power of story through our collaborative research. Thanks also to two anonymous reviewers and to Jay Johnson, Mark Palmer, Anastacia Schulhoff, Matt Jacobson, and Elaine Lawless, all of whom read and provided constructive commentary on earlier versions of this essay.

1. Today, the Dakelh First Nations comprise twenty bands (the Canadian legal term for an Indigenous political unit) occupying an area in north-central British Columbia stretching from roughly the Fraser River in the east to the Hazelton Mountains and Kitimat Ranges of the Coast Mountains in the west. For ethnological source material, see Goldman (1941) and Tobey (1979).

2. The dialogue in this essay was reconstructed from field notes in collaboration with the interlocutors. All block quotations in this essay come directly from interview transcripts.

3. Importantly, historical trauma does *not* denote a single-cause psychological mechanism that applies uniformly to all Indigenous people, but rather refers to the sociopolitical *environment* of forced impoverishment, segregation, and assimilation in which the traumatic psychological experience of oppression takes place (Jordan 2011). The colonial experience does not predetermine adverse psychological states; that is to say, Native communities have been remarkably resilient in the face of colonialism.

4. Contemporary research has explored how storytelling helps people come to terms with trauma by disclosing emotional upheaval in the form of a narrative shared with others.

This process of narrating trauma has been shown to result in disinhibition (e.g., releasing emotional stress), social reconnection, and enhanced cognitive understanding of the traumatic event (Snyder and Lopez 2002; Niederhoffer and Pennebaker 2002).

5. I want to thank an anonymous reviewer of an earlier draft of this essay for this insight, which Garbutt (2006) also has expanded on through an exploration of the settler "autochthonic imaginary" in Lismore, Australia.

6. The phrase is from the Māori word *"tūrangawaewae."* As Johnson (2008, 128) described it, expressing one's standing place is a "first crucial step in building a trusting relationship for Māori (as well as for other Indigenous peoples) and a critical foundation for knowledge production."

References

Basso, K. H. 1996. *Wisdom Sits in Places: Landscape and Language among the Western Apache.* Albuquerque: University of New Mexico Press.

Behar, R. 1997. *The Vulnerable Observer: Anthropology That Breaks Your Heart.* Boston: Beacon Press.

Behar, R., and D. Gordon, eds. 1995. *Women Writing Culture.* Berkeley: University of California Press.

Brave Heart, M., and L. DeBruyn. 1998. "The American Indian Holocaust: Healing Historical Unresolved Grief." *American Indian and Alaska Native Mental Health Research* 8 (2): 60–82.

Brody, H. 1981. *Maps and Dreams.* Vancouver: Douglas and McIntyre.

Cajete, G. 2000. *Native Science: Natural Laws of Interdependence.* Santa Fe, NM: Clear Light.

Cameron, E. 2012. "New Geographies of Story and Storytelling." *Progress in Human Geography* 36 (5): 573–92.

Cerwonka, A., and L. Malkki. 2007. *Improvising Theory: Process and Temporality in Ethnographic Fieldwork.* Chicago: University of Chicago Press.

Christensen, B. 1995. *Too Good to Be True: Alcan's Kemano Completion Project.* Vancouver, BC: Talonbooks.

Christensen, J. 2012. "Telling Stories: Exploring Research Storytelling as a Meaningful Approach to Knowledge Mobilization with Indigenous Research Collaborators and Diverse Audiences in Community-Based Participatory Research." *Canadian Geographer/Le Géographe canadien* 56 (2): 231–42.

Coffey, A. 1999. *The Ethnographic Self: Fieldwork and the Representation of Identity.* London: Sage.

Coombes, B., N. Gombay, J. T. Johnson, and W. Shaw. 2011. "The Challenges of and from Indigenous Geographies." In *A Companion to Social Geography*, edited by V. Del Casino, M. Thomas, P. Cloke, and R. Panelli, 472–89. Malden, MA: Blackwell.

Cruikshank, J. 1990. *Life Lived Like a Story: Life Stories of Three Yukon Native Elders.* Lincoln: University of Nebraska Press.

———. 1998. *The Social Life of Stories: Narrative and Knowledge in the Yukon Territory.* Lincoln: University of Nebraska Press.

Day, R. 2005. *Gramsci Is Dead: Anarchist Currents in the Newest Social Movements.* London: Pluto Press.

Denzin, N., Y. Lincoln, and L. T. Smith, eds. 2008. *Handbook of Critical and Indigenous Methodologies.* Thousand Oaks, CA: Sage.

Duran, E., and B. Duran. 1995. *Native American postcolonial psychology.* Albany: State University of New York Press.

Ellis, C., C. Kiesinger, and L. Tillmann-Healy. 1997. "Interactive Interviewing: Talking about Emotional Experience." In *Reflexivity and Voice,* edited by R. Hertz, 119–49. Thousand Oaks, CA: Sage.

Fabian, J., ed. 1979. "Beyond Charisma: Religious Movements as Discourse." *Social Research: An International Quarterly of the Social Sciences* 46 (1): 1–203.

Fee, M., and L. Russell. 2007. "'Whiteness' and 'Aboriginality' in Canada and Australia: Conversations and Identities." *Feminist Theory* 8 (2): 187–208.

Garbutt, R. 2006. "White 'Autochthony.'" *Australian Critical Race and Whiteness Studies Journal* 2 (1): 1–16.

Gibson-Graham, J. K. 2006. *A Postcapitalist Politics.* Minneapolis: University of Minnesota Press.

Gold, J. 2002. *The Story Species: Our Life-Literature Connection.* Allston, MA: Fitzhenry and Whiteside.

Goldman, I. 1941. "The Alkatcho Carrier: Historical Background of Crest Prerogatives." *American Anthropologist* 43 (3): 396–418.

Goulet, J. G., and B. Miller, eds. 2007. *Extraordinary Anthropology: Transformations in the Field.* Lincoln: University of Nebraska Press.

Johnson, J. T. 2008. "Kitchen Table Discourse: Negotiating the 'Tricky Ground' of Indigenous Research." *American Indian Culture and Research Journal* 32 (3): 127–37.

Johnson, M. 1987. *The Body in the Mind: The Bodily Basis of Meaning, Imagination, and Reason.* Chicago: University of Chicago Press.

Jordan, J. B. 2011. "Indigenous Psychology in North America: Lessons Learned from Neo-Colonialism." In *Progress in Asian Indigenous and Cultural Psychology,* 1:1–31. Yogyakarta, Indonesia: Center for Indigenous and Cultural Psychology, University of Gadjah Mada.

King, T. 2005. *The Truth about Stories.* Minneapolis: University of Minnesota Press.

Kovach, M. 2009. *Indigenous Methodologies: Characteristics, Conversations, and Contexts.* Toronto: University of Toronto Press.

Larsen, S. 2006. "The Future's Past: Politics of Time and Territory among Dakelh First Nations of British Columbia." *Geografiska Annaler* 88B (3): 311–21.

Lassiter, L. 2001. "'Reading over the Shoulders of Natives' to 'Reading alongside Natives,' Literally: Toward a Collaborative and Reciprocal Ethnography." *Journal of Anthropological Research* 57 (2): 137–49.

McKnight, A., G. Hoban, and W. Nielson. 2011. "Using *Slowmation* for Animated Storytelling to Represent Non-Aboriginal Preservice Teachers' Awareness of 'Relatedness to Country.'" *Australian Journal of Educational Technology* 27 (1): 41–54.

Niederhoffer, K., and J. Pennebaker. 2002. "Sharing One's Story: On the Benefits of Writing or Talking about Emotional Experience." In *Handbook of Positive Psychology,* edited by C. Snyder and S. Lopez, 573–83. New York: Oxford University Press.

Pain, R. 2004. "Social Geography: Participatory Research." *Progress in Human Geography* 18 (5): 652–63.

Smith, L. 1999. *Decolonizing Methodologies: Research and Indigenous Peoples.* London: Zed.

Snyder, C., and S. Lopez, eds. 2002. *Handbook of Positive Psychology.* New York: Oxford University Press.

Stephens G., L. Silbert, and U. Hasson. 2010. "Speaker-Listener Neural Coupling Underlies Successful Communication." *Proceedings of the National Academies of Science of the United States of America* 107 (32): 14425–30.

Thornton, T. 2008. *Being and Place among the Tlingit.* Seattle: University of Washington Press.

Tillmann–Healy, L. 2003. "Friendship as Method." *Qualitative Inquiry* 9 (5): 729–49.

Tobey, M. 1979. "Carrier." In *Handbook of North American Indians: Subarctic,* edited by J. Steward, 413–32. Washington, DC: Smithsonian Institution.

Watson, A., and O. Huntington. 2008. "They're Here––I Can *Feel* Them: Epistemic Spaces of Indigenous and Western Knowledges." *Social and Cultural Geography* 9 (3): 257–81.

Young, D., and J. G. Goulet, eds. 1994. *Being Changed by Cross-Cultural Encounters: The Anthropology of Extraordinary Experience.* Toronto: University of Toronto Press.

Rocking the Boat
Indigenous Geography at Home in Hawai'i

KALI FERMANTEZ

> The spears sailed through the air in vain because of the magical
> power of Kamapua'a, the pig deity. As an enormous pig, just one
> of his many *kinolau* (body forms), the enemy had no chance of
> hurting him, but he needed to protect his people. With his back
> wedged against the sheer valley wall, his family climbed up his
> body, out of range of their pursuers. The rain fell freely in the
> lush windward valley called Kaliuwa'a, slowing their climb, but at
> last they made it over the valley ridge, to safety in the uplands.

As Native scholars, we often find ourselves backed against the wall. It is our ability to change shape and form with shifting fluid identities in different contexts,
simultaneously Native and scholar, often with hybrid ancestry, that enables us to
open up safe spaces in the mountains of the academy. This shape-shifting allows
us to mitigate the damage already done and to provide a means of escape from
oppression, depression, and suppression of Indigenous culture and people.

I grew up in Hau'ula on the Windward side of O'ahu, about a mile from
Kaliuwa'a, a place named for the pig god Kamapua'a's outrigger canoe. To this day
the indentation from his back scars the valley wall, a reminder in the landscape of
his heroic feat to save his people from destruction. In my academic career, I, like
Kamapua'a, have taken many forms, and geography is like the canoe *Kaliuwa'a,* the
vessel that has taken me on my academic journey and which has ultimately brought
me safely home.

My intent here is to dive into the depths of what it means to be an Indigenous
geographer who teaches and conducts research at home. It is imperative that we as
Native academics make teaching and research and the academy itself safe for our people (as safe as educating restless Natives can be). As fashionable as it is to trace one's
academic trajectory, hurtling through space at terminal velocity in a linear fashion is

not the right way to express my journey. In Hawaiian, the broad term for history and story is *mo'olelo*, which literally refers to a succession of talk. In Pidgin English, the local vernacular, informal and comfortable conversation is called "talk story." *Mo'olelo* and talk story are more circular, fluid, and roundabout—more well-rounded ways of telling the real stories of Indigenous scholars working in Native communities. I talk story about the politics of being an Indigenous geographer working at home by discussing my career from the perspective of the places I have been. I also share *mo'olelo* of my experiences as a Native Hawaiian working on a PhD, conducting fieldwork, and starting my career as a geographer, all at home in Hawai'i.

Rocking the Boat as Part of the Out-rigor

My view of the world spun 180 degrees as the canoe flipped upside down, and the *ama* (outrigger float) made a circuit through the sky and plunged into the ocean, a path the sun would shortly follow. While clichés of my "world being turned upside down" and being "in over my head" come to mind, my inverted immersion was somehow refreshing, and I made my way out from under the canoe and proceeded to *huli* (turn) the canoe back over. It is essential to know how to flip an overturned canoe back over so you are prepared for when you *huli* in the open ocean. You have to be able to get the canoe back over, bail the water out, and get the canoe moving forward again if you want to return home.

The canoe was a bit heavier when I finally pushed it out of the water onto the beach. I quickly undid the lashings on the *ama* and *'iako* (outrigger boom) and carried the pieces of the canoe to my little station wagon. I had built the canoe while conducting my dissertation research in the marginalized community of Wai'anae on the island of O'ahu. It was built for transportability and affordability and from traditional and modern materials. It was made of plywood and held together with screws and glue, and a coat of epoxy was applied to make it watertight. The old school parts were the hau wood from Hau'ula (where I'm from) used for the *ama* and *'iako*. The style of lashing I used to hold all of the pieces together was the traditional Hawaiian style of lashing.

As Indigenous geographers we are in troubled waters, rocking the boat of the academy and the discipline. These waters can be negotiated by overturning the way we think and using traditional and contemporary knowledge to skillfully maneuver and navigate past the reefs, waves, currents, undercurrents, and creatures of the deep that threaten us. I have used the outrigger canoe conceptually as my course model when I have taught the undergraduate course "Geography of Hawai'i." Native Hawaiian geographers have recently made an important distinction between the "geography of Hawai'i" and "Hawaiian geography," and I use the *wa'a* (canoe) to demonstrate the difference (Andrade 2001; Oliveira 2006). The voyaging canoe has recently become an Oceanic symbol linking the indigenous islanders of the Pacific, especially Polynesians. It has also been a powerful catalyst and teaching tool in the recent revival and reinvigoration of Hawaiian culture.

Unlike the voyaging canoe with its large twin hulls, the smaller outrigger canoe is made up of the main hull and the attached ama, which balances the canoe in the water. Local knowledges and Indigenous geographies are like the ama whereas global knowledge and conventional geography are like the main hull. The breadth of the main hull is wider, carries more volume and weight, and although it also displaces more water, it is part of the breadth we need in the academy. The main hull of my course is the geography of Hawai'i, which is the conventional outsider approach.

Though smaller, the ama is essential in balancing and keeping the *wa'a* afloat; without it, the canoe sinks. The ama of my course is the Hawaiian geography that I present using Native Hawaiian perspectives. Working in the Native context, we have a smaller body of knowledge that is more focused and concentrated and which increasingly continues to be created by our people, being brought forth from the depths of a past space-time and reconfigured in the present. In this way, local and other knowledges help balance global and dominant knowledges and create a dialogue between difference and resonance in ways of knowing. The added rigor of incorporating Indigenous world views into research and teaching is what I refer to as "academic out-rigor."

My ultimate goal is for my course model to eventually become a voyaging canoe with hulls about the same size and weight, and thus equally balanced. In this manner, old and new, Western and Indigenous, global and local knowledges can be lashed together, creating a space of dialogue as we venture into new horizons of uncharted knowledge.

The lashing holding together the *mo'olelo* presented here is a contemporary Indigenous geography that reaches back to the past but is used in the present. Such is the nature of being a Native scholar today, a bit old-fashioned, a bit new, a bit hybrid—a fusion. It is symbolic of a way of knowing that is not in the past tense or temporally fixed. It is updated instead of outdated knowledge that empowers us to quit the bad habit of speaking of ourselves in the third person and in the past tense (Johnson 2008). The homemade vessel is a montage of the twenty-first century that symbolizes the way we as a people can navigate the present and future in the context of the past.

Surfing and Diving: Geographical Breadth and Depth

As geographers, we know that before you can reach depth, you have to deal with the breadth of a discipline that spans the physical and social sciences and whose spatial perspective and technologies permeate. My favorite metaphor referring to breadth and depth was presented by Epeli Hau'ofa, a Pacific scholar who referred to researchers in Oceania as either surfers, who skimmed across surfaces, or divers who took the time to painstakingly explore the depths (Waddell 1993, 67). Of course, as Hau'ofa knew, we need to be both—looking across disciplines, becoming specialized, and then also in the Native context, immersing ourselves in Indigenous world views. From an Indigenous perspective, it is out-rigorous to surf and dive in geography in particular because it is a discipline characterized by its breadth.

I also like to extend the surfing metaphor further by discussing the politics of knowledge from a Native perspective (Fermantez 2007a). Surfers position themselves on a wave as close to the peak as possible because that is where the power is concentrated, and after they "drop in" they skillfully maneuver from the peak to the shoulder of the wave (from center to margins) and then "cut back" to the center. Being too close to the center ("too deep" on the wave) you can get "closed out" and wipe out. If you're too far out on the shoulder of the wave (on the margins away from the center), you can lose the wave altogether and it will pass you by.

Being a Native scholar requires negotiating more dominant knowledges from the center and alternative voices from the margins. There is a requisite balance between the nomothetic, broad universal geographic knowledge and theories, and the ideographic, localized, and particular Indigenous geography. Native scholars need to embrace the politics and struggle for social justice while maintaining balance. There is a fine line between attempting radical maneuvers on the margins and being co-opted by the powers in the center.

Using the metaphors of the outrigger canoe and surfing is helpful in generalizing the relationships between the insider/outsider, Western/Native, center/margin dichotomies. However, I would like to point out that in reality the power dynamics are much more complex, fluid, and contextual. Being an Indigenous scholar requires a fine balance on our surfboards and adept shape-shifting because we have to ride out the treacherous waves and dodge spears from all directions, all along dealing with critique from both sides of another problematic dualism: the academic community on the one side and the ambiguous and amorphous Native community on the other.

Some of the deadliest spears from the academy are those launched from the epistemological stance that the work we do is not valid. This is not surprising given the historic absence of Native voices in geography, and it is about time we are even heard (Louis 2007). It is hard not to sense the feeling that one is meeting some kind of demographic or curricular quota, a supposedly sorry excuse for taking up space in the academy, in the name of diversity. Even when we are able to have a voice, there is still the smug dismissal of work by, for, on, and about Native people because such work is considered somehow less than "real" scholarship. Our work is characterized as being too local, particular, impractical, quaint, antiquated, archaic, irrelevant, unscientific, unobjective, and unrealistic. In response, I argue that the kind of work we do in Indigenous geography between the academy and the cultural community is actually out-rigorous. We must have a healthy balance between academic rigor and community rigor and be fit enough to survive the "scientific rigor (mortis) [that] has infected [the lands] of our ancestors" (Peter Cole, quoted in Johnson 2008, 127). It is difficult and requires extra work to be legitimate scholars and accountable Natives at the same time.

A major part of the out-rigor is the task of being true to our own people. Because Native people are not a monolithic homogenous mass, and because of the basic truth that you can't please everyone, there will always be detractors among our own people who try to pull us down. This is another can of worms, or I should say another basket or bucket of trouble.

Corn in Baskets and Crabs in a Bucket

Jet-lagged and just off the red eye from Honolulu to the 2009 Association of American Geographers Annual Meeting in Vegas—a city that should not exist because of the water, or I should say lack thereof. And it's not just because I'm from an island surrounded by the life-giving substance—it's extreme irony symbolized by the water shows in the city and "water hazards" of thirsty golf courses in a desert, a huge façade symbolic of the hubris that led to the global financial meltdown—an over-the-top built environment, constantly being rebuilt into something new and supposedly improved, yet lacking a solid foundation.

Checked in to the conference hotel and just in time to make it to the Indigenous geography session, or so I thought. I'm late because, of course, the meeting room is way out on the margins, not even in the conference hotel and at the far end of the convention center—the farthest rooms were ours, no surprises there.

The keynote talk by Greg Cajete has already begun. He's talking about different colors of corn all in the same basket—symbolic of diversity working together. Jet-lagged and not in my right mind, I can't

help the metaphor and comment, "While there might be all different kinds and colors of corn, when heated, some kernels expand, rise
above the others, and turn white"—wryly explaining that I'm not sure
what that means. But I really do know what it means.

Sometimes the spears that threaten to impale us come from within our own
Native community. All too often one hears the sentiment that Native scholars are
somehow sellouts, that we've become too educated, Westernized, modernized,
brainwashed, whitewashed, and tainted. In the Pacific context, the term is "co-
conuts, they are brown on the outside but white inside" (Hereniko 1999, 137). In
the Hawaiian context, one can be referred to as *haole* (foreign or white) or simply
"un-Hawaiian."

The metaphor often used in reference to Hawaiians who can't seem to get along,
agree, or come to a consensus is that we are just like "crabs in a bucket" (Tengan
2008, 192). The basic idea is that when one individual seeks to rise up, the rest pull
that one down. If the crabs worked together they could latch onto each other and
climb to safety.

Among Hawaiians in Hawai'i there is an anti-intellectual stance that is at times
subtle and implicit and at other times voiced loudly and clearly. Since I was educated
in the primary and secondary public school system in Hawai'i (which as elsewhere
is a broken system, but it is also among the most broken), the idea that to do "good"
in school is a bad thing is so ingrained in me that I'm almost apologetic and embarrassed today to tell people in my home community that I have a PhD and teach
at the university level. Although I recognize that some of this anti-intellectualism
derives from the conflation of class and race in my marginalized home community,
I don't want to be the crab that seeks self-aggrandizement and seems to think he's
better than everyone else.

This anti-intellectualism, which I still to some degree have internalized, is
understandable given our colonial history and the assimilationist and racist educational system that punished students for speaking our language, suppressed our
culture, and put down Hawaiian ways of thinking and knowing. However, although
this backlash against Western education and scholarship makes sense, in the context of the cultural revitalization movement among Hawaiians today, the persistent
echo of crabs in the bucket weighs heavily on Native scholars who already have
more than enough criticism from the academy.

The way to deal with the crabs and the corn is first to recognize the partial
truths these metaphors suggest. As Linda Smith has explained, the liminal place of
Native intellectuals is problematic because "these same producers and legitimators
of culture are the group most closely aligned to the colonizers in terms of their

class interests, their values and their ways of thinking" (1999, 69). I have felt some ambivalence and irony regarding the way careers have built off of dispossession never experienced by privileged Natives, but also cannot forget the way power and inequity surge through all societies.

As indigenous scholars, we not only rock the boat of the academy or the discipline; part of our boat-rocking has to be an internalized critique of Native communities. As painful and counter to the overromanticized notion of Indigenous consensus and solidarity as it may be, we need to recognize that a critique turned inward on ourselves is a measure of health and vitality, and can be productive. As Greg Cajete suggested, differences of opinion and a variety of colors of corn are signs of diversity and maturity. Being self-critical and reflexive as well as open to new ideas and change can allow Native peoples to be conservatively progressive. This should allow us to move forward or actually, back to the future in a time/ space and worldview where the past is in front of us and the future behind: "It is as if the Hawaiian stands firmly in the present, with his back to the future, and his eyes fixed upon the past, seeking historical answers for present-day dilemmas" (Kame'eleihiwa 1992, 22).

The more we look to the time/space of our Native past, the more we recognize the need to remove ourselves from the buckets and put ourselves into Native baskets. As Sam Ka'ai, one of Ty Kawika Tengan's mentors explained, "The trouble is that the bucket is galvanized; if it was a basket they crawl in and out. . . . I don't think it's the fault of the crabs as it is the fault of the environment" (2008, 193). As Indigenous scholars we must create social spaces and contexts in the academy that are open-ended like baskets, allowing Native communities to crawl in and out. Baskets, as compared to buckets, are more organic, Indigenous, and environmentally friendly—we need to make the academy a friendlier environment for Native people.

Furthermore, we need to recognize the multiplicity of ways that we are all complicit in and consent to our own dispossession. We're not simply in buckets or baskets anyway—we have complex and overlapping relationships, social networks, positionalities, and linkages that confound any simplistic understanding of power dynamics. The point is that we should be critical of ourselves and others and of the power we behold and uphold. As a Native scholar, I have found it difficult to deal with my own people pulling me down as I have sought to rise through educational attainment. However, we should change metaphors here. As one of my students reminded me when I was talking about crabs in a bucket, by climbing the rungs of education, one is actually in a position to lift others. This idea is well articulated in the Native American context by the song "Go My Son," which I sang and signed as a dancer in college at BYU Provo on the continent:

Go my son, go and climb the ladder
Go my son, go and earn your feather
Go my son, make your people proud of you
Work my son, get an education
Work my son, learn a good vocation
Climb my son, go and take a lofty view
From on the ladder of an education
You can see to help your Indian Nation
Then reach my son, and lift your people up with you.
(Burson and Williams 1969)

Temporal Depth in the Academy

"I wouldn't be here if I was writing" rang in my ears, and I lost my appetite. Up to that point the food tasted good. The food is the true measure of success at any luau and everyone seemed to be having an enjoyable time. The comment made by a non-Hawaiian academic friend who happened to be at my niece's first birthday celebration (aka baby luau) was what unsettled my stomach. Being an established academic, he had made similar comments before about saying no, being committed to the academic work, and focused. My mind understood the words he was saying, but I couldn't comprehend the implications of not being there, let alone the taken for granted, given, understood expectation by my ʻohana (extended family) that I would be there—and not simply showing face, but also helping out.

A luau in its modern, local, and even global manifestation is a feast, and is considered "traditional" in Hawaiʻi today. The luau literally is the new shoot of the *kalo* (taro) plant, the traditional staple of Hawaiians. ʻOhana, the word for family, comes from ʻoha, or the offshoot growing from the root, which can be replanted. At the same time a luau is infused with modernity; the coming together of ʻohana and preparing food together in the traditional arduous and time-consuming way brings families and communities together.

That I would go to something trivialized and reduced to being a "baby party" seemed nonsensical to my academic friend. He had made it onto the faculty, knew what it took, and partying wouldn't work. I recently saw that friend again, dissertation written, PhD in hand, and in a tenure-track position. He could see that I made it through, it just took me LONGER.

Part of being a Native scholar is being true to your culture, genealogy, and people. It is also being true to the academy, its values, and its rigor. Satisfying all these demands often means added time depth (spending more time and becoming more deeply involved), which in my experience, meant completing the requirements for a PhD all at home, with all of the support and obligations home entails.

To survive in the academy, added time depth might be required to fill holes in one's less-than-stellar previous academic training. Learning the culture of the academy is likewise an added dimension that comes more easily to some than others. Academic conferences are a perfect example of the learning curve for Indigenous scholars. It's always amusing to go to academic gatherings where there is food, because in the Native context there is a different understanding of what food is and means. I'm not just talking about the types of food, but also the quantity, and how it is eaten. In the Pacific context, it's not good form culturally to stand and eat, but that often happens in the academy. Furthermore, it's rude and impolite to butt in to other people's conversations and simultaneously interrupt and leave someone else hanging, but it happens all the time at conferences. In the Indigenous context, introducing one's self is place-based, and sharing knowledge is often accompanied by protocols that take more time than the fifteen-minute presentation and five-minute question-and-answer session. As pointed out at the AAG annual meeting in Las Vegas in the Indigenous Geography Specialty Group business meeting, we didn't really have the time to honor and respect the Native people of that land in the proper way. Indigenous conferences would need more time and a slower pace than mass-produced, standing and eating, industrial scholarship.

The main idea I want to point out is that time depth in the academy is necessitated by the different learning curves and time constraints Indigenous people have. Not that non-Native scholars don't have lives, family obligations, demands on their time, and learning curves of their own—I would simply point out that the learning curves are different and various obligations seem to take longer precisely because there is a different understanding and experience of time/space. In addition to historical marginalization in the academy and the associated conflation of class and race, there are also the rural versus urban and digital divides that can further marginalize Native people. Anecdotally at least, I can say that getting from point A to point B for many Native scholars seems quite circuitous, while recognizing that the academic trajectory for non-Native scholars is also not exactly a straight line. But this links up nicely to Indigenous epistemology, which is commonly thought of as more circular as compared to the ostensible linearity of Western thought (at the same time I recognize that these binaries are problematic and can be deconstructed).

Grass Roots: Temporal Depth in the Land/Community

E Hawaiʻi e kuʻu one hānau ē
Kuʻu home, kulāiwi nei
ʻOli nō au I nā pono lani ou
E Hawaiʻi, aloha ē

O Hawaiʻi, o sands of my birth
My native home
I rejoice in the heavenly blessings of you
O beloved Hawaiʻi
(Wilcox et al. 2003, 45)

In addition to spending a long time, even a lifetime in the community, temporal depth for Native scholars goes back generations. This, of course, speaks to genealogy and the knowledge that we gain from our ancestors. In the Hawaiian context, the way in which our ancestry is embedded in the land comes in the concepts of *one hānau* (sands of our birth) and *kulāiw*i (bone plain, where the bones of our ancestors are interred). This temporal depth reaches back to the *pō*—which signifies our deep, dark, primordial origins, but also as Ty Kawika Tengan suggested, the (Po)st Colonial—a time/space where we reach back to the past but live in the present with its attendant po-litics (2008).

For non-Native researchers, temporal depth in the Native community requires doing one's homework, which includes background research and especially spending time in the community to gain trust and to come to an understanding of cultural protocols, values, and ethics. For Native researchers in general, although rapport is more easily gained and cultural understandings are more obvious, the long-term commitment requires another kind of time depth. Fortunately this is changing, and a critical mass is developing, but because Native scholars have been few and far between historically, time depth means being pulled in various directions simultaneously, especially by one's own family and indigenous community as well as by an academic community desperately lacking what they call "diversity." Being pushed and pulled by winds, waves, tides, and currents often leaves Native scholars in too deep and out of breath.

To fix my position in the shifting sea as I surf, I alternately line up two or more points on land. This allows me to be at the right place at the right time in the water. Similarly, triangulation in research is used to fix the validity and sea/see worthiness of the research by using different points of reference. This triangulation is geared to fixing not *the* truth, but instead *a* truth established by rigorous research. The four

major types of triangulation are multiple sources, methods, theories, and investigators (Bradshaw and Stratford 2000). An inherent triangulation also accompanies
work in Native communities, which requires time depth. The iterative nature of
research is enhanced as the work cycles from reflexive self, to the Indigenous community, to the academic community, and back to the researcher. Triangulated in
these ways, research is time-consuming and needs to be validated by the input of
both of these very different communities. This weight added to the ethics and rigor
of the academy is the out-rigor the community requires.

Part of our job in researching in Native communities (whether we're Native or
not) is to ensure that the research we do is safe for the people, or in other words we
follow the fundamental ethic to do no harm. I was recently talking to a non-Native
student who was planning to interview *kupuna* (elders). I made the point to this
student (who happens to be headed to law school), that above and beyond legal
and human subjects research requirements, it is important that what we intend to
do is *pono* (right, proper, correct). The people whom we gather information from
should be okay with what they are on record as saying and should know what their
knowledge, words, images, and identities will be used for. In this added dimension of triangulation in the Native community, the research ethics of *pono*, like the
university's internal review board, determine the proper research protocols and
structure the ways in which research can and should be conducted in Hawaiian
communities. The Hawaiian geographer Kapa Oliveira warned of these added
kuleana (rights and responsibilities) Native Hawaiian researchers carry: "We must
answer to our Kanaka Maoli community to be fully accepted. Only those who are
pono (righteous) can achieve such status. Those who fail to be *pono* are stripped
of their *mana*" (2006, 25). While the stakes may seem higher for Indigenous researchers, the opportunities to empower and build the *mana* (power/efficacy) of
our communities should outweigh reservations.

When it comes to accountability, a difficult question is defining exactly who
the grassroots or Native community is. There is a scalar factor in defining "community" in the Hawaiian context, which can range from small rural communities
to districts, individual islands, groups of islands, and even worldwide. In this age
of increased mobility we need to be accountable to both roots and routes, and
this entails understanding how cultures are embedded in place but also transcend
space through mobility and technology (Clifford 2001). In the Hawaiian context
there is a rural and outer island bias contrasted with urban areas in the islands
and the diaspora in "mainlands" and global cities. Part of understanding the
depth and breadth of Indigenous communities is recognizing the currents and
countercurrents flowing between Hawai'i and communities "off-island" (Kauanui
1998). However we define community, and I prefer being context-driven and as

inclusive as possible, our role should not merely be to protectively avoid causing harm. We should actively try to do good.

"Talk Story" Approach: Participatory Action Research

When I heard that a class of Wai'anae High School Hawaiian studies students was planning a hike to the top of Mount Ka'ala, I knew I had to go. Our young family had just moved to the Wai'anae Coast from the opposite side of the island of Oahu a few short weeks earlier, so this was a great opportunity for me to get acquainted with the mountain for which my community partner organization was named, as well as to participate in one of Ka'ala Farm's cultural education programs.

We had made it halfway up the mountain in good time, and I was surprised and disappointed when the students decided not to hike all the way to the top. Instead they decided to head back down, leaving the hike only half completed. I decided to finish the hike alone. There's something about mountains, and this trek gave me time to think and reflect on being immersed in the field and trying to do Participatory Action Research (PAR).

I had always wanted my research to be meaningful and relevant to the community but was also somewhat skeptical about it actually trickling down to the grassroots. I found in PAR an approach whose goal was not for research to trickle down at all, but for research to actually sprout bottom up from the grassroots. As I struggled with the demands of PAR, that my research needed to be participatory and involve action, I saw that in developing my research, I had actually met the community partner halfway up the mountain. I could see that my research had its own trail before coming into contact with Ka'ala Farm, and it became our research when we sat down and "talked story" about what the community wanted to see from my research and what questions they wanted answered.

By doing PAR, I'm translating and mediating between the grassroots and the academy. I work with the community on the ground and meet the community halfway, but I also have to head up the mountain to commune with the pantheon of gods in the academy. The gods of the academy can only be placated by the timely completion of the sacrificial offering, otherwise known as the dissertation, while the community on the ground, at the grassroots, is appeased by the practical application of the research.

    A few months later, a visit by students from a graduate seminar at the University of Hawai'i helped me express my experience of doing PAR with Ka'ala Farm. We had just done a Hawaiian chant in preparation for entering the organization's cultural learning center and were preparing to cross the stream marking its boundary. One of the students asked me about my research experience, and I pointed to the plank spanning the small stream and said, "I'm like that plank." I was trying to balance and bridge my research between the rigorous demands of the academy on the one hand and the practical needs of the community on the other. Situated in the middle of the stream, I was just beginning to comprehend what happened upstream in the community and trying to grasp community dynamics. While trying to comprehend the past and present, I also recognized that while standing midstream, my actions and research would have impacts downstream, and it was a bit daunting to realize that. (Fermantez 2004)

    Just as I descended from Ka'ala's lofty heights back down to sea level, the approach to my research on the ground would be to see level, to see eye-to-eye and face-to-face with my research partners and community. "Talk story" has been used by geographers and other social scientists as an appropriate research method that has proven successful as an unthreatening and comfortable way of accessing information in the local Hawaiian context (Andrade 2001; 2008; Suryanata and Umemoto 2003). Despite the contrived nature of qualitative research in general, this kind of approach can enable "more 'natural' interactions and responses to occur" (Kearns 2000, 109). In my dissertation research, I tried to take the home field advantage by conducting field work at home in Hawai'i. Even though Wai'anae is not my home community, as a *kama'āina* (child of the land) I am *kama'āina* (familiar) with the local situation. While recognizing that my local understanding would allow "more natural" interactions to occur, I also needed to be reflexive, constantly analyzing my own situatedness in the process, recognizing that research is a power-laden endeavor that enabled me to become a powerful PhDeity.

    Although I will briefly discuss Participatory Action Research (PAR) as an appropriate approach for Indigenous geographers, I would like to point out that any research on, about, for, and with Native peoples should have a participatory component. Both Native and non-Native researchers need to go through the proper academic as well as cultural protocols to conduct research, and this initial kind of talk story dialogue should mark the beginning of conducting research among Indigenous people.

Many researchers working in Indigenous communities have been doing PAR without calling it that. Discovering PAR was eye-opening to me because research that is from the "bottom up" and "for and with" instead of "on or about" a group of people makes sense in Native communities. Not surprisingly, PAR is an approach on the margins. Its validity is challenged because unlike supposedly "pure" research, PAR is biased and has an agenda. It is considered by some to lack validity for the very reasons it is considered valid in the Native context. I like the fact that instead of trying to be objective and emotionally distant, PAR embraces the politics and seeks to invert the power relationships, thus bringing the power to the people, to the grassroots.

PAR is a convergence of the Participatory Research and Action Research traditions, both of which have complex genealogies (Greenwood and Levin 1998; Herr and Anderson 2005). The research is participatory in that the researcher forms a partnership with a group, organization, or community, and they collaboratively design, implement, and analyze research. Not merely descriptive or simply for knowledge's sake, action in PAR comes through both process and product as the research is a catalyst and instrument of positive social change. In "true'" or ideal forms of PAR, participants are actively engaged in all aspects of the research, and their lives are tangibly improved through the process. These overlapping aspects come with an impressive range of philosophical, historical, theoretical, practical, and methodological implications (Park et al. 1993; McTaggart 1997; Stringer 1999; Reason and Bradbury 2001).

Recognizing the inherent spatiality of participation, geographers have recently come to embrace PAR, creating a critical mass of participatory geographies (Pain and Kindon 2007). This "participatory turn" in geography has evolved from a focus on research to pedagogical concerns and the inclusion of PAR in teaching and learning (Kindon and Elwood 2009, 20). PAR is especially appropriate for doing Indigenous geography because the temporal depth required enables access to Indigenous knowledge that can then be privileged and given voice. Precisely because it is time-consuming and characterized by its "ambiguity and messiness," it is fitting for the dynamic flux of Native communities (Herr and Anderson 2005, 127). Pyrch and Castillo explain that when working to recover ancestral wisdom, a dialogic and pragmatic orientation is enabled by PAR, which by its nature is flexible and responsive to the ebb and flow of life in Indigenous communities:

> In PAR it is accepted as simple and straight-forward that we are only one blade of grass, but that we are rooted to the next blade, which is rooted to the next, and so on. All those blades are working together, holding each other up in order to achieve a common objective. . . .

> We plan our activities as we go along—adapting them to the rhythm which is formed among the participants, the rhythm which creates the movement. . . . We do not simply plan activities. We are always preparing for surprise, for unanticipated learning, which becomes as powerful as the anticipated. (Pyrch and Castillo 2001, 381)

Work among the grassroots enables PAR because it provides the requisite solidarity and pliability to cope with the challenges and empowerment that come from engaging with Indigenous communities.

In my research among the grassroots in Wai'anae I was able to get to a deeper sense of place as I used PAR as a talk-story approach to explore the way in which reconnecting to a Hawaiian sense of place and cultural identity, what I call re-placement, empowered Native Hawaiians in this marginalized community (Fermantez 2007b). The methods used to access this depth of place were also talk-story qualitative methodologies: participant observation, semistructured interviews, and a focus group (group interview). We also need to talk story with our communities in the way we present our research.

Kaona: Depth in Writing/Re-Presenting Our Work

> "You were writing to a Hawaiian audience," one of my students commented after she read excerpts from my dissertation. Kind of thinking she was stating the obvious, I said, "Yes, but I was writing in English to an academic and general audience as well."

We need to have depth in the way we write and speak to different audiences simultaneously. In my research, descriptions of Hawaiian culture resonate differently and are more meaningful to Native Hawaiians, just as the academic jargon used is better understood by a scholarly audience. Thus, a balancing piece of the out-rigor attached to research in indigenous communities is the way research is communicated in writing or other forms. In Hawaiian, the idea of having double or multiple meanings is called *kaona.* I like to tell my classes that while a hula (dance) may be about the *manu* (bird) visiting the *pua* (flower), metaphorically it might actually be about "the birds and the bees." Hula can be used as a metaphor to express how culturally significant ways of transmitting knowledge can enable research to reach our people. There needs to be a Native depth in the way we present our research, especially because formal written form is perhaps the least accessible to the majority of Indigenous people. Speaking directly to our people in alternative modes of communication in our work is in no way dumbing-down the work. Quite the opposite, it is out-rigorous and difficult to present research that is both academic and creative, that satisfies the demands and academic rigor of a Western academy and is also legible and accessible to a Native community.

We need to speak in the language of the people because the work must be understood at the grassroots to be empowering. In Hawai'i, in addition to English and 'ōlelo Hawai'i (the Hawaiian language) the language of the people includes Pidgin, often called "broken English" (known formally as Hawaiian Creole English—I like Pidgin better). A quintessential marker of "local" culture in Hawai'i as well as a signifier of class, I often refer to Pidgin as my "native tongue" at the same time that I am learning Hawaiian. For Hawaiians today, speaking and writing in 'ōlelo Hawai'i is vital because it is part of the larger cultural revitalization movement.

Our work must be legible to the people whose lived experiences are recorded and who have a stake in the work. In writing my dissertation and subsequent articles, including this one, I have spent time in a kind of writing I had never done before (personal, reflexive, and first person—a kind of writing that in the past was discouraged) to convey "meaning emerging out of articulation—the oral, the vernacular, the chant, the popular verse . . . [as] essences of experience" (Murray Chapman, personal communication, May 2007). Working in Native communities lends itself to experimenting with alternative ways of presenting research to make it resonate and reverberate with lived experience.

Reaching various audiences can also be enhanced by delving into the areas of culture, arts, and media technology. For example, my familiarity with some of our oral traditions and contemporary Hawaiian music has been mobilized in my research to present an oral literature built on a deep oral tradition. Performative, oral, and audiovisual modes of sharing knowledge should also be explored as creative ways of making our work accessible and meaningful. Likewise, contemporary fictional literature can also be used to provide an added dimension by building on oral traditions and fleshing them out in high definition. Experimentation with alternative ways of presenting research can lead to the creation of new mo'olelo (stories/histories) that have multiple meanings for a diverse audience.

From "Sink or Swim" to Professional Development

In their majesty, the peaks of the massive mountains wreathed in clouds appeared, rising above the developing storm below as we flew into Hilo on the Big Island of Hawai'i. Just the day before, I had arisen to the highest peak education can offer, enjoying my apotheosis at the University of Hawai'i at Mānoa, as a PhDeity, wreathed in lei. The pomp of wearing regalia and getting hooded for graduation seemed almost an afterthought to a long arduous journey.

Hilo is famous for its rains, which have their own names, and the runway was wet as the plane touched down. This was to be my first day of orientation as a new faculty member at the University of Hawai'i at Hilo. But instead I was disoriented that day. Hurricane Flosse was on its way, closing in on the southeastern part of the Big Island, right where our house was. Not even unpacked with a new baby on the way, we were definitely not ready for the cyclone. But I guess we were used to being in a whirlwind, frenetically writing while teaching a heavy load at the community college to finish my dissertation in time.

Just as I was taping up windows and we were settling in for the storm, the house started shaking—kind of surreal, I wondered what next? I guess you get used to earthquakes when living on an active volcano, and this must have been the fire goddess Madam Pele's welcome to us. I think she was also warning us that getting my first real job, a tenure-track position in geography at UH Hilo, would prove to be an earthshaking whirlwind.

Having bounced between two University of Hawai'i institutions, Mānoa the flagship and little sister Hilo, I was fortunate to be a part of geography departments that are "user friendly" for Indigenous scholars. In a deliberate effort to recruit Hawaiian and Pacific scholars, UH Mānoa's geography graduate program has been able to attract many up-and-coming indigenous scholars. Similarly, UH Hilo is particularly friendly to Hawaiian scholarship given its position as a center of Hawaiian language and culture. These programs helped break me in to the discipline, the profession, and the culture of the academy. Approaching geography in general, and Indigenous geography in particular, in open and welcoming environments has enabled me and others to thrive and/or survive in the discipline and academy, making a long voyage a little more comfortable.

Having departments and especially faculty that are supportive of Indigenous scholars is key in helping spawn a critical mass in Indigenous geography. Part of this support involves training Indigenous scholars through both formal and informal mentoring and faculty development. In addition to being indebted to the individuals who mentored me, such as my adviser (Brian Murton), dissertation committee members (Carlos Andrade, Murray Chapman, Jon Goss, Vilsoni Hereniko), department chair (Jim Juvik), and colleagues (Kathryn Besio, Nan Elmer, Sonia Juvik, Drew Kapp, Jon Price), I was also fortunate to participate in a few faculty development workshops while I was at UH Hilo.

During the summer of 2008, I had the opportunity to participate in the Geography Faculty Development Alliance (GFDA) Workshop at the University of Colorado, Boulder. Organized to move away from the old school sink-or-swim mentality, and to instead mentor and actively develop young geography faculty, the workshop provided me with a deeper understanding of how to manage various aspects of the culture shock of being on the faculty. I was impressed specifically by the alliance's foresight in trying to address diversity in the discipline as was exemplified in the broad cross section of geographers who exchanged a range of experiences at the workshops. Feelings of inadequacy, whatever flavor or pigmentation one may be, appear to be fairly universal among new faculty, but as mentioned previously, there seems to be a different learning curve for Indigenous scholars.

In the fall back at UH Hilo, I had the opportunity to do faculty development Hawaiian style. Organized by the university's Kīpuka Native Hawaiian Student Center, the Uluākea (profound knowledge) program was designed to teach faculty members Hawaiian culture so that they could incorporate Indigenous ways of knowing into their teaching. With place- and culture-based workshops and field trips, Uluākea enabled faculty participants to incorporate Hawaiian culture into the curriculum. It is good geography to teach faculty working in Native lands the host culture and ingenious to encourage the incorporation of Indigenous knowledge across disciplines. As one of the few Native Hawaiian faculty members on campus and in the program, I gained insights as to how it is out-rigorous for non-Indigenous scholars to add this depth to their teaching.

For me it is only natural and sometimes unconscious to incorporate local knowledge and Hawaiian culture into my teaching. By sharing stories, anecdotes, idioms, music, mannerisms, and jokes, I try to make my classroom come alive (or at least keep my students awake). When at UH Hilo I loved teaching the local demographic who are in the majority on campus, and who often caught my jokes. The pushback I've gotten when sharing this knowledge is not that my jokes are bad, but that generally the pigmentally challenged continental students didn't always get or appreciate my jokes. They feel that I'm favoring the locals and don't appreciate the power/knowledge inversion of a local/Native professor on home turf teaching Indigenous and local knowledge. They don't appreciate needing a glossary or Hawaiian dictionary, having to work and study harder on assignments that are easier for those in the know. I love the inversion: Welcome to our world of out-rigor. For too long in Hawai'i, there has been a non-Native and nonlocal bias in teaching, so much so that Hawaiians and locals are used to the bias and being the ones left out of the joke. Just as the clown, jester, or trickster is allowed to temporarily invert power relationships, Indigenous scholars are in a position to turn the tables and disrupt what is considered common sense and taken-for-granted knowledge.

Nativity: Return to the Sands of My Birth

Hiki mai e nā pua i ka la'iē
Ke pi'i a'ela i ka mauna ki'eki'e
Ha'a mai nā kama me ka makua
He wehi pūlama a o ke kupuna
E ka'i mai ana e ka'i mai ana
E hahai I ka leo o ka Haku ē
Aloha ē, Aloha ē, Aloha ē

Come forth children in the calm of the day
Ascending the mountain heights
Humbly arise, children with your parents
As cherished adornments of your ancestors
Leading forward, dancing in step
Following the voice of the Lord
Forever exchanging the breath of life.[1]

My tenure at UH Hilo was a sudden and brief earthshaking whirlwind, and I left after two short years. Unfortunately, I never got my feet planted, and for personal and family reasons I returned home. I am indebted to a geography department and institution that welcomed me, was very supportive and collegial, and wanted me to succeed. Most would have said leaving was not a good move as far as an academic career is concerned, but just like going to a luau when I should have been writing, my career is shaped by my family, culture, and identity, which all come together in place.

The *oli* (chant) *Hiki Mai E Nā Pua,* is the oli of the Hawaiian studies program at Brigham Young University Hawai'i, where I now teach. It speaks of climbing the mountain of education, and thereby honoring our ancestors and God. I have returned to my home community and shape-shifted again, working not explicitly in geography, but in a Hawaiian and Pacific studies context. Returning full circle, I now reflect on geography, the canoe that has brought me home to teach and research in the place of my nativity.

Like Kamapua'a, the shape-shifting pig god, I've changed my identity once again, re-creating myself, no longer disciplined by geography. With a Native studies orientation I feel somewhat comfortable because I've always thought that geography is a perfect fit for Indigenous knowledge. Considered both a strength and a weakness, its breadth is shared by programs like Hawaiian studies and Pacific Islands studies, which can involve anything Hawaiian or Oceanic. In fact, in addition to geography departments that have welcomed me, as a Native scholar it is easy to see how the discipline itself, which allows for surfing and diving breadths and depths, can and should likewise be welcoming to Indigenous scholarship. Further, the place-centered orientation of geography is a near-perfect fit for Hawaiian studies, as evidenced by the growing number of Hawaiian geographers who not coincidentally find themselves in Hawaiian studies positions.

One of the drawbacks is that because I am not shielded by the disciplinary department, I have to take the full brunt of the spears that come my way. When Indigenous anger was leveled at academics in the past, it was easy to sidestep and hide behind geography, at the same time deflecting the spears to a discipline like anthropology, an easy target. Many don't know what geography is, not to mention the identity crises the discipline has survived—geography has many *kinolau* (body forms) that can confuse both friend and foe. Anthropology, in contrast, fairly or unfairly, is perhaps too well known for its historic problematic treatment of Indigenous people and culture. Geography is clearly not innocent in the way it has similarly dealt with (or not dealt with) Native people, but the discipline lacks the infamous notoriety that anthropology has—such is the nature of disciplined knowledge and power. For me personally, geography has been an amiable, welcoming, and nonconfrontational field that has been a good fit for my Indigenous community (these qualities are very Hawaiian).

Now that I'm not a geographer who happens to be Native, but instead a professor of Hawaiian studies, I'm supposed to be an expert on everything Hawaiian. I feel the burden of an Indigenous community in a Native studies context in my home community much more than if I were in a geography department.

So now here I sit, back in my home community, at times like Kamapuaʻa with my back against the wall. I can see that geography has allowed me to understand my place as a Native scholar more deeply and has been the vessel that brought me home. It has been a vehicle, or a canoe, that has allowed me to fulfill my *kuleana* (rights and responsibilities) to academic and Indigenous communities. Changing form like Kamapuaʻa, as I leave the canoe *Kaliuwaʻa*, I see it is still with me. I realize that in one way, shape, or form, everything about where I am now living, teaching, and researching, coalesces with my own sense of place, identity, and culture.

Note

1. "Hiki Mai E Nā Pua" was composed in 1997 by Kumu Hula (dance master) Cy Bridges and taught by "Uncle Bill" William Wallace, director of the Jonathan Nāpela Center for Hawaiian Language and Cultural Studies at BYU-Hawaiʻi. My translation.

References

Andrade, C. L. 2001. *Ha'ena, ahupua'a: Towards a Hawaiian Geography.* PhD thesis. Geography, University of Hawai'i at Mānoa.

———. 2008. *Hā'ena: Through the Eyes of the Ancestors.* Honolulu: University of Hawai'i Press.

Bradshaw, M., and E. Stratford. 2000. "Qualitative Research Design and Rigour." In *Qualitative Research Methods in Human Geography*, edited by I. Hay, 37–49. South Melbourne, Victoria, Australia: Oxford University Press.

Burson, C., and A. Williams. 1969. *Go My Son.* Sheet music. School of Music, Brigham Young University, Provo, UT. Distributed by Tantara Records.

Clifford, J. 2001. "Indigenous articulations." *Contemporary Pacific* 13 (2): 467–90.

Fermantez, K. 2004. "Staying on Par and the Home/Field Advantage in Wai'anae, Hawai'i." *Regeneration* 4 (2): 2–4.

———. 2007a. *Between the Hui and Da Hui Inc.: Incorporating N-Oceans of Native Hawaiian Resistance In Oceanic Cultural Studies.* Special publication, Center for Pacific Island Studies, University of Hawai'i at Mānoa.

———. 2007b. "Re-Placing Hawaiians: Sense of Place and Identity in Wai'anae." PhD thesis. Geography, University of Hawai'i at Mānoa.

Greenwood, D. J., and M. Levin. 1998. *Introduction to Action Research: Social Research for Social Change.* Thousand Oaks, CA: Sage.

Hereniko, V. 1999. "Representations of Cultural Identities." In *Inside Out: Literature, Cultural Politics, and Identity in the New Pacific*, edited by V. Hereniko and R. Wilson, 137–66. Lanham, MD: Rowman and Littlefield.

Herr, K., and Gary Anderson. 2005. *The Action Research Dissertation: A Guide for Students and Faculty.* Thousand Oaks, CA: Sage.

Johnson, J. T. 2008. "Kitchen Table Discourse: Negotiating the 'Tricky Ground' of Indigenous Research." *American Indian Cultural and Research Journal* 32 (3): 127–37.

Kame'eleihiwa, L. 1992. *Native Land and Foreign Desires: Pehea la e pono ai?* Honolulu: Bishop Museum Press.

Kauanui, J. K. 1998. "Off-Island Hawaiians 'Making' Themselves at 'Home': A [Gendered] Contradiction in Terms?" *Women's Studies International Forum* 21 (6): 681–93.

Kearns, R. 2000. "Being There: Research through Observing and Participating." In *Qualitative Research Methods in Human Geography*, edited by I. Hay, 103–21. South Melbourne, Victoria, Australia: Oxford University Press.

Kindon, S., and S. Elwood. 2009. "Introduction: More Than Methods—Reflections on Participatory Action Research in Geographic Teaching, Learning, and Research." *Journal of Geography in Higher Education* 33 (1): 19–32.

Louis, R. 2007. "Can You Hear Us Now? Voices from the Margin: Using Indigenous Methodologies in Geographic Research." *Geographical Research* 45 (2): 130–39.

McTaggart, R. ed. 1997. *Participatory Action Research: International Contexts and Consequences.* Albany: State University of New York Press.

Oliveira, K. A. 2006. "Ke alanui kike'eke'e o maui: na wai ho'i ka 'ole o ke akamai, he alanui i ma'a i ka hele 'ia e o'u mau makua." PhD thesis. Geography, University of Hawai'i at Mānoa.

Pain, R., and S. Kindon. 2007. "Participatory Geographies." *Environment and Planning A* 39 (12): 2807–12.

Park, P., M. Brydon-Miller, B. Hall, and T. Jackson, eds. 1993. *Voices of Change: Participatory Research in the United States and Canada*. Westport, CT: Bergin and Garvey.

Pyrch, T., and M. Castillo. 2001. "The Sights and Sounds of Indigenous Knowledge." In *Handbook of Action Research: Participatory Inquiry and Practice*, edited by P. Reason and H. Bradbury, 379–85. London: Sage.

Reason, P., and H. Bradbury, eds. 2001. *Handbook of Action Research: Participative Inquiry and Practice*. London: Sage.

Smith, L. T. 1999. *Decolonizing Methodologies: Research and Indigenous Communities*. New York: St. Martin's Press.

Stringer, E. T. 1999. *Action Research*. 2nd ed. Thousand Oaks, CA: Sage.

Suryanata, K., and K. Umemoto. 2003. "Tension at the Nexus of the Global and Local: Culture, Property and Marine Aquaculture in Hawai'i." *Environment and Planning A* 35 (2): 199–213.

Tengan, T. 2008. *Native Men Remade: Gender and Nation in Contemporary Hawai'i*. Durham, NC: Duke University Press.

Waddell, E. 1993. "Jean-Marie Tjibaou: Kanak Witness to the World." In *The Margin Fades: Geographical Itineraries in a World of Islands*, edited by E. Waddell and P. Nunn, 66–91. Suva, Fiji: Institute of Pacific Studies, University of the South Pacific.

Wilcox, C., K. Hussey, V. Hollinger, and Puakea Nogelmeier. 2003. *He Mele Aloha: A Hawaiian Songbook*. Honolulu: 'Oli'Oli Productions.

REIMAGINING LANDSCAPE, ENVIRONMENT, AND MANAGEMENT

Kaitiakitanga
Telling the Stories of Environmental Guardianship
JAY T. JOHNSON

> Place has dropped out of sight in the "globalization craze" of recent
> years, and this erasure of place has profound consequences for
> our understanding of culture, knowledge, nature, and economy.
> —Arturo Escobar, "Culture Sits in Places"

My decision to travel to Aotearoa/New Zealand to explore Māori self-determination in resource management did not start out as an exploration of place. Perhaps naively, I was so preoccupied by my central goal of uncovering how the New Zealand government's commitment to biculturalism was playing out in 2001, a decade into their revolutionary and perhaps vain experiment with holistic resource management in the form of the Resource Management Act of 1991 (RMA), that the politics of place within which these struggles over resource management were playing out was not at the forefront of my mind. Perhaps, as many an academic is wont to do, I was privileging my intellectual pursuits over embodied learning and knowing as I tripped through place. Luckily, I had guides who took me out of the library and archive to explore the beach, the harbor, and the river, to see firsthand what was being struggled over. Hopefully I was not so lost in the "globalization craze" to quote Escobar (2001, 141) that I was totally disconnected from understanding the role of place in Māori struggles and in understandings of culture, knowledge, nature, and economy, but it was finally in place that all I had read and heard from those *kaitaiki* (guardians) began to make sense.

As I have already stated elsewhere (Johnson 2008), my engagement with Māori concerning their self-determination over the management of valued community resources is founded in my own epistemological and ontological understandings, based within both Native American and Western ways of seeing and knowing the world. My Native American heritage provided me with related, although at times very different, understandings of the environment I was encountering with my Māori guides. Grounding oneself through connections to rivers, villages, and ancestors was all very familiar, but being from the Great Plains, the connections to mountains were as unfamiliar as were some significant Māori concepts such as *mana*. Unbeknown to me, I was learning not just about Māori self-determination and biculturalism but also about a new way of understanding the environment and the significant places contained within it. To accomplish this, though, I had to begin to understand an ontology that was completely new to me. I had to break out of the "hall of mirrors," the reflection of the academic perpetually speaking to himself or herself, and begin down an uncanny path, which at times was unsettling, to say the least (see Howitt and Suchet-Pearson 2003).

Although the path I had set out to walk was largely focused on describing Māori self-determination in an effort to discover whether it provided a successful model for other Indigenous nations around the world, it was very academic in its orientation. I was, after all, setting out to write a dissertation and receive a doctorate of philosophy in geography from the University of Hawai'i; "academic" was what was expected. Soon I realized, though, that to record and understand the stories of guardianship (*kaitiakitanga*) of the environment that I was receiving meant that I would have to open myself to the metaphysical and to seeing the environment as holistic instead of dualistic in nature. I would have to appreciate the "more-than-human" environment, the agency of a vast array of biotic, abiotic, and metaphysical entities (see Whatmore 2002; Ingold and Ingold 2006). Where does one begin in learning a new ontology? How far back do you have to go? As a Māori research collaborator said to my adviser when he questioned why I was exploring Māori cosmologies instead of material he deemed to be more pertinent to my research, "You leave him alone; he's doing it the right way; he's starting at the beginning!"

Learning a New of Way of Seeing and Relating to the Environment

As Eric Schwimmer has observed, Māori cosmology has "the distinction of peering most deeply into the infinite darkness that existed before life began" (Schwimmer 1966; quoted in Roberts, Norman, et al. 1995, 8). It is within this "infinite darkness" that Māori *whakapapa*, or genealogies, have their foundation. According to Māori cosmology, everything has evolved from Te Kore, the realm of potential being through the long and everlasting night (Te Pō) into the world of light and knowing (Te Ao Mārama) (see Marsden and Royal 2003). It is within this world of light that the biotic and abiotic world is created through the union of Papatūānuku (Mother Earth) and Ranginui (Father Sky). The *whakapapa* of everything around us traces back to this union, which led to the birth of the many children who became the gods, or *atua*, and who in turn serve as the progenitors of "all known phenomena, living and nonliving" (Roberts, Haami, et al. 2004, 3). Important among these atua are Tāne, the god of forest trees, birds, insects, rocks, and in some tribal traditions, humans; Tangaroa, the god of the sea and all creatures related to marine and fresh water; Rongo, the god of cultivated foods and peace; and, Haumia, the god of uncultivated or wild foods. These atua not only serve as the progenitors of every component of the environment but also as kaitiaki, or guardians, of all they create. Much like attentive parents, they continue to oversee their children.

Within the Māori language this understanding of the universe is referred to as Mātauranga Māori, which can be defined in a traditional context to mean "the knowledge, comprehension or understanding of everything visible or invisible that exists across the universe, including language, traditional environmental knowledge and traditional cultural knowledge" (National Library of New Zealand 2006). This conceptualization of the universe as an all-encompassing genealogy means that no distinction is made to compartmentalize insects and humans or even stars and ferns within this cosmology, all are inextricably related. To truly embrace this ontology, I had to call into question a number of powerful modernist juxtapositions such as natural/supernatural, culture/nature, and living/nonliving (see Roberts, Haami, et al. 2004). Although this construct of the universe as one genealogy was new to me, it fit well within my Native American understandings of an interrelated universe with humans in the role of younger sibling. What was more challenging was the idea that I would need to bring the supernatural into my academic work.

Kaitiakitanga

Seeking to understand any concept within the Māori language requires some basic understanding of the *whakapapa*, or genealogy, of the concept, an idea also common in Michel Foucault's work (see Foucault and Rabinow 1984). My journey to understand the term *kaitiakitanga*, a key Māori environmental concept that has been included and defined within the RMA as part of an effort to give voice to Māori efforts at protecting their valued resources, started with a purely academic understanding but eventually came back to cosmological roots.

As Merata Kawharu describes it, the word "kaitiankitanga" may be recent, coming into common usage only in the 1980s, but "the underlying values and cultural convictions have been key facets of Māori life for generations in the management of resources and the promotion of identity" (Kawharu 2000, 350). Kaitiakitanga describes a resource-management regime based within a universe ordered by a genealogical descent-time within a kinship-space. It is a guardianship founded within human genealogical connections to places and expressed within the politics of chieftainship (*rangatiratanga*). Since the signing of the RMA in 1991, it has also become a term defined within the New Zealand legal code as "the exercise of guardianship by the tangata whenua (aboriginal people) of an area in accordance with the tikanga Māori (customary law) in relation to natural and physical resources; and includes the ethic of stewardship" (Resource Management Act 1991). It is a concept that this same legislation requires the national, regional, and local governments to "have particular regard to." How significant its influence actually is, is a matter of much debate by Māori and resource managers throughout New Zealand (cf. Beverly 1997; McShane 1999; Skelton and Memon 2002; Tomas 1994). Many have argued that this rather simplistic definition found within the RMA removes the concept from its ontological framework and has turned it into a rather hollow shell, particularly since the legislation does not include reference to its place within the traditional knowledge of Māori, Mātauranga Māori (Hayes 1998).

Māori have not relied on legislation, though, to permit them to continue to act as guardians of their treasured resources. The role of kaitiaki has been an honored position with significant responsibilities since long before the RMA, or the Treaty of Waitangi for that matter. To defend a valued resource through actions or words is to assert one's *mana*, or "lawful permission" delegated by atua (gods), received through one's ancestors or demonstrated by one's accomplishments (see Marsden and Henare 1992). With or without the legal recognition of the state, Māori continue to act as kaitiaki over those resources which they have been invested to protect. The relationship between the kaitiaki and the resource protected is one of "reciprocal appropriation" (Momaday 1976, 80). The guardian invests his *mana* into the preservation of the resource and in turn derives from the resource *mana*, spiritual life and food to feed his or her community (Johnson 2003).

The humans serving in the role of kaitiaki over various resources across Aotearoa/New Zealand are only one form of guardian, though. As mentioned previously, the offspring of Papatūānuku and Ranginui also serve as spiritual guardians over their offspring. Tāne keeps watch over the trees in the forest, along with many of the animals that inhabit the forest, and Tangaroa guards the fish of the sea, lakes, and rivers. Yet these atua serve as only one form of spiritual guardian. Taniwha, or water spirits taking the form of giant lizards, also serve as guardians of particular harbors or stretches of rivers. All these spiritual guardians have their genesis in the *poutiriao*, supernatural preservers of the welfare of all things within creation. As the universe emerged from the cosmic night (Te Pō), the poutiriao were created to maintain balance in creation by guarding every heaven, realm, and division of nature (Best 1913, 101). Acting in concert, the spiritual and human kaitiaki serve to protect the resources of the physical and spiritual world.

Knowing this on an intellectual level was only the beginning of what became a transformation of my way of understanding environmental guardianship. Growing up as a mixed-race Native American, I had some understanding that guardianship over the environment was an expectation, but as an urban Indian, I did not have a great deal of practical experience with what that should mean in my daily life. The clichéd example of the "crying Indian" portrayed by the Italian American actor who took the name, Iron Eyes Cody, lamenting the trash dumped at his feet in public service ads produced in the United States in the 1970s, has become an enduring modern American example of Indigenous environmental guardianship. This was definitely not the sort of "caring for the land" I was beginning to grasp through my research in Aotearoa/New Zealand.

Walking the Beach

> Movement . . . is not adjunct to knowledge, as it is in the educational theory that underwrites classroom practice. Rather, the movement of walking is itself a way of knowing. A knowledgeable person is distinguished from a novice not by the sheer amount of information packed into his or her head—information that would in any case be perpetually obsolescent in an ever-changing environment—but by observational acuity and an awareness of the consequences of actions.
> —Tim Ingold and Jo Lee Vergunst, Introduction in *Ways of Walking:*
> *Ethnography and Practice on Foot*

Naively, I thought my research work in Aotearoa/New Zealand was complete; I was done. I had spent the previous months looking through material in the archives. I had attended resource consent consultations with Ngati Wairere hapū and Mighty River Power over the company's desire to raise and lower the river levels more rapidly than their current consent allowed. There had been the mediation hearings, ordered by the Environment Court, between Tainui hapū and the Waikato District Council over the council's current sewage disposal scheme for the small city of Raglan, which was dumping only partially treated sewage into Whāingaroa/Raglan Harbor. There were the interviews I had conducted all around the North Island including a trip to Lincoln University on the South Island to meet with Professor Hirini Matunga about his work on Māori resource management. I honestly thought I had reached the end of what I could reasonably learn about Māori self-determination and the RMA! Unfortunately, arrogance had once again reared its ugly head.

My dissertation adviser, Brian Murton, had traveled from Honolulu to Hamilton, my research base, in part to see how I was doing with my research. He listened with his usual patience to my description of what I had learned and how I thought I would write up the research. He nodded knowingly and suggested that I accompany him to visit some of his cousins who live in Dargaville on the north end of the Kaipara Harbor. He was not sure that I would learn anything new, but along the way we could stop and visit some of the individuals from Te Uri o Hau hapū he had worked with on their Waitangi Tribunal claim. I was particularly interested in learning more about the tribunal claims process and jumped at the chance.

After months of fog and cold in Hamilton I was very glad to be heading north toward sunny, fine weather. Our visit at Maungatoroto with the folks from Te Uri o Hau went well, and I did indeed learn more about their particular claims process and its resolution. We left that meeting with a bag of oysters given to Brian and headed on to Dargaville and his cousins. They were very welcoming and glad to see the oysters we had with us. After hearing about my research interests, they decided that I should meet another cousin who lives in the area, Jim Te Tuhi, who serves as kaitiaki on a long stretch of beach claimed by Te Uri o Hau hapū.

Jim came to visit me the next morning, and I really had no idea what to expect. He brought several notebooks full of material he had been collecting about his work on Ripiro Beach, which runs from Pouto to Maunganui Bluff along the Tasman Sea (figure 8). While he ran an errand in town, he left me with the notebooks so that I could have time to look through them before he returned. Once back from town, Jim decided that I should actually see the beach, walk the beach, so that I could understand his work as kaitiaki firsthand.

We drove out to the beach in Jim's pickup, while he told me stories about the *taonga*, or treasured resource, he is most interested in protecting, the *toheroa*, or giant surf clam. Jim had at that point started working with marine researchers from several different universities and organizations on the life cycle of the toheroa. Although the clam had once been a valuable foodstuff, once even canned for export, there has been a ban on harvesting the clams on most beaches, especially in Northland, since 1971 (Stace 1991; Murton 2006). Prior to the rapid decline in numbers in the 1960s, the clams could be found in the millions on beaches around Dargaville and at lengths exceeding 140–200 millimeters. Despite the decline in numbers over the last several decades, it is only since the late 1990s that significant research has been done into the life cycle and health of the toheroa.

As we walked the beach, Jim told me the story of the life cycle of the toheroa according to Mātauranga Māori. This valuable *kaimoana*, or shellfish, has been a significant foodstuff since the ancestors of Māori first arrived in the islands. Jim told me that Māori believe that the toheroa breed in early spring, moving up from the deeper waters off the beach to the high-water mark where females lay their eggs and males fertilize them. Once the young have hatched, they are blown by the stiff onshore winds up the sand dunes and into the pingao grass, also known by Māori as the eyebrow of Tāne. Jim tells me that the replacement of the native pingao grass with spinifex grass from Australia, a common grass used in sand dune restoration projects throughout New Zealand, has contributed to the steep decline in toheroa numbers. He believes that the spinifex grass does not provide a hospitable home for

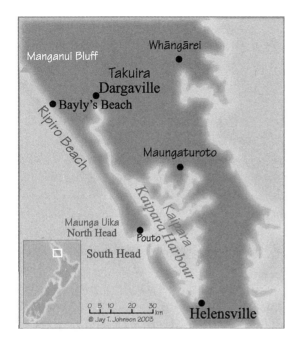

Fig. 8. Ripiro Beach Map

the young fry and states that areas of the dunes where there is still pingao grass are the areas with the largest populations of clams. While lodged in the pingao grass, Jim informs me, the young fry mature, awaiting easterly winds that generally arrive in September and push the fry back down the beach into the surf during the high spring tides, where they dig into the sand and continue to mature (see Te Tuhi and Gregory 2008). This life-cycle story is widely told among Māori and can even be read in one version or another in newspaper accounts of the clams ("Toheroa" 1927; "Tohera Breeding" 1950).

Western science has a very different account of the life cycle of the giant surf clam, despite the fact that it has only recently engaged in research on the topic. The scientific account makes no mention of Māori deities and does not connect at all on several key points with the story Jim told me. Glenys Stace recounts the scientific version of the giant surf clam's life cycle for *New Zealand Geographic* as a fertilization that occurs in the ocean, where the small fry "live and grow in the plankton for about 20 days before being eventually washed up on the beach as miniature toheroa smaller than a pinhead by incoming tides" (Stace 1991, 22). The Western version of the story provides no role for the beach grasses, indigenous or alien, in the life cycle of the clams. This disconnect between the Western scientific account and the Indigenous ecological account is not limited to the life cycle of toheroa on New Zealand beaches. The arrogance of Western science has relegated Indigenous ecological knowledge to the level of myth over the past several centuries as it has placed itself at the pinnacle of global intellectual pursuits (see Johnson and Murton 2007). As Turnbull (2000) has observed, all knowledge is local knowledge, and Jim's work with the marine biologists has helped them over time to integrate Māori perspectives into the research on toheroa, although they continue to discount the role of beach grasses in the life cycle.

Walking the beach with Jim and hearing him recount his work protecting the toheroa was less in the end about the giant surf clams and much more about me finally seeing and understanding environmental guardianship as enacted by a kaitiaki. Jim's dedication to his guardian role for the beach and the toheroa has sometimes required that he break the laws of the government of New Zealand, particularly since the government considers the clam a protected species. Jim sees his role as guardian requiring an involved and active propagation of the species that led him to relocate toheroa from densely populated beds to areas where there are few of the creatures in an effort to help the species survive. He also sees his guardianship extending to stopping poachers from taking illegal harvests using whatever nonviolent means are at his disposal. From the government's perspective, the guardianship of the beach and protected species is the purview of the Ministry of Fisheries and its field officers, and is governed by the laws of the nation-state. For the government, this is about the exercise of sovereignty.

For Jim and Te Uri o Hau, guardianship is about the exercise of Indigenous self-determination over their resources. Although the government recognizes that Māori have a customary right to take toheroa for cultural purposes, it has failed to recognize Māori rights to protect and actively manage this resource. Jim allowed me to have a copy of a letter he had sent to the (then) Minister of Fisheries, the Right Honorable Mr. Hudson, in which he outlines his work to save the toheroa and serve as kaitiaki on the beach. He takes it upon himself to educate the minister concerning the meaning of several key words contained in his letter as well as the RMA including *kaitiaki, kaitiakitanga,* and *taonga.* The primary purpose of the letter was to request official recognition from the government of his right to serve as kaitiaki. Jim describes in the letter that "this appointment of Kaitiaki means . . . that I believe that I have the right to disturb Toheroa and see that they are there for future generations" (Te Tuhi 2000). After several years of letter writing, Jim was successful and received a highly prized license from the Ministry of Fisheries outlining his right to exercise his *iwi,* or tribally, granted authority. Jim's diligence contributed to the government's creating a formal category that recognizes kaitiaki throughout the country. His work has also led to a Māori-language children's book describing his guardianship of the toheroa (Te Awa and New Zealand Ministry of Education 2008).

A Deeper Sense of Place . . .

The time I spent walking the beach with Jim helped me gain a greater understanding of *kaitiakitanga* and of the actions I had witnessed by Māori throughout Aotearoa/ New Zealand in protecting their treasured environmental resources. Sometimes small and simple, other times complex and based within the legal constructs of court cases, these acts were all geared toward a guardianship founded within Mātauranga Māori, an ontology that orders the universe through genealogical connection and interrelatedness.

Māori guardianship is a form of Indigenous self-determination they enact upon the landscapes of their ancestors. As they do so, they are maintaining the *mana* they receive from the land by continuing to speak and act on its behalf. This reciprocal relationship necessitates their active engagement, not only to maintain balance within the ecosystem, but also to maintain individual and community identities. The Māori word for land, *whenua*, is the same word used for placenta. A Māori child's afterbirth is buried in the land to which they belong so that literally to look after the land and its resources is to "look after" one's self as well.

These acts of self-determination in defense of lands and resources do not play out within a Māori-controlled political environment. Despite the promise laid out in the Treaty of Waitangi to protect the rights of Māori to continue their self-determination over "their lands, villages and all of their treasures," sovereignty over the islands eventually became exclusively the domain of the settler-state (Kawharu 2011). These acts of self-determination then occur outside of and frequently in conflict with the state. Whereas the apparatus of state sovereignty is plainly visible, Fleras and Spoonley have observed that, "only the exercise of tino rangatiratanga [Māori self-determination] provides tangible evidence of its existence" (Fleras and Spoonley 1999, 27). In order to see this evidence one must read the landscape and hope to glimpse places outside of the hegemonic control of the settler-state (Johnson 2010).

To see the evidence of Māori self-determination over their lands and resources, I had to look outside of the library and archive and walk the beach. In walking the beach I did indeed glimpse the exercise of Māori self-determination; in fact, I was able to see it firsthand. Learning while I walked with Jim afforded me an embodied experience that was grounded in an inherently sociable engagement, not only with Jim but also with the landscape. This form of fieldwork, as Jo Lee and Tim Ingold (2006, 68) observe, allows for ethnographic work to become auto-ethnographic in nature. In the end, I was able not only to describe Jim's guardianship of the beach but I have also had the opportunity to discuss how this experience has affected my understandings of environmental guardianship. Certainly, this embodied engagement with the beach has provided me with a deeper sense of the place-based knowledge Jim had to share. It also allowed me a firsthand experience of the place-based struggles to protect the beach and its treasured resources. Although these kinds of experiences are not unique in geographic research, it is worth considering how this embodied learning changes us as researchers.

To walk alongside those who hold the "deep spatial knowledge" of the places we research is to open ourselves up to being transformed by the experience (Wildcat 2009, 83). But we must open ourselves to this transformation or our experience is more likely to produce no new paradigm-altering experience. To open ourselves to a new ontology is perhaps the most uncanny experience our research can provide but perhaps also the most rewarding. Breaking out of the "hall of mirrors" and glimpsing the everyday lived experiences of others can provide us with a more profound sense of dwelling and caring about the places we encounter on every walk we take.

References

Best, E. 1913. "The Cult of Io, the Concept of a Supreme Deity as Evolved by the Ancestors of the Polynesians." *Man* 13:98–103.

Beverly, P. 1997. "The RMA and the Protection of Māori Interests: Recent Developments." *Resource Management Bulletin* 2 (7): 76–80.

Escobar, A. 2001. "Culture Sits in Places: Reflections on Globalism and Subaltern Strategies of Localization. *Political Geography* 20 (2): 139–74.

Fleras, A., and P. Spoonley. 1999. *Recalling Aotearoa: Indigenous Politics and Ethnic Relations in New Zealand*. Auckland: Oxford University Press.

Foucault, M., and P. Rabinow. 1984. *The Foucault Reader*. 1st ed. New York: Pantheon Books.

Hayes, S. 1998. "Defining Kaitiakitanga and the Resource Management Act 1991." *Auckland University Law Review* 8 (3): 893–99.

Howitt, R., and S. Suchet-Pearson. 2003. "Ontological Pluralism in Contested Cultural Landscapes." In *Handbook of Cultural Geography*, edited by K. Anderson, 557–69. Thousand Oaks, CA: Sage.

Ingold, J. L., and T. Ingold. 2006. "Fieldwork on Foot: Perceiving, Routing, Socializing." In *Locating the Field: Space, Place and Context in Anthropology*, edited by S. Coleman and P. Collins, 67–85. Oxford: Berg.

Ingold, T., and J. L. Vergunst. 2008. Introduction to *Ways of Walking: Ethnography and Practice on Foot*, edited by T. Ingold and J. L. Vergunst. Aldershot, England: Ashgate.

Johnson, J. T. 2003. "Biculturalism, Resource Management. and Indigenous Self-determination." PhD thesis. Geography, University of Hawai'i at Mānoa, Honolulu.

———. 2008. "Kitchen Table Discourse: Negotiating the 'Tricky Ground' of Indigenous Research." *American Indian Cultural and Research Journal* 32 (3): 127–37.

————. 2010. "Indigenenity's Challenges to the Settler State: Decentring the 'Imperial Binary.'" In *Making Settler Colonial Space: Perspectives on Race, Place, and Identity*, edited by T. Banivanua-Mar and P. Edmonds, 273–94. Houndmills, Basingstoke, Hampshire: Palgrave Macmillan.

Johnson, J. T., and B. Murton. 2007. "Re/placing Native Science: Indigenous Voices in Contemporary Constructions of Nature." *Geographical Research* 45 (2):121–29.

Kawharu, H. S. 2011. *Translation of the Māori Text of the Treaty of Waitangi 1840.* Webpage. New Zealand E-Government Unit 1987 (cited September 8, 2011). Available from http://www.waitangi-tribunal.govt.nz/treaty/kawharutranslation.asp.

Kawharu, M. 2000. "Kaitiakitanga: A Māori Anthropological Perspective of the Māori Socio-Environmental Ethic of Resource Management." *Journal of the Polynesian Society* 109 (4): 349–70.

Marsden, M., and T. A. Henare. 1992. *Kaitiakitanga: A Definitive Introduction to the Holistic World View of the Māori.* Wellington, NZ: Ministry for the Environment.

Marsden, M., and T. A. u. C. Royal. 2003. *The Woven Universe: Selected Writings of Rev. Māori Marsden.* Otaki, NZ.: Estate of Rev. Māori Marsden.

McShane, O. 1999. "Māori Issues and the RMA." *New Zealand Law Journal* (September): 346–47.

Momaday, N. S. 1976. "Native American Attitudes to the Environment." In *Seeing with a Native Eye*, edited by W. H. Capps, 79–85. New York: Harper and Row.

Murton, B. 2006. "'Toheroa Wars': Cultural Politics and Everyday Resistance on a Northern New Zealand Beach." *New Zealand Geographer* 62 (1): 25–38.

National Library of New Zealand. 2011. *Mātauranga Māori.* National Library of New Zealand 2006 (cited August 17, 2011). Available from http://www.natlib.govt.nz/collections/online-exhibitions/matauranga-maori.

Resource Management Act. New Zealand Parliament 069. October 1, 1991.

Roberts, M., B. Haami, R. A. Benton, T. Satterfield, M. L. Finucane, M. Henare, and M. Henare. 2004. "Whakapapa as a Māori Mental Construct: Some Implications for the Debate over Genetic Modification of Organisms." *Contemporary Pacific* 16 (1): 1–28.

Roberts, M., W. Norman, N. K. Minhinnick, D. Wihongi, and C. Kirkwood. 1995. "Kaitiakitanga: Māori Perspectives on Conservation." *Pacific Conservation Biology* 2 (1): 7–20.

Schwimmer, E. 1966. *The World of the Māori.* Wellington, NZ: A. H. and A. W. Reed.

Skelton, P., and P. A. Memon. 2002. "Adopting Sustainability as an Overarching Environmental Policy: A Review of Section 5 of the RMA." *Resource Management Journal* 10 (1): 1–10.

Stace, G. 1991. "The Elusive Toheroa." *New Zealand Geographic* 18–34.

Te Awa, M., and New Zealand Ministry of Education. 2008. *James Henare Te Tuhi: te kaitiaki toheroa.* [Wellington, NZ]: Huia.

Te Tuhi, J., and R. Gregory. 2008. *Toheroa.* [Wellington, NZ]: Huia Education.

Te Tuhi, J. H. 2000. *Toheroa Relocation and Survey of Riprio and Rangatira Beaches.* Te Kopuru, NZ, 17 April 2000.

"Toheroa." 1927. *The Dominion*, April 21.

"Toheroa Breeding Knowledge Would Be Useful In Discussions." 1950. *Northland Times,*
    September 8.

Tomas, N. 1994. "Implementing Kaitiakitanga under the RMA." *New Zealand Environment
    Law Reporter* 1 (2): 39–42.

Turnbull, D. 2000. *Masons, Tricksters, and Cartographers: Comparative Studies in the
    Sociology of Scientific and Indigenous Knowledge.* Australia: Harwood Academic.

Whatmore, S. 2002. *Hybrid Geographies: Natures, Cultures, Spaces.* Thousand Oaks, CA:
    Sage.

Wildcat, D. R. 2009. *Red Alert!: Saving the Planet with Indigenous Knowledge.* Golden, CO:
    Fulcrum.

From Landscape to Whenua
Thoughts on Interweaving Indigenous and Western Ideas about Landscape

BRIAN MURTON

In this essay I reflect on the understanding that Māori, the Indigenous people of Aotearoa/New Zealand, have of "landscape." Although a quintessentially European term, "landscape" is widely used throughout the world today, even among peoples whose homelands have been settled by Europeans and especially where English is the dominant language. The essay arises out of my experiences in a number of research projects among Māori during the 1990s and early 2000s, and especially one that dealt with "landscape transformation" in the late eighteenth century and early nineteenth, in which, on occasion, the participants seemed to be "talking past" one another, especially when using common English words that are also academic concepts, such as "landscape." It became apparent that many Māori participants had a very different understanding of the term "landscape," although they were quite willing to use the term when speaking English. At the same time, primarily through teaching a graduate cultural geography seminar at the University of Hawai'i, I became intrigued by the parallels between Māori understandings of place, another key geographical idea, and how some Western scholars (philosophers, anthropologists, geographers, for example) were writing about it, and about landscape, from a phenomenological perspective.

I began to explore both Māori and Western understandings of "landscape" in seminars and with students, many of Indigenous background, at the University of Hawai'i, in discussions with Māori scholars and academics at meetings in Aotearoa, and in a number of conference papers. As my own understanding grew, I realized that much of my uneasiness resulted from the way in which "landscape" was being "represented" by Māori participants in the "landscape transformation" project in relationship to the way in which it is portrayed in most scholarly writing. Edward Casey (2002, xv) notes that representation is not problematic because it happens, but in how it happens. This provides the focus for my reflections: If Māori think differently about "landscape," how do they "represent" it? This led me to consider two further questions: Did Māori in the period under consideration (1769–1840) have a conception of "landscape" as a unified scene? And is it appropriate to even use the term "represent" to describe Māori understandings of the entities in their environment?

The next section of this chapter gives further background on the places and contexts from which the conceptual "tensions" emerged. This is followed by a brief synopsis of the European landscape idea, a more extended discussion of how landscape has been represented, and especially, the dimensions underlying the European representation of Bay of Islands "landscapes," 1769–1840. I then raise the question of whether "landscape" can be considered a valid Māori concept and introduce the phenomenological premise that it is speech that creates "landscape." This is followed by a more extensive examination of how Māori know "landscape" through language, especially the spoken word. The section titled "Simultaneous Landscapes: The Face of Place" deals with how naming created the Māori world. It focuses on the role of named places, which along with named people, I argue constitute Māori "landscapes." The concluding section reflects on whether it is possible to integrate Māori and European understandings of "landscape" in a single text and whether the use of the term "representation" is appropriate.

Conceptual "Tensions"

My reflections on the landscape idea emerge from three different places and contexts. First, during the late 1990s and early 2000s, I was teaching a seminar in cultural geography at the University of Hawai'i and began to focus on the intersection of concepts, such as landscape, place, identity, imperialism, and colonialism. We directed our attention to whether and how cultural geography could resonate with Indigenous understandings of the world. Many students in the seminar were grappling with the "colonial" nature of the discipline and with how they might overcome some of the biases they saw in Western research. These concerns were often underlined by their experiences in other classes and seminars in which Indigenous perspectives were ignored, and sometimes denigrated.

Over time, the seminar came to engage with the question of knowledge in cultural geography, especially with ontological binaries such as nature and culture, individual and society, and space and place, features absent in most Indigenous knowledge systems. In particular, participants, many of whom were nongeographers, began to reflect on how they might break out of the "hall of mirrors" (Howitt and Suchet-Pearson 2003, 557), in which self-consciously postcolonial theory mirrors its own views rather than engaging with alternate ontologies when working with Indigenous communities. The experience of teaching so many talented students was a constant goad to reframe my ideas. A cohort of master's and doctoral students constantly struggled to remedy my ignorance about their knowledge systems. I am grateful to them and hope their verdict will be of my recent writings: "making some progress." From a different perspective I hope that they learned of the importance of critically engaging European ideas, methodologies, and theories, to not only show how they have marginalized, distorted, and ignored Indigenous voices, but to show how Indigenous philosophies can engage with European philosophy to make a difference politically and intellectually (see Turner 2006).

The ideas examined in this seminar proved to be especially valuable when I came to grapple with issues emerging from research I was engaged in after 1995 to support claims to the Waitangi Tribunal, the body established by legislation in 1975 to provide Māori with judicial means to address breaches by the Crown of the Treaty of Waitangi of 1840, in Aotearoa/New Zealand. While engaged in this research (1995–2005) I spent three to four months each year on site, participating in *hui* (meetings), many held on *marae* (meeting house), giving testimony at tribunal hearings as an expert witness, and having many discussions about not only my own research, but traditional history, environment, and resource management issues, contemporary economic development, Māori language (Te Reo) issues, health issues, and Māori politics. Much of this time I was immersed in Māori ways of thinking, reminiscent of time spent with my grandmother when I was young, and to say that I learned, perhaps remembered, a tremendous amount is an understatement. During this time I also renewed and reaffirmed my Māori family connections in *Tai Tokerau*, the far north: I am partially of Māori descent, being *Te Popoto* and *Te Honihoni* of *Ngāpuhi* and *Te Ihutai, Ngāti Kuri* and *Waiariki* of *Te Rarawa*.

Then in 2004 I became involved in a collaborative project dealing with "landscape" change, 1769–1840, in the Bay of Islands in the northern part of the country. The project went through several iterations, during which it became both bicultural and multidisciplinary. I became involved through a cousin in 2003 after elders of *Ngāti Hine*, an *iwi* (tribe) whose territory is in the southern part of the Bay of Islands, endorsed a revised proposal. The project was premised on the idea that although European voices have spoken frequently and loudly about events leading up to the signing of the Treaty of Waitangi in 1840, Māori perspectives have virtually been ignored, especially with regard to the rapidly changing landscape in which the treaty was signed. Collaborative work of this sort is always difficult, as indicated by the now abundant literature on the subject, including that produced by geographers (see Hodge and Lester 2006; Kindon, Pain, and Kesby 2007; Louis 2007; Tipa, Panelli, and the Moeraki Stream Team 2009), and I will not detail it here. Rather, I want to turn to collaborative difficulties of another sort.

The Bay of Islands "landscape" transformation project was structured around five hypotheses, three of which focus directly on "landscape" change. Moreover, the project intended that these hypotheses/questions were to be scrutinized from both Māori and European perspectives, using a "two-sided historical ethnography" of the type endorsed by Anne Salmond (2003, 431). It was at this juncture that the project encountered a fundamental difference in the way knowledge, especially history, is constructed, perhaps best described in the title of the article by Judith Binney (1987), "Māori Oral Narratives, Pakeha Written Texts."

Given such differences, many of the senior Māori participants had reservations about working in conjunction with the lenses imposed by Western scholarship, and this was especially the case with regard to a hypothesis which stated that *whenua* (land, country, ground, placenta) shifted to "landscape" in the study period. Even if the use of this term is seen as metaphorical, Māori members have subsequently realized that alone they would never have contemplated its inclusion, as it implies that the worldview of the *tangata whenua* (people of the land) of the Bay of Islands underwent a total transformation between 1769 and 1840, and that such a suggestion, including the use of the term "landscape," reflects a markedly Western perspective.

The European Landscape Idea

"Landscape" is a term once used primarily in art, art history, "landscape" architecture, and geography, but it now has resonance well beyond academia and is part of our everyday vocabulary. The word has become a well-worn metaphor, and there are a confusing array of usages, including the "legal landscape," the "religious landscape," "landscape ecology," the "leisure landscape," the "cultural landscape," and even the "changing landscape of bladder augmentation" (Cresswell 2003, 269). Because "landscape" is used by so many different people for such a variety of purposes, it is an ambiguous term. There are problems of translation and uncertainties of exact meaning both within and between languages, so it is not surprising that no single clean and clear definition exists to satisfy all.

A number of scholars have reviewed how the term "landscape" was used in Europe since it became a word in common usage in the fifteenth and sixteenth centuries (see Appleton 1975; Schama 1995; Casey 2002; Cosgrove 1998; Olwig 2002). These writers have emphasized that the idea of "landscape" emerged in Europe as a particular way of seeing in which some Europeans represented to themselves and to others the world about them and their relationships with it (Cosgrove 1998, 1). Most commentators on the "landscape" idea point out that it is only since the nineteenth century that there has been any technical or academic discussion of the meaning of "landscape" (Relph 1981, 23).

Vision and "Landscape": One Way of Representing Bay of Islands "Landscapes"

Numerous scholars have grappled with the idea of "representation," a word that has many meanings (see "Web definitions for representation," wordnetweb.princeton. edu). Most are not pertinent to our purpose, but two have relevance: "a presentation to the mind in the form of an idea or image" and "a creation that is a visual or tangible rendering of someone or something." Both of these involve what Martin Jay (1992) calls a "resolute ocularcentrism" in which the eye is the primary way of sensing the world, the development of the methods of perspective in art, which in turn helped define and delimit relations between observer and the world, and create an "optic" for framing "objective science" emerging in the seventeenth century, the separation of humanity from nature. It also involves the Cartesian subject-object and mind-body separation, in which the mind contained two elements, representations of the external world and the scanning activity of what Macnaughten and Urry (1998, 110) call the "Inner Eye." In this abstract and disembodied Western approach, the starting point is the self-centered subject, which confronts a domain of isolable objects, entities, which a perceiver first has to make sense of, rendering them intelligible by categorizing them, and assigning to them meanings or functions, before they can be made available for use (Ingold 2000, 168–69). The truth of any reality exists only in the representations of it and thus in the domain of the mind, not out there in the world being looked at.

Thus there is a close association between "knowledge" and the rise of the "subject" as an identifiable entity, autonomously capable of interpreting the world (Strohmayer 2003, 523). It is the role of the modern subject to represent truths about the world that subsequently, once they have been rendered communicatively available, take on a life of their own. This taken-for-granted nature of the construction of knowledge in Western societies privileging the "eye" over and against other forms of connecting to the world also delegitimizes alternate ways of knowing. Further, based on the idea that artificial perspective was the "natural" form of representation, a "transparent window" (Duncan 1993, 41), perspectival painting came to be seen as offering a mimetic reproduction of the world of experience, and this spread from art to other forms of knowledge within Europe by the eighteenth century. It came to be thought that mimesis was best captured visually and that the language closest to replicating the mimetic qualities of realist art was a dispassionate objective language of science that could both describe the visual qualities of objects and classify them in relation to other objects. The focus on vision and the discourse of mimesis marginalized other modes of representation, creating what Derek Gregory (1994, 15) calls the "problematic of visualization," with sight regarded as the noblest of senses and the basis for modern epistemology.

Martin Heidegger (1977, 115–54) in his essay "The Age of the World Picture" contends that the "metaphysical ground" of modern science is the idea of the world conceived and grasped as a picture. This "world picture" is dependent on four basic factors, summarized by Casey (2002, 233–37) as the world-as-picture; the world-as-enframed; the world as populated by represented objects that stand within horizons and over against us; and our own position as the sole source of all representations. These, Casey (2002, 237) tells us, together specify the conceptual foundations of the modern era as a age in which everything exists in order to be represented, indeed, only exists as represented. These metaphysical ideas, the world-as-picture and en-framing, turn on a distinction between representation and reality, the key duality put in place, through the process of enframing, which endows the modern viewing subject, constructed as a disembodied and distanced observer, with the exclusive privilege and the extraordinary power to discover the "real" world order.

The conceptual ordering outlined above, deriving from visual ways of knowing, permeates the European descriptions in the late eighteenth and early nineteenth centuries of Bay of Islands "landscapes": in paintings, sketches, maps, textual materials from a variety of sources, as well as the categorization of plants and animals through the lens of natural history. "Landscapes" were framed, ordered as compositions of elevations and planes, effectively creating a grid within which objects could be isolated and enumerated (see T. Mitchell 1988; Willems-Braun 1997). In a similar manner the observable structure of the natural world was placed into conceptual grids logically derived, extracting species from their particular surroundings, from their organic and ecological relations with each other, as well as their places in other peoples' economies and knowledge systems (Pratt 1992, 31). By the late eighteenth century the "certainty of truth" found in the European-generated sources dealing with the Bay of Islands was made to turn on the need to establish a distance between observer and observed so that order could be discovered and re-presented. These ways of representing "landscapes" also dominate the scholarly and popular interpretations of the Bay of Islands in the period immediately before the signing of the Treaty of Waitangi in 1840. As the Bay of Islands "landscape" transformation project was intended to use a European perspective in part, this was not a problem for this aspect of the project. However, the question of how to do this in conjunction with a Māori perspective proved more troublesome.

"Landscape" and Speech: An Alternate Mode of Representation

That Māori in the late eighteenth and early nineteenth centuries had a very different conception of themselves and their world is unquestionable (see Salmond 1997).

Further, a number of commentators, in considering the term "landscape" in various parts of the world, suggest that while every society has been historically aware of environment, "landscape," the idea of a unified scene, may not be universal, and requires careful consideration when used (Corner 1999; Burenhalt and Levinson 2008). Nonetheless, there is evidence that Māori did have a notion of "landscape." This emerges from interpretations of early nineteenth-century European paintings containing Māori (W. J. T. Mitchell 2002, 22–27), from observations of early ethnographers (Best [1942] 1977, 28), from other types of Māori visual material (Neich 1994, 16–17), and from the Māori language, which does contain several words which provide connotations of "landscape" (Williams [1844; 1971] 1992, 424). A review of this evidence led me to conclude that in the past Māori did view their environment, gaze upon it, and may even have had a number of terms for "landscape" as a whole, but that the profound visuality of Western ways of understanding the world is subversive of Māori modes of knowledge, its acquisition, revelation, and articulation (Murton 2011). I suggest that the concept of "landscape" as it is commonly used in Western scholarly and popular representations is inappropriate to apply to the "Māori landscapes" of the Bay of Islands before 1840, because although Māori did have a notion of "landscape" in a visual sense, it was not as a dominant mode of representation.

Edward Casey (2002, xv) notes that representation is integral to the perception of "landscape" itself. Casey (1993; 1996; 1997; 2001; 2002) has argued extensively for an alternate perspective on "landscape," one that humans can only grasp by being bodily there, and which can be construed as the "face of place, its expressive faces or sensuous surface" (Casey 1996). Coupled with the writings of Indigenous scholars such as Gregory Cajete (2000, 23, 25), who notes that phenomenology parallels the approach of Indigenous understandings of the world, these ideas led me to examine phenomenological approaches to "landscape" as a possible way of framing and structuring research that permitted Māori philosophy, principles, language, and custom to engage with European philosophy in a way sometimes described as Kaupapa Māori research (see Smith 1999; Pihama 2003).

The limited amount of phenomenological work carried out in Indigenous societies by non-Indigenous scholars (for example, Myers 1986; Weiner 1991, 2001; Basso 1988, 1996a, 1996b; Thornton 2008) that draws on the concept of "dwelling" as articulated by Martin Heidegger (1971) and the idea of the "body-subject" derived from the work of Maurice Merleau-Ponty (1962) further supports my contention that such an approach can be fruitfully applied to the pre–Treaty of Waitangi "Māori landscapes" of the Bay of Islands. This approach insists that humans first of all find themselves enmeshed in a world and in a set of relationships, and that it is only subsequent to this that they begin to separate out a sense of themselves and a sense of things as they are apart from them: according to Heidegger human existence cannot be construed as coming before (either temporally or ontologically) the encounter with other things or persons (Malpas 2006, 51–52).

Most significantly for any exploration of how Māori understand "landscape" is that for those scholars pursuing phenomenological interpretations, what creates the world, bringing forth the earth as a collection of human places, is speech. Among geographers, Yi-fu Tuan (1991) argued cogently that named places illustrate the unity of language and place, and as David White (1978, 25) observes, "Names bestow what Heidegger calls a measured command over entities." Names are considered to be part of the things (entities) labeled. Language, therefore, is laid out as a property of the world and not as a coding of the world, as in approaches based on Cartesian separations (Weiner 2001, 89–90). David Abram (2010), in writing about the "sensuous world" (the creaturely world directly encountered by humans' animal senses), notes that it is through spoken language that preliterate, oral societies speak not about the world, but directly to the world, acknowledging animals, plants, and even landforms as expressive subjects with whom they might expect to find themselves in conversation. Language for oral societies is thus not a specifically human possession but rather a property of the animate earth, in which humans participate. Language is part of an active perceptual engagement with the animate and inanimate world, and the world is full of active entities with whom humans engage, the "participation mystique" of the French anthropologist, Lucien Levy-Bruhl (Abram 1996, 57).

How Māori Know "Landscape"

Māori see knowledge as involving an inseparable relationship between the world of matter and the world of spirit. In Māori understandings of the world, the Cartesian dichotomy between an observing, thinking self and the outside cannot exist. There are many dimensions of this worldview (see Salmond 1985; Shirres 1997; Roberts 1998; Roberts and Wills 1998; Mead 2003 for in-depth discussions of *tikanga* and Mātauranga Māori), but here my focus is on how Māori bring "landscapes" into being.

In Māori understanding, creation is viewed as a process of continuous action, in which particular forms of sound and thought play an essential role (Salmond 1985; Stewart-Harawira 2005, 37–38). Stewart-Harawira (2005, 38) puts it this way:

> The cadences of ancient songs, of ritual calls, of sacred chants, through which the world is sung into existence, the flesh is sung onto the bones, and the relationships are sung which bind all together within

the cosmos . . . (breathe) life into the network of subtle interconnections between human beings and the entire natural world.

Thought and spoken words exist together for Māori, with sound being the original foundation for thought to be conceptualized and expressed in words. According to Salmond (1985, 246) the primal energy surge produces thought, memory, the mind, then desire. From desire, ancestral knowledge generates darkness, and then Te Kore, the primal power of the cosmos, the void or negation, yet containing the potentiality of all things afterwards to come. From Te Kore space emerges, and then light, land, the gods, and humans. This cosmic generative power, this common dynamic process in which all things unfold, already contains the form of every possible being. Consequently, all things in the phenomenal world unfold their nature (*tipu*), live (*ora*), and have form (*āhua*) and so come to possess a body (*tinana*), and immaterial self (*wairua*), an essence of divine power, a unique living force (*mauri*), and a characteristic vitality (*hau*) (Roberts and Wills 1998, 49).

One northern Māori tradition, notes the *tohunga*, scholar, writer, healer, Anglican minister, and philosopher, Māori Marsden (Royal 2003, 16–23), has it that it is through recitation by a supreme entity, Io, that all things come into being. Marsden states that it was through the *mana* of the creative word that everything has come into existence, including the phenomenal world, after the children of the primal parents, Ranginui (the Sky Father) and Papatūānuku (the Earth Mother), separated their parents and created the world of light (Te Ao Mārama). The spoken word connects the breath of people to that of the world and animates, brings life to place.

What orders the visible and invisible world brought to life by thought and speech is genealogy (*whakapapa*), which provides a cognitive template and is the means by which Māori "know" the phenomenal world. In its literal translation *whakapapa* means "to place layers, one upon another." Genealogy provides a framework for understanding historical descent, pattern, and linkages, whereby everything, animate and inanimate, is connected into a single family tree or "taxonomy of the universe" (Roberts 1998; Roberts and Wills 1998; Roberts et al. 2004). In some traditions genealogy begins with the primal parents who then produce many offspring, deified as gods (*atua*), who in turn act as the progenitors and personification of all known phenomena, both living and nonliving. Knowledge associated with the individuals, be they deity, demigod, human, plant, animal, rock, is the "flesh" for the epistemological "bones" provided by genealogy. This knowledge is primarily in the form of narratives: songs, chants, proverbs, prophetic sayings, stories about ancestors. As in oral cultures elsewhere, extensive use is made of personification and metaphor (Roberts and Wills 1998, 53). Further, because Māori conceptions of time are nonlinear, represented by a double spiral (*koru*) which symbolizes that the past, present, and future, and space and time exist simultaneously, the conception of genealogy is spatial, or perhaps holographic, rather than involving descending vertical lines (Salmond 1985, 247).

Māori conceive of the cosmos as a gigantic "kin," with humans powerfully linked to both the natural and supernatural worlds, all the elements and deities of which have agency and identity. The Māori view of self is markedly nonindividu-alistic, involving the kinship group which reaches both backwards and forwards in time, and includes deities, as reflected in the proverb, *He tangata, he tipua, he atua rānei?* (Am I human, demigod, or god?), a rhetorical question, the answer to which is I am all three (Tau 2001, 139). More distantly, the Māori self is related to all other named entities. It is useful to note that Casey (2001, 693) suggests that the way he conceives of self as a phenomenologist is not restricted to the human self, as animals and perhaps plants possess their own equivalent of embodiment and emplacement. This idea is certainly true for Māori.

Thus, Māori understandings of how things or entities come to be known is through the spoken word. To quote Vincent Vycinas (1961, 270), in his work inter-preting Martin Heidegger, "To say something is to bring it to life." Speech enables Māori to create their world as a collection of human places. But as well as being the vehicle for thought and language, sound has deep metaphysical and creative connotations that go beyond its use as the practical instrument of ordinary com-munication. Names expose things in their being.

Language, especially sound and speech, replaces the prominent visuality of Western ways for Māori. Māori create the world in speech and through the act of naming. Names were the great object of Māori oral scholarship in the past, be they of ancestors, places, treasures (*taonga*), or events, and naming remains significant today, although new forms of visual representation have emerged. The genealogical recitation of names identified illustrious ancestors and the battles that made them famous, their journeys of discovery, and their ordinary day-to-day activities. These tribal histories recounted the relationships between named entities in the genealo-gies and stories about how such relationships were made, changed, or broken.

"Simultaneous Landscapes": The Face of Place

For Māori, I suggest that named entities constitute "landscape," the sensuous sur-face of place, its named or nameable parts, its condensed and lived physiognomy (Casey 1996, 28). Māori name places as part of the broader process of naming and ordering the world. According to the linguist and Māori language scholar, Richard Benton (2007), there is no Māori term equivalent to "place-name," other than mod-ern artificial constructions. Benton states that the term *ingoa* (name, namesake, acquire distinction) covers the names for people, places, and *taonga* (property, anything highly prized), and as identity and status are bound up in a name, a place is its name, and the name is the place. He also notes that when a name changes, a place may well become a different one in Māori conceptualization.

Sources for named places are reasonably abundant, even for the distant past. There remain many knowledgeable Māori in rural areas who can walk through such "landscapes," pointing out named places and recounting their stories, and these provided one source of information for the Bay of Islands project. There is also handwritten manuscript material, from both the nineteenth and early twentieth centuries, usually belonging to elders, which documents genealogy and associated narratives (for the inland Bay of Islands see Sissons, Wi Hongi, and Hohepa 2001).

Māori oral accounts contained in the Minute Books of the Native (Māori) Land Court written down in the late nineteenth century contain much detail on named places, genealogy, and resources in pre-European and early contact times. These are informative and detailed despite problems arising from being translated into English after being spoken in Māori and being sometimes slanted in favor of one particular group over another. Because the records contain a genealogically based chronology, the activities of ancestors—clearing forest for gardens, founding settlements, battling intruders, gathering flax, capturing birds in certain kinds of trees, constructing eel weirs—can be broadly dated, especially at the local level. The named features associated with these activities were the outcomes of immersion in place through the Māori self/body's involvement with the environment as part of their normal business of life, what Casey (2001, 689) calls "habitation," Heidegger (1962, 100) the "work world," and Ingold (2000, 193) the "taskscape." Such places are known to those who live there, and when the names are spoken, the places and the ancestors who named them are animated, brought to life, reflecting "idiolocalism," which invokes the subject who incorporates and expresses a particular place (Casey 2001, 689). From this perspective the body/self is an integral part of a close-knit harmony of organic parts united to the cosmos and the world (Casey 2001, 689). The experience of making a living in an environment is central to what it means to inhabit a place, to dwell in it. Such places can be named by those who continue to live there, and the act of naming places not only brings them to life, but also the ancestors who had made and named them.

For the inland Bay of Islands (especially the area known as Waimate and Taiāmai, and around Lake Ōmāpere, the location of especially fertile soil derived from basaltic lava flows and dotted with striking volcanic cones), the information is especially rich for the period 1770 to 1840 (see Northern Minute Book, 2, 1875, Waihōanga; Northern Minute Book, 3, 1879, Ōmāpere; Northern Minute Book, 23, 1897, Ahuahu; Northern Minute Book, 28, 1898, Whakataha). The area comprising the various Motatau blocks is also rich in place-names and genealogical material, though much of this refers to events before 1770 (see Northern Minute Book, 36, 1904, Kaikou; Northern Minute Book, 38, 1905, Motatau No. 2; Northern Minute Book, 40, 1906, Motatau No. 3).

Māori naming practices thus impressed ancestors and deities into the "landscape," and they were thus immediate and available (Stewart-Harawira 2005, 41), locking together the kin groups' understanding with the entities themselves so that a place and its knowledge could not be separated. More than this, this is one of the ways the earth, which is an entity very much like a human and is imbued with human characteristics, can speak to Māori, a feature common to other Indigenous peoples as well (Fair 1997; Basso 1996a, 1996b; Cajete 2000, 23, 25, 185). As Rose Pere of Waikaremoana reminds us, *I whakatangatahia te whenua* (the land is imbued with human characteristics) (cited in Wiri 2001, 34). This idea is similar to the phenomenological view that the body has a relationship to the world though two dimensions, "outgoing" where the lived body participates and is active in the world, and "incoming" where places come into the body, "placializing" through "tenacity" or the lasting impressions that places make on people, and "subjection," the idea that people are subject to places, that places constitute people as subjects (Casey 2001, 688). *Pepeha,* identity axioms, which link land and people into a whole in such as way as to make them inseparable, do this for Māori.

Named places not only record and express important mythological and historical aspects of people, but by the virtue of the knowledge contained in the names, they and the places they represent, are the physical manifestations of the group, just as the group is the manifestation of the land. This is why Te Maire Tau (2001) calls Māori knowledge "mirror knowledge."

After all, Papatūānuku, the Earth Mother, and all of her descendants lie directly in front of the people. With the understanding that actions are incorporated into the earth, and into the minds of people, for Māori the phenomenal world, the world of things and objects, is a "simultaneous landscape" (Simmons 1996, 23), a reflection of themselves, a metaphoric extension of the body, just as they are a reflection of their "landscape." Like many other peoples (see Weiner 2001, 16–30; Thornton 2008, 27, 70), Māori also imagine sequences of named places as the "footsteps of the ancestors" (*Ngā tapuwae o ngā matua tupuna*), paths or trails followed for a variety of purposes.

Many Māori place-names can be understood only through their connection to other names and other places, and whole series of names belong together in groups, commemorating journeys of exploration by an ancestor, the understanding of how the land was made by gods and demigods, or a series of events and people relationships (Davis, O'Regan, Whiting and Wilson 1990, xiii).

Final Thoughts

Fundamentally, in this essay I have argued that although Māori "saw" things in the world, such things became visible primarily through language. What replaces the profound visuality of Western ways of understanding the world for Māori is sound and speech. Māori create the world in speech and through the act of naming. Naming places is but part of the overall naming process, which for Māori involves genealogy as the way of ordering the phenomenal world.

I have suggested that named places are the "face of place," or "landscape." For Māori existence cannot be construed as coming before (whether temporally or ontologically) the encounter with other things or persons. A dynamic mode of narration that locates the narrator inside the story emphasizes this. Existence is "there" and is not something separate from the place, the world in which it finds itself. Names are part of the things they label, and place-names illustrate the unity of language and place. Naming places is an integral part of active perceptual engagement with the animate and inanimate world, a world that is in perpetual creative motion. A knowledge of "landscape" in this sense in conjunction with genealogy gives life to Māori identity and binds kin groups to their resources.

The chapter has attempted to articulate in English and through the written word the differences (and perhaps similarities) between Māori and European conceptions of "landscape." This accords with Māori Marsden's model for understanding Māori worldviews in the contemporary world, in which he emphasizes the use of the written word as well as comparisons with other wisdom traditions (see Royal 2003). In another context Turner (2006, 114) has argued that there is a need for Indigenous academics to weave Indigenous thinking into Western philosophical traditions and vice versa, creating a dialogue between Indigenous philosophy and the theories and methodologies of the social sciences and humanities. However, while there are aspects of Māori understandings of "landscape" that resonate with some Western conceptualizations, notably some deriving from phenomenology, caution is required. After all, in Aotearoa/New Zealand two cosmologies, two "landscapes" coexist, one sensing that nature and people are separate, the other that they are inseparable (Ihimaera 1977, cited in Park 1995, 323). Perhaps the only sensible way to present these very different representations of "landscape," especially for the period 1770–1840, is as parallel texts, one using Māori sources and following Māori modes of representation, the other using European sources and associated modes of representation.

Whether the term "represent" is appropriate in this context is also questionable. Written words and other images laid out on flat surfaces (paper, canvas, stone, wood, computer screens) make us forget that they are sustained by the animate earth. We begin to imagine that their primary task is to provide us with a representation of the world (as though we are outside of, and not really a part of the world), unlike Māori and all oral peoples, for whom language's primary gift is not to re-present the world, but to call ourselves into the vital presence of that world, and to call it into ourselves. This is especially true when we seek to understand Māori worlds in past times, before the coming of Europeans and even thereafter. Although many Māori rapidly became literate and familiar with other forms of representation, the spoken language continued to be the primary way of calling the world into being.

References

Abram, David. 1996. *The Spell of the Sensuous: Perception and Language in a More-Than-Human World.* New York: Vintage Books.

———. 2010. *Becoming Animal: An Earthly Cosmology.* New York: Pantheon.

Appleton, Jay. 1975. *The Experience of Landscape.* London: John Wiley and Sons.

Ballara, Angela. 1998. *Iwi: The Dynamics of Māori Tribal Organisation from c. 1769 to c. 1945.* Wellington, NZ: Victoria University Press.

Basso, Keith H. 1988. "Speaking with Names: Language and Landscape among the Western Apache." *Cultural Anthropology* 3 (2): 99–130.

———. 1996a. *Wisdom Sits in Places: Language and Landscape among the Western Apache.* Albuquerque: University of New Mexico Press.

———. 1996b. "Wisdom Sits in Places: Notes on Western Apache Landscape." In *Senses of Place*, edited by Steven Feld and Keith H. Basso, 53–90. Santa Fe, NM: School of American Research Press.

Benton, Richard. 2007. Personal communication. April 13, 2007.

Best, Elsdon. (1942) 1977. *Māori Forest Lore.* Wellington, NZ: Government Printer.

Binney, Judith. 1987. "Māori Oral Narratives, Pakeha Written Texts: Two Forms of Telling History." *New Zealand Journal of History* 21 (1): 16–28.

Burenhult, Niclas, and Stephen C. Levinson. 2008. "Language and Landscape: A Cross-Linguistic Perspective." *Language Science* 30 (2–3): 135–50.

Cajete, Gregory. 2000. *Native Science. Natural Laws of Interdependence.* Santa Fe, NM: Clear Light Publishers.

Casey, Edward S. 1993. *Getting Back into Place: Toward a Renewed Understanding of the Place-World.* Bloomington: Indiana University Press.

———. 1996. "How to Get from Space to Place in a Fairly Short Stretch of Time: Phenomenological Prolegomena." In *Senses of Place*, edited by Steven Feld and Keith H. Basso, 13–52. Santa Fe, NM: School of American Research Press.

———. 1997. *The Fate of Place: A Philosophical History.* Berkeley: University of California Press.

———. 2001. "Between Geography and Philosophy: What Does It Mean to Be in the Place-World?" *Annals of the Association of American Geographers* 91 (4): 683–93.

———. 2002. *Representing Place: Landscape Painting and Maps.* Minneapolis: University of Minnesota Press.

Coombes, Brad, Nicole Gombay, Jay T. Johnson, and Wendy S. Shaw. 2011. "The Challenges of and from Indigenous Geographies: Implications for Openly Transcultural Research." In *The Companion to Social Geography*, edited by Vincent J. del Casino, Mary E. Thomas, Paul Cloke, and Ruth Panelli, 472–89. New York: Wiley-Blackwell.

Corner, James. 1999. "Introduction: Recovering Landscape as a Critical Cultural Practice." In *Recovering Landscape. Essays in Contemporary Landscape Architecture*, edited by James Corner, 1–26. New York: Princeton Architectural Press.

Cosgrove, Denis E. 1998. *Social Formation and Symbolic Landscape.* Madison: University of Wisconsin Press.

Cresswell, Tim. 2003. "Landscape and the Obliteration of Practice." In *Handbook of Cultural Geography*, edited by Kay Anderson, Mona Domosh, Steve Pile, and Nigel Thrift, 269–81. Thousand Oaks, CA: Sage.

Davis, Te Aue, Tipene O'Regan, Cliff Whiting, and John Wilson. 1990. *He Kōrero Pūrākau Mo Ngā Taunahanaha a Ngā Tūpuna. Place Names of the Ancestors. A Māori Oral History Atlas.* Wellington: New Zealand Geographic Board.

Duncan, James. 1993. "Sites of Representation: Place, Time, and the Discourse of the Other." In *Place/Culture/Representation*, edited by James Duncan and David Ley, 39–56. New York: Routledge.

Fair, Susan W. 1997. "Inupiat Naming and Community History: The Tapqaq and Saninaq Coasts near Shishmaref, Alaska." *Professional Geographer* 49 (4): 466–80.

Gregory, Derek. 1994. *Geographical Imaginations.* Cambridge, Mass.: Blackwell.

Heidegger, Martin. 1962. *Being and Time.* New York: Harper and Row.

——. 1971. "Building Dwelling Thinking." In *Poetry, Language, Thought*, translated and with introduction by Alfred Hofstadter, 141–60. New York: HarperCollins.

——. 1977. "The Age of the World Picture." In *The Question concerning Technology and Other Essays*, translated and with an introduction by William Lovitt, 115–54. New York: Harper and Row.

Hodge, P., and P. Lester. 2006. "Indigenous Research: Whose Priority? Journeys and Possibilities of Cross-Cultural Research in Geography." *Geographical Research* 44:41–51.

Howitt, Richard, and Sandra Suchet-Pearson. 2003. "Contested Cultural Landscapes." In *Handbook of Cultural Geography*, edited by Kay Anderson, Mona Domosh, Steve Pile, and Nigel Thrift, 557–69. Thousand Oaks, CA: Sage.

Ihimaera, Witi. 1977. "The Māori Landscape. Editorial." *The Listener*, July 30, cited in Geoff Park (1995), *Nga Uruora: The Groves of Life: Ecology and History in a New Zealand Landscape.* Wellington, NZ: Victoria University Press.

Ingold, Tim. 2000. *The Perception of Environment: Essays in Livelihood, Dwelling, and Skill.* London: Routledge.

Jay, Martin. 1992. "Scopic Regimes of Modernity." In *Modernity and Identity*, edited by S. Lash and J. Friedman, 178–95. Oxford: Blackwell.

Kindon, S., R. Pain, and M. Kesby. 2007. *Participatory Action Research Approaches and Methods: Connecting People, Participation, and Place.* New York: Routledge.

Louis, Renee Pualani 2007. "Can You Hear Us Now? Voices from the Margin: Using Indigenous Methodologies in Geographic Research." *Geographic Research* 45 (2):130–39.

Macnaughten, Phil, and John Urry. 1998. *Contested Natures*. Thousand Oaks, CA: Sage.

Malpas, Jeff. 2006. *Heidegger's Topology. Being, Place, World*. Cambridge, MA: MIT Press.

Mead, Hirini Moko. 2003. *Tikanga Māori: Living by Māori Values*. Wellington, NZ: Huia Publishers.

Merleau-Ponty, Maurice. 1962. *The Phenomenology of Perception*. London: Routledge and Kegan Paul.

Mitchell, Timothy. 1988. *Colonizing Egypt*. Cambridge: Cambridge University Press.

Mitchell, W. J. T. 2002. "Imperial Landscape." In *Landscape and Power*, edited by W. T. J. Mitchell, 5–34. Chicago: University of Chicago Press.

Murton, Brian. 2011. "Embedded in Place: 'Mirror Knowledge' and 'Simultaneous Landscapes' among Māori." In *Landscape in Language: Transdisciplinary Perspectives*, edited by David M. Mark, Andrew G. Turk, Niclas Burenhult, and David Stea, 73–100. Amsterdam: John Benjamins.

Myers, Fred. 1986. *Pintupi Country, Pintupi Self: Sentiment, Place, and Politics among Western Desert Aborigines*. Washington, DC: Smithsonian Institution Press.

Neich, Roger. 1994. *Painted Histories: Early Māori Figurative Painting*. Auckland, NZ Auckland University Press.

Northern Minute Book. 1875. Native (Māori) Land Court. No. 2 Waihoanga.

Northern Minute Book. 1879. Native (Māori) Land Court. No. 3 Omapere.

Northern Minute Book. 1897. Native (Māori) Land Court. No. 23. Ahuahu.

Northern Minute Book. 1898. Native (Māori Land Court). No. 28. Whakataha.

Northern Minute Book. 1904. Native (Māori) Land Court. No. 36. Kaikou.

Northern Minute Book. 1905. Native (Māori) Land Court. No. 38. Motatau No. 2.

Northern Minute Book. 1906. Native (Māori Land Court). No. 40. Motatau No. 3.

Olwig, Kenneth R. 2002. *Landscape, Nature, and the Body Politic: From Britain's Renaissance to America's New World*. Madison: University of Wisconsin Press.

Pihama, Leonie. 2003. "Asserting Indigenous Theories of Change." In *Sovereignty Matters: Locations of Contestation and Possibility in Indigenous Struggles for Self-Determination*, edited by Joanne Barker, 191–210. Lincoln: University of Nebraska Press.

Pratt, Mary Louise. 1992. *Imperial Eyes: Travel Writing and Transculturation*. New York: Routledge.

Relph, Edward. 1981. *Rational Landscapes and Humanistic Geography*. London: Croom Helm.

Roberts, Roma Mere. 1998. "Indigenous Knowledge and Western Science: Perspectives from the Pacific." In *Science and Technology, Education and Ethnicity: An Aotearoa/ New Zealand Perspective*, edited by Derek Hodson, 59–75. Royal Society of New Zealand Miscellaneous Series 50. Wellington: Royal Society of New Zealand.

Roberts, Roma Mere, and Peter R. Wills. 1998. "Understanding Māori Epistemology: A Scientific Perspective." In *Tribal Epistemologies: Essays in the Philosophy of Anthropology*, edited by Helmut Wautischer, 43–77. Aldershot: Ashgate.

Roberts, Roma Mere, Brad Haami, Richard Benton, Terre Satterfield, Melissa L. Finucane, Mark Henare, and Manuka Henare. 2004. "Whakapapa as a Māori Mental

Construct: Some Implications for the Debate Over Genetic Modifications of Organisms." *Contemporary Pacific* 16 (1): 1–28.

Royal, Te Ahukaramū Charles. 2003. *The Woven Universe. Selected Writings of Rev. Māori Marsden*. Otaki, NZ: Estate of Rev. Māori Marsden.

Salmond, Anne. 1985. "Māori Epistemologies." In *Reason and Morality*, edited by Joanna Overing, 240–63. New York: Routledge.

———. 1997. *Between Worlds. Early Exchanges between Maori and Europeans, 1773–1815*. Auckland, NZ: Viking Penguin.

———. 2003. *The Trial of the Cannibal Dog: Captain Cook in the South Seas*. Auckland, NZ: Penguin.

Schama, Simon. 1995. *Landscape and Memory*. London: Harper and Collins.

Shirres, Michael P. 1997. *Te Tangata. The Human Person*. Auckland, NZ: Accent Press.

Simmons, David. 1996. "The Spiritual Landscape." Unpublished Lecture, University of Auckland.

Sissons, Jeffrey, Wiremu Wi Hongi, and Patrick W. Hohepa. 2001. *Ngā pūriri o Taiamai: A Political History of Ngā Puhi in the Inland Bay of Islands*. Auckland: Reed Books, in association with the Polynesian Society.

Smith, Linda Tuhiwai. 1999. *Decolonizing Methodologies: Research and Indigenous Peoples*. New York: Zed Books.

Stewart-Harawira, Makere. 2005. *The New Imperial Order:Indigenous Responses to Globalization*. New York: Zed Books.

Strohmayer, Ulf. 2003. "The Culture of Epistemology." In *Handbook of Cultural Geography*, edited by Kay Anderson, Mona Domosh, Steve Pile, and Nigel Thrift, 520–31. Thousand Oaks, CA: Sage.

Tau, Te Maire. 2001. "The Death of Knowledge: Ghosts on the Plains." *New Zealand Journal of History* 35 (2): 131–52.

Thornton, Thomas F. 2008. *Being and Place among the Tlingit*. Seattle: University of Washington Press.

Tipa, Gail, Ruth Panelli, and the Moeraki Stream Team. 2009. "Beyond 'Someone Else's Agenda': An Example of Indigenous/Academic Research Collaboration." *New Zealand Geographer* 65 (2): 95–106.

Tuan, Yi-fu. 1991. "Language and the Making of Place: A Narrative-Descriptive Approach." *Annals of the Association of American Geographers* 81 (4): 684–96.

Turner, Dale. 2006. *This Is Not a Peace Pipe: Toward a Critical Indigenous Philosophy*. Toronto: University of Toronto Press.

Vycinas, Vincent. 1961. *Earth and Gods: An Introduction to the Philosophy of Martin Heidegger*. The Hague: Martinus Nijhoff.

Weiner, James. 1991. *The Empty Place*. Bloomington: Indiana University Press.

———. 2001. *Tree Leaf Talk. A Heideggerian Anthropology*. New York: Berg.

White, David. 1978. *Heidegger and the Language of Poetry*. Lincoln: University of Nebraska Press.

Willems-Braun, Bruce. 1997. "Buried Epistemologies: The Politics of Nature in (Post) Colonial British Columbia." *Annals of the Association of American Geographers* 87 (1): 3–31.

Williams, H. W. (1844; 1971) 1992. *Dictionary of the Māori Language.* 7th ed. Wellington, NZ: GP Publications.

Wiri, Robert K. J. 2001. "The Prophecies of the Great Canyon of Toi: A History of Te Whāiti-Nui-A-Toi in the Western Urewera Mountains of New Zealand." PhD diss. Sociology, University of Auckland.

Toward a Paradigm of Indigenous Collaboration for Geographic Research in Canadian Environmental and Resource Management

DEBORAH McGREGOR

In the decade since the publication of Māori scholar Linda Smith's book *Decolonizing Methodologies*, there has been a remarkable emergence of Indigenous research scholarship. Groundbreaking work by both Indigenous and non-Indigenous scholars around the world has created a community of scholars locally, nationally, and internationally who share research ideologies, theories, approaches, and methods (Archibald 2008; S. Wilson 2008). Indigenous research paradigms are informed by a number of principles and values that seek to decolonize past and current research approaches and advance Indigenous ones (Louis 2007). In Canada, Aboriginal organizations, Indigenous scholars, funding agencies, and non-Indigenous scholars alike have begun to articulate such research paradigms more clearly (Kovach 2009; McGregor 2010).

This essay provides insights into how place-based research involving Aboriginal peoples in the environmental and resource management (ERM) area has responded to the overall paradigm shift in Indigenous research in Canada. I draw on my own experience in this area as an Indigenous scholar, teacher, and practitioner. Thus the chapter progresses from a discussion of Traditional Knowledge (TK)[1] in existing Canadian environmental resource management to a consideration of shifting Indigenous research paradigms in Canada, to a more specific look at Aboriginal research in geography.

The State of Traditional Knowledge in Environmental and Resource Management in Canada

Indigenous peoples all over the world have called for the incorporation of traditional knowledge in the decision-making processes that affect their lives, lands, and waters. The recognition of the unique role of Indigenous peoples in achieving sustainable development goals obligates governments and other actors such as

environmental nongovernmental organizations (ENGOs) to work more cooperatively with Indigenous peoples. Recognition of Indigenous peoples' unique perspectives, knowledge systems, and concerns with respect to environmental issues goes
back decades into the early 1980s when the International Union for Conservation
of Nature (IUCN) established a working group on traditional ecological knowledge,
chaired by Graham Baines (Williams and Baines 1993). These early international
initiatives were supported by a serious of workshops and symposiums examining
the value of TEK for natural resource management. The 1987 Report of the United
Nations World Commission on Environment and Development (the "Brundtland
Report") emphasized the important role of Indigenous peoples in sustainable
development and served as a catalyst for increased recognition of TEK (WCED
1987). Five years later, at the United Nations Conference on Environment and
Development, the Convention on Biodiversity (CBD) was signed, one of two legally
binding agreements to arise out of that conference. The CBD reiterated the vital
role of Indigenous people and their knowledge for achieving sustainability. The
CBD has had significant influence in terms of putting traditional ecological knowledge on the map in Canada in environmental and resource management over the
past two decades, though there remain significant gaps and barriers between such
policy and actual practice (McGregor 2008a; White 2006). For countries that have
signed the Convention on Biological Diversity, including Canada, the consideration
of TK in environmental management is important and has been one the main driv-
ers for governments to include TK in environmental and resource management
decision making in Canada (Higgins 1998). The recognition of the unique role
that Indigenous peoples have in achieving sustainable development goals in such
agreements also obligates governments and other actors (e.g., ENGOs) to strive to
work more cooperatively with Indigenous peoples. In many respects these trends,
gaining strength since the 1990s, represent opportunities for the involvement of
Indigenous peoples in sustainable development.

In Canada, international agreements have had significant influence in terms
of putting traditional knowledge on the environmental management map in efforts to achieve environmental sustainability (Higgins 1998; Settee 2000). There are
several factors that have shaped Canada's approach to TK. Recent court decisions
have played a key role in steering policy and legislative frameworks toward greater
involvement of Aboriginal peoples (Doyle-Bedwell and Cohen 2001; J. Wilson
and Graham 2005). Recognition of Aboriginal and treaty rights has shaped land
claims policy, particularly modern-day treaty making, and has entrenched TK as an
integral part of many ERM co-management regimes in northern Canada (Bocking
2005; Spak 2005; White 2006). In Canada, TK discussions exist primarily within
the context of increasing Aboriginal control over lands and resources through

self-government agreements, comprehensive land claims, and other mechanisms. This trend represents a considerable opportunity for the expression of TK in ERM as part of new and more progressive systems of management. Aboriginal people in general have a strong desire to see their knowledge and traditions inform the decision making that affects their lives and lands (AFN 1993; Borrows 2005). The study of TK is, therefore, not just an esoteric or academic exercise; it can be, and has been, utilized as a powerful tool in the establishment of Aboriginal influence in ERM regimes (Houde 2007; Menzies and Butler 2006).

Despite such progress, Indigenous voices remain conspicuously absent or muted; they are often still ignored by more established, mainstream scholars (Louis 2007). In general, therefore, issues in the field of TK research are frequently framed from a Western, non-Indigenous perspective rather than from the perspective of Indigenous peoples, the actual holders and practitioners of the knowledge (Howitt and Suchet-Pearson 2006). So concerned are they about the appropriation of their knowledge that Aboriginal peoples have sought to protect their intellectual property, especially TK (Brascoupe and Mann 2001; Crowshoe 2005; NAHO 2007). Aboriginal people have become reluctant to share their knowledge because they fear it will be exploited or used against them. One of the main messages being put forward is that from an Aboriginal perspective, TK is embodied in the people who hold the knowledge both individually and collectively. According to this worldview, TK cannot appropriately be "removed" or "extracted" and owned by someone else, especially by those who do not practice it (McGregor 2004).

Aboriginal people have also expressed concern that TK is not valued as highly as Western science (Battiste and Henderson 2000; Nadasdy 2006; Roberts 1996). This represents a significant barrier for the respectful consideration of TK in ERM, as does the lack of understanding of Aboriginal worldview, knowledge, and perspective (Howitt and Suchet-Pearson 2006).

The consideration of TK in ERM is characterized by imbalances in the power relationship between Aboriginal and non-Aboriginal peoples (Butler 2006; Ellis 2005; McGregor 2004). Political relationships represent a major factor in continuing such imbalances, but so are the underlying assumptions embedded in Western ERM discourses (Howitt and Suchet-Pearson 2006). In Canada, it has become the state's goal to incorporate TK in Western systems of ERM. Aboriginal peoples, however, wish to make self-determination a reality by employing their *own* systems of ERM based on Indigenous worldviews, traditions, values, and knowledge. The field of TK in ERM is thus a dynamic one, sometimes reflecting the contrasting goals of various actors. Despite the many outstanding issues, there are also considerable opportunities for ensuring the appropriate consideration of TK in ERM (McGregor 2008a). The field is becoming more responsive to Aboriginal aspirations as

Aboriginal peoples gain more control of lands and resources. Furthermore, the research methods to support TK work are also changing to reflect self-determination in research (Schnarch 2004).

Indigenous peoples represent one of the most researched cultural groups in the world. The methods used for "studying" Aboriginal people over time have often contributed to their oppression through ongoing processes of colonization. Howitt and Suchet-Pearson (2006) caution that research remains related to processes of continued colonization, dispossession, and control. The underlying epistemologies, paradigms, approaches, and methods for such research remain problematic in terms of both the outcomes of the research and the treatment of Aboriginal people (McGregor 2010; Smith 1999). As Aboriginal people begin to exert more control over the events that affect them, and as their desire to have their interests advanced through scholarly work increases, researchers are pushed toward altering their research relationships with Aboriginal peoples (Brant Castellano 2004). Not only is there a movement to decolonize research approaches, but there is an equally important movement to advance Indigenous approaches and methods of research (Archibald 2008; Kovach 2009; Steinhauer 1999; Weber-Pillwax 2001).

The broader shift in relationships between Aboriginal and non-Aboriginal peoples and institutions has played a significant role in decolonizing research relationships. An important aspect of asserting self-determination is assuming greater control over research agendas (RCAP 1993; Schnarch 2004).

Research involving Aboriginal peoples in geography has begun to respond to this paradigm shift (Johnson et al. 2007). This is due in part to increased Aboriginal involvement in geography, in particular the establishment of the Indigenous Peoples' Knowledge and Rights Commission (IPKRC) with the International Geographical Union. The IPKRC is a catalyst for raising concerns and providing a space for dialogue for Indigenous-academic geographic research. This organization has a wealth of experience to draw on as the discipline of geography tries to adapt to rapidly changing expectations with regard to research involving Aboriginal peoples.

Paradigm Shifts in Research Involving Aboriginal Peoples

The Cree scholar Margaret Kovach (2009) explores the theoretical and epistemological basis of Indigenous methodologies. Kovach advocates for the centrality of "tribal epistemologies to Indigenous research frameworks" (56). Progress toward this goal was begun by the Royal Commission on Aboriginal Peoples (RCAP), which since the 1990s has advocated different research approaches to address the concerns, interests, and values of Aboriginal peoples. RCAP released its final report in several volumes in 1993, which called for research to be conducted in an "integrated, holistic" manner rather than one fragmented along the lines of conventional academic disciplines (RCAP 1993). In the effort to meet its own standards, RCAP ensured that during the fulfillment of its mandate, "appropriate respect [was] given to the cultures, languages, knowledge and values of Aboriginal peoples, and to the standards used by Aboriginal peoples to legitimate knowledge" (RCAP 1993, 37).

The research agenda set by RCAP provided an important foundation from which many scholars, Aboriginal organizations, and funding agencies advanced an Indigenous research paradigm in Canada. Furthermore, much of the background research for RCAP's deliberations was conducted by scholars involved in research with Aboriginal peoples in Canada. Spanning five years, this exercise alone initiated a transformation in research involving Aboriginal peoples. In 2002, the Social Science and Humanities Research Council of Canada (SSHRC), a federally funded research agency, undertook extensive consultations and developed a program specifically designed to advance Aboriginal research. McNaughton and Rock (2004) summarized findings from these consultations and found that a transformation of Aboriginal research was needed, a paradigm shift that called for research conducted *by and with* Aboriginal peoples as opposed to research *for and on* Aboriginal peoples. This research approach was institutionalized through SSHRC's strategic grants program from 2004 to 2009.

Indigenous and non-Indigenous scholars committed to a paradigm of Aboriginal research have advocated respect for traditional knowledge and also for its careful consideration in research. It is important to note that there is no single Aboriginal research paradigm in Canada, although a number of principles, values, and characteristics are shared. Aboriginal peoples are diverse in governance, culture, language, and tradition, and research paradigms must reflect this diversity. Kovach (2009) simply states that "Indigenous knowledges can never be standardized, for they are in relation to place and person," while adding that "at the same time, Indigenous methodologies are founded upon Indigenous epistemology, and they will or ought to be evident in such frameworks, revealing shared qualities that can be identified as belonging to an Indigenous paradigm" (56).

Kovach's (2009) observations reveal a tension in the continuing transformation of Indigenous research. Diversity among Indigenous nations means there are a multitude of intellectual traditions that shape research theories, paradigms, and practices. Practically, it is challenge to describe all Indigenous traditions that contribute to the framing of Indigenous research paradigms. Instead, it is useful to characterize these paradigms by a common set of principles and objectives, assuming as its primary goal benefits to the Indigenous communities in support of self-determination. The research objectives must reflect the lived reality of the people in the community and be supported by them. The research practices are process-oriented and require a high degree of accountability and responsibility on the part of the researcher. Indigenous voices, experience, and lives are privileged in this research as well the recognition that Indigenous knowledges are distinct and relevant (Rigney 1999; Martin 2003).

Another important aspect of Aboriginal research paradigms constitutes the high ethical standards expected of researchers as part of the research relationship. Policies, guidelines, and toolkits exist that address traditional knowledge and the protection of such knowledge. Some Aboriginal organizations have developed specific policies to protect TK. For example, NAHO has published a toolkit for traditional knowledge called *Sacred Ways of Life: Traditional Knowledge* (Crowshoe 2005) with guidance provided for governance and policies to protect knowledge. Regional Aboriginal organizations are also developing specific TK policies and guidelines (e.g., Council of Yukon First Nations, *Traditional Knowledge Research Guidelines* [CYFN 2000] and the Gwich'in Renewable Resources Board's *Working with Gwich'in Traditional Knowledge in the Gwich'in Settlement Region* [GRRB 2004]).

Given such developments in Indigenous research in Canada, how has ERM responded? How have Indigenous research paradigms influenced the field of natural resource management, particularly within the discipline of geography?

Asserting an Indigenous Geographic Research Paradigm

It can be argued that there has always been an Indigenous aspect to geographic research (Johnson et al. 2007). However, much of the history of geographic research is tied to the history of colonial expansion (Shaw, Herman, and Dobbs 2006). The transformation of geography's interactions with Indigenous peoples through the emerging discipline of Indigenous geography is dependent on a new and entirely different focus, the intention of which is to "encourage respectful, reciprocal research relationships between geographers and Indigenous communities; relationships that recognize the struggles of Indigenous peoples to preserve and further their knowledges and the affirmation of their rights to sovereignty over political, economic and cultural resources" (Johnson et al. 2007, 119). With such notions at its ideological center, Indigenous geography has begun to receive enthusiastic promotion over the past few years, resulting most notably in the creation of the Indigenous Peoples' Knowledges and Rights Commission (IPKRC) of the International Geographical Union and its first meeting in Brisbane in 2006. At that meeting, the commission declared as one of its primary aims the need to "bring Indigenous geographies from the margins of the discipline and into greater focus, particularly with regard to our efforts to decolonize the discipline by recognizing the historical and contemporary ramifications of Geography's service to colonialism" (Johnson 2008, 3). More recently, at the 2008 Association of American Geographers' conference in Boston, a symposium titled "Indigenous Geographies of Struggle and Self-Determination" was designed to bring the discipline "in from the margins" (Richardson 2008). Perhaps most significantly, the IPKRC has been granted observer status as an academic organization by the United Nations Permanent Forum on Indigenous Issues (Johnson 2008, 4). This provides an important mode of international support for Indigenous peoples' quest for self-determination.

As is the case for any subdiscipline, Indigenous geography continues to evolve. The critical question from an Indigenous perspective has come to focus on ascertaining Indigenous peoples' understandings of and aspirations for this discipline. The Indigenous activist Jose Barriero describes Indigenous geography as "a proactive and uniquely Indian-led and conceptualized discipline that has grown from practical community-based needs" (Barriero 2004, 4). He adds that Indigenous geography can help Indigenous peoples "to recover traditional cultural knowledge, to assert legal rights to territories and natural resources, to negotiate co-management agreements and to introduce their young people to their identity in the land" (Barriero 2004, 4). A community-based perspective on Indigenous geography emphasizes what the discipline has to offer Indigenous peoples as they "articulate their own perception of their own lands and territories . . . based on their own traditional knowledge branches" (Barriero 2004, 1).

The mainstream discipline of geography has as one of its core concepts place and peoples' relationships to place, whether physical or spiritual, local or global, cultural, or even virtual. These, of course, are not new or unusual concepts to Indigenous peoples, and therefore they understand them as critical components of Indigenous geography as well. In Indigenous geography, however, topics of specific concern include treaty rights, environmental and resource management, sustainable development, environmental justice, globalization, traditional knowledge, and self-determination (IPKRC 2007). Through my scholarly and professional activities, these are all topics that I have been engaged in researching and teaching for more than two decades. Thus, I have a view of Indigenous geography from both community-based and mainstream scholarly perspectives, and this has formed, and continues to form, the basis of my work. My cross-appointment in geography and Aboriginal studies provides fertile ground for advancing such concepts in Indigenous geography.

In Canada, the term "*Aboriginal* geography" is sometimes used, and leadership in the field is currently emerging from the University of Victoria's Department of Geography, which itself is responding to a larger university-wide initiative to build institutional capacity for Indigenous teaching and research. There is also recognition in British Columbia that First Nations are regaining control over environmental and natural resources, including the use of geographic tools and information in managing such resources (e.g., Aboriginal mapping exercises). Similarly, there is some national recognition that Aboriginal peoples are regaining control over lands and resources through land claims, self-government processes, and assertions of Aboriginal and treaty rights. Geographers in Canada such as Evelyn Peters (2006) and Peter Usher (2000) have also been advancing scholarly and applied work in Indigenous geography. The University of Northern British Columbia (UNBC) offers Aboriginal geography courses, again responding to the broader political climate in British Columbia. At the University of Toronto, I offer three courses addressing Aboriginal geography at the undergraduate and graduate levels in both geography and Aboriginal studies. I also supervise and train students, generate scholarly work, and serve the Aboriginal community through this discipline.

Geographic-related research will further evolve as the broader context for research continues to find expression in formal policies, guidelines, and protocols. Researchers will be expected by funding and Aboriginal agencies, organizations, and communities to respect Indigenous theories, paradigms, and approaches to research. This overall trend has slowly begun to permeate Indigenous geography, although it has not been formalized. The next section will highlight actions necessary for bringing researchers in step with current broader initiatives in Aboriginal research in Canada.

Decolonizing Geographic Research

In the late 1990s, when I was writing my doctoral thesis, there was very little published literature upon which to draw to develop research frameworks and methods for traditional knowledge and ERM research relating to Aboriginal people. It was my intention at that time to root my work in an Indigenous worldview, my own experience, and my cultural traditions, but I found overall Indigenous theoretical frameworks to be lacking in the environmental and natural resource management sciences literature. I therefore decided to ground my work in the Aboriginal research frameworks described in the research plan and ethical guidelines set out by RCAP (1993).

In my experience, the sciences have been slower to take up the project of decolonizing their disciplines. To effectively decolonize such firmly entrenched areas of study, there needs to be active engagement in Aboriginal scholarship and with Indigenous scholars. The current lack of engagement is evident in the published geography-related literature, where there are only a small number of Indigenous and non-Indigenous scholars who engage with Indigenous scholarship. Even in the community-based, collaborative work conducted by some researchers, there is little engagement with Indigenous scholarship. Few if any references are made to Indigenous thinkers—such as the late Vine Deloria Jr., Gregory Cajete, Marie

Batistte, Sa'ke'j Henderson, John Borrows, Dale Turner, LeRoy Little Bear, Jean Tiellet, Darlene Johnston, and Taiake Alfred—who theoretically frame environmental and resource management issues from Indigenous perspectives

Connecting with Indigenous scholarship and scholars is essential for the decolonizing process in geography. Aboriginal Studies in Canada is constantly evolving in response to the needs of Aboriginal communities. Furthermore, as Indigenous scholars begin to occupy leadership positions in academia while retaining ties to their communities, we will begin to see more rapid and positive changes. Respect for traditional knowledge and Aboriginal language is a core aspect of Aboriginal research. Aboriginal people need to be recognized for their role in knowledge production, not just as research participants but also for their intellectual contributions, for which others often take credit.

Shaping Indigenous Theoretical and Methodological Frameworks

> Indigenous Peoples have their own philosophies, which they apply when articulating their understanding of the world. Indigenous philosophies are rooted in oral traditions, which generate explanations of the world expressed in indigenous normative languages. But the legal and political discourses of the state do not use indigenous philosophies to justify their legitimacy. The asymmetry arises because indigenous peoples must use the normative language of the dominant culture to ultimately defend world views that are embedded in a completely different normative framework. The dominant culture does not face this hurdle. (Turner 2006, 83)

Turner goes on to stipulate that "greater participation in the intellectual culture of the dominant culture is a good thing, because having our voices heard is the first step towards having a greater say in shaping the normative language of contemporary Aboriginal politics" (Turner 2006, 93). Turner, an Anishinaabe scholar, expresses the difficulty Indigenous scholars have in engaging the "intellectual landscape" of academia. It is not only that we must gain voice; it is also *how* we must do it. Turner's words speak well to my work. A common strand running through my research activities, particularly because I am engaged in emerging disciplines, is the attention I must pay to Indigenous theoretical frameworks, epistemologies, paradigms, knowledges, and concerns over how to reconcile them with dominant discourse. As my work is rooted in asserting that Indigenous voice matters in such landscapes, I must also articulate what this "voice" says. At the same time, I am not *the* voice of Indigenous peoples, so I must rely on community-based research and service to provide the guidance and insights required to do this work with credibility.

I first began to tackle this task of defining Indigenous ways of knowing, the process of mediating between two intellectual traditions, while working on my PhD dissertation. The research approach and methods I utilized then remain central to the current dialogue on questions concerning the nature of the conceptual frameworks underlying Aboriginal research, the nature of Aboriginal research itself, and appropriate methods for investigating questions important to Aboriginal people in academic settings.

It is a challenge for anyone in academia to determine appropriate approaches to issues that involve Aboriginal peoples, knowledge, tradition, and values. The challenge of the current research, therefore, is to contribute not only to the body of knowledge but also to the methodology involved in investigating such a question in the first place. The ongoing paradigm shift in geographic research creates an environment of uncertainty in examining research questions; however, it also creates a climate of opportunity. It is a time of excitement, creativity, growth, and innovation. As Kovach states, "We need to delve in to the possibilities" (2009, 38). The Indigenous research approach aims to describe an approach to dealing meaningfully with Aboriginal worldviews, epistemologies, knowledge, and modes of knowledge acquisition and production. The next section discusses ways in which the two systems may be able to come together utilizing a "coexistence" model based on Indigenous conceptual frameworks.

Indigenous Theory for Research Based on Coexistence

Indigenous-academic research is in many ways cross-cultural. It is an attempt to make sense of or to bridge two worldviews and two ways of knowing. If it is to be useful, this research must represent Aboriginal reality in an authentic manner, despite the difficulties in communication between Aboriginal and non-Aboriginal societies. For academic research to be relevant and practical within Indigenous contexts, Kovach states that "there is a need for methodologies that are inherently and wholly Indigenous" (2009, 13). She adds that "Indigenous methods do not flow from western philosophy; they flow from tribal epistemologies. If tribal knowledges are not referenced as a legitimate knowledge system guiding the Indigenous methods and protocols within the research process, there is a congruency problem" (36).

As noted earlier, the aim of Indigenous research theories and paradigms is to center Indigenous knowledges, goals, and objectives and does not necessarily reject academic research paradigms. Indigenous research seeks to create space within the academy for the generation, innovation, and production of knowledge relevant to Indigenous peoples. In fact, as will be described, Indigenous intellectual traditions explicitly create space for difference among nations, peoples, knowledges, traditions, and values. It is rooted in Indigenous intellectual traditions (e.g., Anishinaabe, Haudenosaunee) but also recognizes there are other traditions.

The challenge is to rise above the colonial relationship that still exists and move toward a more equal sharing of knowledge in Indigenous-academic research. In my PhD research approach, I used both Western scientific (including social scientific) and Aboriginal traditions in investigating my research question. More fundamentally, I based my overall research approach within an Aboriginal worldview and investigative framework, applying the concept of "coexistence" that embodies principles of mutual recognition, respect, and sharing (RCAP 1993).

My greatest challenge in this regard was selecting a theoretical perspective, an appropriate methodology consistent with and reflective of the epistemological underpinnings of a research question that required a cross-cultural framework and legitimized an Indigenous worldview and knowledge. The nature of reality and how we try to understand it is a critical foundation for the research. Scholars generally acknowledge that Aboriginal and Western worldviews and epistemology are significantly different (Deloria 1999; Kovach 2009; Turner 2006). These differences are much less of a problem than the fact that Aboriginal knowledge is often regarded as less valid or acceptable than information obtained through the Western scientific tradition (Battiste and Henderson 2000). This, too, is part of the larger context in which my research found itself.

Choosing a research framework and methodology consistent with Aboriginal modes of investigation, one that would also fulfill the academic requirements of my research from a Western institutional standpoint, was no easy task. I chose to embrace the "coexistence" concept as the overriding paradigm for my research. This concept illustrates how the theoretical perspective embraced both Western and Aboriginal intellectual traditions and formed the context for the research process.

Although the idea of coexistence has been around and its methods practiced since time immemorial, it is now beginning to enjoy a resurgence. The concept has been passed on through oral tradition and is symbolically represented in the Gus-Wen-Tah or Two Row Wampum of the Haudenosaunee peoples. Although in recent years the concept has been used in reference to treaty making and as a way to honor treaties already made, it has application in other areas as well. One such application involves the coexistence of Western and Aboriginal intellectual traditions. Coexistence can be viewed as a way to have two worldviews and knowledge systems interact in an equitable fashion. This notion is summarized in a report by the Royal Commission on Aboriginal Peoples (RCAP 1993, 45):

> The widespread concerns for authentic Aboriginal voice, for authentic representation of Aboriginal experience and history, are continuing

legacies of the colonial past. They underline the power relationship between Aboriginal and non-Aboriginal people in Canada. A related concept recurring throughout is the necessity of parallel development, perhaps best captured symbolically in the Two Row Wampum belt. Hamelin advocates a process of intercultural convergence and cohabitation:

> There is symbolism in the train that enhances its value—added by using two rails that are independent yet associated for the task. Writers will think of independent canoes moving along the same body of water without colliding. Still others will envision a dog sled team on the tundra, each animal using its own track to jointly pull the sled. These metaphors imply that the mutual regime would include both independent and communal traits.

Whether in justice, social services, education, or government structures and processes, efforts to "indigenize" the dominant, non-Aboriginal institutions are seen largely as failures. Parallel institutions and systems, in which authentic voice and representation can be asserted, are seen as more promising avenues of development. Writers repeatedly urged the Royal Commission to study diverse existing examples of parallel development under Aboriginal direction, with the goal of finding out what works. On the basis of such research, models may be developed and communicated for broader application.

The description above aptly describes the perspective I chose for my dissertation research. Neither the Aboriginal nor the Western system of knowledge is subordinate or dominant; both are legitimate and run parallel, each with its own forms of validity and reliability and standards for legitimizing knowledge. This perspective will hopefully find broader application in other interdisciplinary fields of study over time.

Although the concept of coexistence has been part of Aboriginal tradition for many centuries, it finds its most prevalent expression in political and legal theory (e.g., treaties). The ideology suggests that "together, side by side, we go down the river of life in peace and friendship and mutual co-existence" (Lyons 1988, 20; see also Borrows 2010, 75–76). Colonial rule undermined the notion of coexistence as the basis of relationships between Aboriginal and non-Aboriginal peoples. In more recent years, the principles signified by the Two Row Wampum are reemerging in environmental and resource management discourse (McGregor 2008a; Ransom and Ettenger 2001; Stevenson 2006) and also in political and legal theory (Borrows 2010; Turner 2006). Coexistence and the principles it embodies have returned to the forefront as a way of describing how two groups of people can peacefully coexist despite having different worldviews, knowledge systems, and ways of knowing.

John Mohawk, a Haudenosaunee scholar, observes that the Two Row Wampum also embodies intellectual traditions. He states that "the wampum represents the people's best thinking into belts. . . . It was a symbol of a people's successful accomplishment of coming to one mind about how they were going to go on . . . in a permanent relationship of peace and tranquility between two sides" (1988, xiv). The Two Row Wampum is thus a metaphor for the relationship historically desired by Aboriginal people with non-Aboriginal people. Hope for the establishment of this relationship continues to the present day.

The concept of coexistence was of such importance that it formed the basis for many early treaties. As Mohawk suggests, it also has application for intellectual traditions, which is of particular interest here. The Mohawk scholar Marlene Brant Castellano asserts:

> For Aboriginal people the challenge is to translate the well-honed critique of colonial institutions into initiatives that go beyond deconstruction of oppressive ideologies and practices to give expression to Aboriginal philosophies, worldviews and social relations. For non-Aboriginal people the challenge is to open up space for Aboriginal initiative in schools and colleges, work sites and organizations so that indigenous ways of knowing can flourish and inter-cultural sharing can be practised in a *spirit of co-existence and mutual respect*. (Brant Castellano, 2000, 32; italics added)

In the spirit of coexistence, my research uses a theoretical perspective that respects and applies both Aboriginal and non-Aboriginal intellectual traditions. Understanding the context for my research process requires an appreciation of the "subjugation of Aboriginal people and the discounting of their ideas" (Ermine 1995, 3). Over time, Aboriginal worldviews, epistemologies, knowledges, and ways of acquiring information have been negated, ignored, deliberately excluded, and ridiculed (Brant Castellano 2000; Howitt and Suchet-Pearson 2006). Vine Deloria Jr., a Sioux scholar who has written prolifically on this topic, observes that "in fact, tribal peoples are as systematic and philosophical as Western scientists in their efforts to understand the world around them. They simply use other kinds of data and have goals other than determining the mechanical functioning of things" (Deloria 1999, 41).

Appreciating Aboriginal Knowledge

Increasingly, changes are occurring that indicate a move toward greater appreciation of Aboriginal systems of knowing. In relation to the substantive area of my research, there are some major forces at work supporting Indigenous research approaches and methods.

The establishment of Aboriginal-related journals reflects increased interest and activity in Indigenous research, teaching, and community work. There is also an increase in the number of Aboriginal organizations that incorporate research as a key component of their organizational mandate and objectives. The National Aboriginal Health Organization's *Journal of Aboriginal Health*, established in 2004, is an excellent example. Operated out of the University of Alberta, *Pimatisiwin* is an example of another recently established journal utilizing both academic and community peer reviewers to ground its writing. Such journals expand the scope of what constitutes "research" and recognize that traditional knowledges form a key aspect of sharing knowledge and research. They also illustrate the essential idea that inviting submissions from community-based researchers is a valid way of contributing to our understanding; universities are not the only sites of Indigenous scholarship and research.

There are a growing number of Indigenous scholars who bring their community ties, responsibilities, obligations, and networks to bear on their research projects. Many Indigenous scholars volunteer with Aboriginal communities and organizations (e.g., by serving as member of a board of directors). Such service links the academy and Aboriginal communities in novel ways. Indigenous knowledge gained collaboratively means that academia and Aboriginal communities are co-creators of knowledge as opposed to the countervailing scenario where communities are seen as sites for research. By engaging Aboriginal communities in multiple ways, scholars are beginning to take up the challenge of incorporating Indigenous epistemologies in their research.

Place and Indigenous Research

Margaret Kovach discusses the importance of place for framing Indigenous research approaches. A key aspect of place is language. Kovach notes that "the ability to craft our own research stories, in our own voice, has the best chance of engaging others." She adds that by situating oneself in place, "the visitation of anecdotes, metaphors, and stories about place make cerebral, academic language accessible and reflect holistic epistemologies" (Kovach 2009, 60). Fundamentally, this means that Indigenous research approaches and methods must reflect our relationships to the environment, land, and ancestors (Cardinal 2001; Pelletier-Sinclair 2003; S.

Wilson 2008). There is a sacredness to this type of research that is grounded in the natural world (Colorado 1988, 5). Indigenous research encompasses a range of codes of conduct and canons of behavior (Pelletier-Sinclair 2003, 128). The scope for Indigenous research, then, is broad; it is fundamentally about our relationships, not just to our research topic or the people we wish to work with, but also to Creation and our responsibilities thereto. The Cree scholar Stan Wilson adds:

> An Indigenous paradigm comes from the fundamental belief that knowledge is relational. Knowledge is shared with all of Creation. It is not just interpersonal relationships, not just with research subjects I may be working with, but is a relationship with all of Creation. It is with the cosmos, it is with the animals, with the plants, with the earth that we share this knowledge. It goes beyond the idea of individual knowledge to the concept of relational knowledge. (S. Wilson 2001, 177)

An Indigenous conceptual framework envisions relationships not only to what we see around us, but also to what came before (our ancestors), to what will come after (those yet to be born), and to the spirit world. Ethically, we work to recognize and live these relationships. In an Indigenous research paradigm, our ethics always include the environment, no matter the research question or topic. Indigenous research paradigms are about place. Kovach adds that:

> Place links present with past and our personal self with kinship groups. What we know flows through us from the 'echo of generations,' and our knowledges cannot be universalized because they arise from our experience with our places. This is why name-place stories matter: they are repositories of science, they tell of relationships, they reveal history, and they hold our identity. (Kovach 2009, 61)

Wilson further explains:

> Indigenous people's sense of self is planted and rooted in the land. The sacred bond with the land is more substantial than a propertied relationship and entails responsibility to all living forms that are sustained from the soil: grasses, medicinal plants, fruit bushes. . . . As an Aboriginal person I am constituted by my individual self and by my ancestors and future generations, who will originate in and have returned to the land. My relationship to the grass, to the trees, to the insects, to the birds, and even to the hunter animals derives from the

fact that my ancestors now are part of the ground. Because the life surrounding me is part of me through my ancestors, I must consider and care for all its constituents. (S. Wilson 2001, 91)

Such approaches to knowledge are thousands of years old (Archibald 2008; Cardinal 2001; Colorado 1988; S. Wilson 2008). As Cardinal observes, "Indigenous research methods and methodologies are as old as our ceremonies and our nations. They are with us and have always been with us. Our Indigenous cultures are rich with ways of gathering, discovering and uncovering knowledge" (Cardinal 2001, 182). In an Indigenous context, then, research is about "living systems" and our relationship and responsibilities to them (Weber-Pillwax 2001).

Indigenous Research Paradigm: Anishinaabe Action Research

Recognition of my responsibilities as an Anishinaabe person has explicitly shaped my research over the past dozen years. In 2000, while I was conducting research for a First Nation organization on traditional perspectives on water, I visited a group of women from Bkejwanong Territory–Akii Kwe. They spoke of their efforts, guided by Anishinaabe spiritual traditions that governed their advocacy and activist work in relation to water. As part of my work with the Akii Kwe I learned that as an Ansihinaabe-kwe woman, I had a responsibility to speak for water (McGregor 2005). This revelation completely changed the focus of my research in terms of approach, responsibility, and focus. I have devoted myself to sharing my work over the years. Advocating for the inclusion of Anishnaabe knowledge and perspective in various capacities has been and continues to be part of my responsibility to all my family, community, and nation—to all my relations and to Creation as a whole (McGregor 2009).

An Anishinaabe research paradigm has been in existence since time immemorial; it is not new, although it has transformed to meet present-day challenges. Anishinaabe intellectual traditions have informed research methods that shape why and how knowledge or power is sought and enacted. Anishinaabe intellectual traditions are fundamentally about relationships— relationships not only among people, but rather among all our relations, including all living things, the spirit world, our ancestors, and those yet to come. Anishinaabe knowledge is derived from our relationship with Creation. This means that Anishinaabe knowledge comes from lived experience (relationships) and in particular relationships with Creation. It is not just knowledge; it is the way that we conduct ourselves and relate to other beings in Creation. Anishinaabe knowledge is about ensuring sustainability, living a good life, and realizing our potential. The research that is enacted to pursue these goals is informed by an "ethic of responsibility": how we conduct ourselves matters on the physical, emotional, intellectual, and spiritual planes. Anishinaabe language, culture, and traditions matter and are inscribed on the geographic landscape (spiritual and otherwise). Anishinaabe theoretical frameworks have informed our stories (McGregor 2012).

Anishinaabe action research for an Anishinaabe-kwe means I have a responsibility to speak for water. As a scholar, I enact this through my research, teaching, and writing. As a community member, I realize this through my policy, governance, and advocacy work with First Nation organizations (McGregor 2008b). As a member of family, community, and nation, I carry out my responsibilities through my lived experience, which forms a fundamental part of who I am.

As noted above in the Anishinaabe tradition, women are seen as having a unique relationship with water (Anderson 2000; Anderson, Clow, and Haworth-Brockman 2011). This is an example of Anishinaabe action research: you must enact it, not just research and write about it. This approach requires acknowledgment of various intellectual traditions that may or may not be Indigenous, and it certainly does not require the rejection of other perspectives.

Future Directions: Indigenous-Academic Collaborations

I believe one of the most important steps for moving toward a paradigm of coexistence in Indigenous-academic collaborations for research is to recognize that there is a *need for* Indigenous methodologies. Kovach sums up the challenge aptly:

> As the academic landscape shifts with an increasing Indigenous presence, there is a desire among a growing number of non-Indigenous academics to move beyond the binaries found within Indigenous-settler relations to construct new, mutual forms of dialogue, research, theory, and action. . . . The infusion of Indigenous knowledge systems and research frameworks informed by the distinctiveness of cultural epistemologies transforms homogeneity. It not only provides another environment where Indigenous knowledges can live, but changes the nature of the academy itself. (Kovach 2009, 13)

Indigenous knowledge is part of the lived experience of a person, family, clan, nation, or people, and even of Creation. Making this understanding of Indigenous knowledge a reality in the academy means that Indigenous people who are part of the academic community (faculty, students, staff, community members) must be able to live their Indigenous knowledge in this context. It is not sufficient to simply talk about it, to study and write about it; one has to actually live its principles, values, and purpose. Indigenous knowledge thus brings considerable responsibility and obligations to bear on its participants. This is an enormous challenge for Indigenous scholars, and space is required to enable Indigenous scholars and their knowledges to flourish.

For non-Indigenous scholars and researchers the question becomes one of how to become engaged in Indigenous research. The role of the non-Indigenous scholar will evolve as Indigenous scholarship continues to grow. Supporting and allying oneself with Indigenous scholarship and engaging with it is one step in the process. Renee Paulani Louis, in her article "Can You Hear Us Now? Voices from the Margin: Using Indigenous Methodologies for Geographic Research" (2007), provides various strategies that include using Indigenous methodologies in geographic curriculum, supporting Indigenous faculty and students, establishing academic allies with non-Indigenous faculty, ensuring that Indigenous communities have a voice in research, and challenging review criteria that privilege Western research and knowledge production. Kovach expands on the role of non-Indigenous scholars by encouraging decolonizing work on oneself and one's institutions. She suggests supporting Indigenous scholars and students by mentoring Indigenous scholars on the intellectual aspects of academia and its operational requirements, and by encouraging and fairly evaluating Indigenous scholarship on its own, not Western, standards (Kovach 2009, 171–72).

One of the most important points raised by Kovach is that non-Indigenous scholars must engage with Indigenous peoples. Such relational work is critical and fundamental to Indigenous scholarship. Establishing and continuing dialogue as the intellectual landscape continues to change are essential strategies for effectively embracing Indigenous scholarship and research. Hopefully, the work of the IPKRC will continue to provide space for dialogue by bringing together Indigenous and non-Indigenous scholars. As Kate Berry (2008, 3) points out, simply having the dialogue will "identify pathways for new approaches and ideas."

Note

1. Although no consensus has been reached as to the appropriate terminology for describing Indigenous peoples' relationships with Creation, I will utilize traditional knowledge (TK) throughout the paper to be consistent with the UN *Declaration on the Rights of Indigenous Peoples* and the *Convention on Biological Diversity*.

References

AFN (Assembly of First Nations). 1993. *Reclaiming Our Nationhood: Strengthening Our Heritage*. Report to the Royal Commission on Aboriginal Peoples. Ottawa, ON: AFN.

Anderson, K. 2000. *A Recognition of Being: Reconstructing Native Womanhood*. Toronto: Second Story Press.

Anderson, K., B. Clow, and M. Haworth-Brockman. 2011. "Carriers of Water: Aboriginal Women's Experiences, Relationships and Reflections." *Journal of Cleaner Production.* In press.

Archibald, J. 2008. *Indigenous Storywork: Educating the Heart, Mind, Body, and Spirit.* Vancouver: University of British Columbia Press.

Barriero, J. 2004. "Indigenous Geography as Discipline Arrives." http://indiancountrytodaymedianetwork.com/ictarchives/2004/03/31/indigenous-geography-as-discipline-arrives-93411.

Battiste, M., and J. Henderson. 2000. *Protecting Indigenous Knowledge and Heritage: A Global Challenge.* Saskatoon: Purich Publishing.

Berry, K. 2008. "Introduction: Mainstreaming Indigenous Geography." *American Indian Culture and Research Journal* 23 (3): 103.

Bocking, S. 2005. "Scientists and Evolving Perceptions of Indigenous Knowledge in Northern Canada." In *Walking a Tightrope: Aboriginal Peoples and Their Representation*, edited by U. Lischke and D. McNab. Waterloo, ON: Wilfred Laurier University Press.

Borrows, J. 2005. *Crown Occupations of Land: A History and Comparison.* Office of the Attorney General. Government of Ontario. Prepared by the Ipperwash Inquiry. http://www.attorneygeneral.jus.gov.on.ca/inquiries/ipperwash/policy_part/research.

———. 2010. *Canada's Indigenous Constitution.* Toronto: University of Toronto Press.

Brant Castellano, M. 2000. "Updating Aboriginal Traditional Knowledge." In *Indigenous Knowledge in Global Contexts: Multiple Readings in Our World*, edited by S. Dei, B. Hall, and D. Goldin-Rosenberg, 21–36. Toronto: University of Toronto Press.

———. 2004. "Ethics of Aboriginal Research." *Journal of Aboriginal Health* 1 (1): 98–114.

Brascoupe, S., and H. Mann. 2001. *A Community Guide to Protecting Indigenous Knowledge.* Ottawa, ON: Minister of Public Works and Government Services.

Butler, C. 2006. "Historicizing Indigenous Knowledge: Practical and Political Issues." In *Traditional Ecological Knowledge and Natural Resource Management*, edited by C. Menzies, 107–26. Lincoln: University of Nebraska Press.

Cardinal, L. 2001. "What Is an Indigenous Perspective?" *Canadian Journal of Native Education* 25 (2): 180–82.

Colorado, P. 1988. "Bridging Native and Western Science." *Convergence* 21 (2/3): 49–64.

Crowshoe, C. 2005. *Sacred Ways of Life: Traditional Knowledge.* Ottawa, ON.: National Aboriginal Health Organization.

CYFN (Council of Yukon First Nations). 2000. *Traditional Knowledge Research Guidelines: A Guide for Researchers in the Yukon.* Prepared by Council of Yukon Indians, Whitehorse, Yukon.

Deloria, V. 1999. *Spirit and Reason: The Vine Deloria Jr. Reader.* Golden, CO: Fulcrum.

Doyle-Bedwell, P., and F. Cohen. 2001. "Aboriginal Peoples in Canada: Their Role in Shaping Environmental Trends in the Twenty-first Century." In *Governing the Environment: Persistent Challenges: Uncertain Innovations,* edited by E. Parsons, 169–206. Toronto: University of Toronto Press.

Ellis, S. 2005. "Meaningful Consideration? A Review of Traditional Knowledge in Environmental Decision Making." *Arctic* 58 (1): 66–77.

Ermine, W. 1995. "Aboriginal Epistemology." In *First Nation Education in Canada: The Circle Unfolds,* edited by M. Battiste and J. Barman, 101–12. Vancouver: University of British Columbia Press.

GRRB (Gwich'in Renewal Resources Board). 2004. *Working with Gwich'in Traditional Knowledge in the Gwich'in Settlement Region.* Inuvik, NT: Gwich'in Renewal Resources Board. www.grrb.nt.cal/pdf/GTCTKpolicy.pdf.

Higgins, C. 1998. "The Role of Traditional Ecological Knowledge in Managing for Biodiversity." *Forestry Chronicle* 7 (3): 323–26.

Hill, R. 1990. "Oral Memory of the Haudenosaunee: Views of the Two Row Wampum." *Northeast Indian Quarterly* 11 (1): 21–30.

Houde, N. 2007. "The Six Faces of Traditional Ecological Knowledge: Challenges and Opportunities for Canadian Co-Management Arrangements." *Ecology and Society* 12 (2): 34. www.ecologyandsociety.org/vol12/iss2 (accessed July 2008).

Howitt, R., and S. Suchet-Pearson. 2006. "Rethinking the Building Blocks: Ontological Pluralism and the Idea of Management." *Geografiska Annaler B* 88 (3): 323–35.

IPKRC (Indigenous Peoples Knowledges and Rights Commission). 2007. *The Meeting of IGU Commission on IPKR.* http://www.unl.edu/geography/IPKRC.

Johnson, J. 2008. *2004–2008 Report on the Indigenous Peoples' Knowledges and Rights Commission.* International Geographic Union. http://www.unl.edu/geography/IPKRC. s

Johnson, J., G. Cant, R. Howitt, and E. Peters. 2007. "Creating Anti-Colonial Geographies: Embracing Indigenous Peoples' Knowledges and Rights." *Geographic Research* 45 (2): 117–20.

Kovach, M. 2009. *Indigenous Methodologies: Characteristics, Conversations, and Contexts.* Toronto: University of Toronto Press.

Louis, R. 2007. "Can You Hear Us Now? Voices from the Margins: Using Indigenous Methodologies in Geographic Research." *Geographical Research* 45 (2): 130–39.

Lyons, O. 1988. "Land of the Free, Home of the Brave." In "Indian Roots of American Democracy: Cultural Encounter 1," edited by J. Barreiro. *Northeast Indian Quarterly* 4 (4) and 5 (1): 18–20.

Martin, K. 2003. "Ways of Knowing, Ways of Being and Ways of Doing: A Theoretical Framework and Methods for Indigenous Research and Indigenist Research." *Journal of Australian Studies* 27 (76): 203–14

McGregor, D. 2004. "Coming Full Circle: Indigenous Knowledge, Environment and Our Future." *American Indian Quarterly* 28 (3/4): 385–410.

———. 2005. "Traditional Ecological Knowledge: An Anishinabe-Kwe Perspective." *Atlantis: A Women's Studies Journal* 29 (2): 103–9.

———. 2008a. "Linking Traditional Ecological Knowledge and Western Science: Aboriginal Perspectives on SOLEC." *Canadian Journal of Native Studies* 28 (1): 139–58.

———. 2008b. "Water Quality in the Province of Ontario: An Aboriginal Traditional Knowledge Perspective." In *Integrated Water Management in Environmental History,* edited by E. Herman, 543–62. Quebec: Les Presses de L'Universite Laval.

———. 2009. "Honouring Our Relations: An Anishinabe Perspective on Environmental Justice." In *Speaking for Ourselves: Constructions of Environmental Justice in Canada,* J. Agyeman, R. Haluza-Delay, C. Peter, and P. O'Riley, 27–41. Vancouver: University of British Columbia Press.

———. 2010. "Traditional Knowledge, Sustainable Forest Management, and Ethical Research Involving Aboriginal Peoples: An Aboriginal Scholar's Perspective." In *Aboriginal Policy Research: Voting, Governance and Research Methodology*, edited by P. White, J. Peters, D. Beavon, and Peter Dinsdale, 10:227–44. Toronto: Thompson Educational Publishing.

———. 2012. "Anishinabe Knowledge and Water Governance in Ontario: Honouring Our Responsibilities." In *Anishinaabewin Niizh: Culture Movements, Critical Moments*, edited by A. Corbiere, D. McGregor, and C. Migwans, 24–39. McChigeeng, ON: Ojibwe Cultural Foundation.

McNaughton, C., and D. Rock. 2004. "Opportunities in Aboriginal Research: Results of SSHRC's Dialogue on Research and Aboriginal Peoples." *Native Studies Review* 12 (2): 37–60.

Menzies, C., and C. Butler. 2006. "Introduction: Understanding Ecological Knowledge." In *Traditional Ecological Knowledge and Natural Resource Management*, edited by C. Menzies. Lincoln: University of Nebraska Press.

Mohawk, J. 1988. "A Symbol More Powerful Than Paper." In "Indian Roots of American Democracy: Cultural Encounter 1," edited by J. Barreiro. *Northeast Indian Quarterly* 5 (1): 13–17.

Nadasdy, P. 2006. "The Case of the Missing Sheep: Time, Space and Politics of Trust in Co-Management Practice." In *Traditional Ecological Knowledge and Natural Resource Management*, edited by C. Menzies, 127–52. Lincoln: University of Nebraska Press.

NAHO (National Aboriginal Health Organization). 2007. *Handbook and Resource Guide to the Convention on Biological Diversity*. Ottawa, ON: National Aboriginal Health Organization.

Pelletier Sinclair, R. 2003. "Indigenous Research in Social Work: The Challenge of Operationalizing Worldview." *Native Social Work Journal* 5:117–35.

Peters, E. 2006. "We Do Not Lose Our Treaty Rights Outside the Reserve: Challenging the Scales of Social Service Provision for First Nations Women in Canada Cities." *Geojournal* 65 (4): 315–27.

Ransom, R., and K. Ettenger. 2001. "Polishing the Kaswetha': A Haudenosaunee View of Environmental Cooperation." *Environmental Science and Policy* 4:219–28.

RCAP (Royal Commission on Aboriginal Peoples). 1993. *Integrated Research Plan*. Ottawa, ON: Minister of Supply and Services Canada.

———. 1996. "Lands and Resources." In *Report of the Royal Commission on Aboriginal Peoples*, vol. 2: *Restructuring the Relationship*. Ottawa, ON: Canada Communication Group.

Richardson, D. 2008. "Indigenous Geographies of Struggle and Self-Determination." *Newsletter of the Association of American Geographers* 43 (1): 2–15.

Rigney, L. 1999. "Internationalization of an Indigenous Anticolonial Cultural Critique of Research Methodologies: A Guide to Indigenist Research Methodology and Its Principles." *Wicazo Sa Review* 14 (2): 109–21.

Roberts, K. 1996. *Circumpolar Aboriginal People and Co-Management Practice: Current Issues in Co-Management and Environmental Assessment*. Conference proceedings. Arctic Institute of North America and Joint Secretariat-Inuvialuit Renewable Resources Committees. Arctic Institute of North America, University of Calgary, Alberta.

Schnarch, B. 2004. *Ownership, Control, Access and Possession (OCAP) of Self-Determination Applied to Research: A Critical Analysis of Contemporary First Nations Research and Some Options for First Nations Communities.* Ottawa, Ont.: First Nations Centre, National Aboriginal Health Organization.

Settee, P. 2000. "The Issue of Biodiversity, Intellectual Property Rights, and Indigenous Rights." In *Expressions in Canadian Native Studies,* edited by R. Laliberte, P. Settee, J. Waldram, R. Innes, B. Macdougall, L. McBain, and F. Barron, 459–90. Saskatoon: University of Saskatchewan Extension Press.

Shaw, W. R. Herman, and R. Dobbs. 2006. "Encountering Indigeneity: Re-Imagining and Decolonizing Geography." *Geografiska Annaler B* 88 (3): 323–35.

Smith, L. 1999. *Decolonizing Methodologies: Research and Indigenous Peoples.* London: Zed Books.

Spak, S. 2005. "The Position of Indigenous Knowledge in Canadian Co-Management Organizations." *Anthropologica* 47 (2): 233–46.

Steinhauer, E. 1999. "Thoughts on Indigenous Methodology." *Canadian Journal of Native Studies* 26 (2): 69–81.

Stevenson, M. 2006. "The Possibility of Difference: Rethinking Co-Management." *Human Organization* 65 (2): 167–80.

Turner, D. 2006. *This Is Not a Peace Pipe: Toward a Critical Indigenous Philosophy.* Toronto: University of Toronto Press.

Usher, P. 2000. "Traditional Ecological Knowledge." *Environmental Assessment and Management* 53 (2): 183–93.

WCED (World Commission on Environment and Development). 1987. *Our Common Future.* Oxford: Oxford University Press.

Weber-Pillwax, C. 2001. "Coming to an Understanding: A Panel Presentation: What Is Indigenous Research?" *Canadian Journal of Native Education* 25 (2): 166–77.

White, G. 2006. "Cultures in Collision: Traditional Knowledge and Euro-Canadian Governance Processes in Northern Land-Claim Boards." *Arctic* 59 (4): 401–14.

Williams, N., and G. Baines, eds. 1993. *Traditional Ecological Knowledge: Wisdom for Sustainable Development.* Centre for Resources and Environmental Studies, Australian National University.

Wilson, J., and J. Graham, J. 2005. *Relationships between First Nations and Forest Industry: The Legal and Policy Context. A Report for the National Aboriginal Forestry Association, Forest Products Association of Canada, First Nations Forestry Program.* Ottawa, ON: Institute on Governance.

Wilson, S. 2001. "Self-as-Relationship in Indigenous Research." *Canadian Journal of Native Education* 25 (2): 91–92.

———. 2008. *Research Is Ceremony: Indigenous Research Methods.* Blackpoint, NS: Fernwood.

Indigenous and Western Science Partners in Climate Change Assessment and Adaptation in Alaska

SARAH F. TRAINOR

Alaska is "ground zero" for climate change in the United States. Statewide, average annual temperatures have increased 3°F since 1949, with the greatest warming occurring in the winter months, averaging nearly 6°F warming. Alaska's Indigenous peoples are arguably disproportionately affected by a changing climate in part because of their close connection to the land for nutrition and cultural identity (Trainor, Chapin, et al. 2007; Trainor, Godduhn, et al. 2009). Ecological conditions are changing, affecting subsistence hunting, fishing, and gathering (Huntington and Fox 2005). Sea ice extent, thickness, and dynamics are changing, affecting subsistence hunting and coastal erosion, which threatens homes and community infrastructure (Markon, Trainor, et al. 2012). Lakes are draining and drying, affecting water fowl and fish habitat (Riordan, Verbyla, and McGuire 2006). River and stream temperatures are changing, which can contribute to fish disease and stress (Kyle and Brabets 2001). The timing and character of seasons are changing, affecting subsistence hunting, gathering, and fishing and creating unsafe travel conditions on partially frozen rivers and bays (Berner and Furgal 2005; Krupnik and Jolly 2002). People are observing insects, plants, and animals that they have not seen before in their home regions (Krupnik and Jolly 2002).

During a year-long process to create climate change adaptation policy recommendations, a dedicated Health and Culture Adaptation Advisory Group[1] was part of the Governor's Sub-Cabinet on Climate Change. Much attention and publicity have been focused on Shishmaref, Kivalina, and Newtok, communities that are among those in need of immediate relocation (Lempinen 2006). However, more attention to the Indigenous perspective in discussion of climate change policy and adaptation is needed.

I compiled the information presented here from a series of workshops, video conferences, and discussions focusing on climate change impacts and adaptation in Native communities, hosted by the Alaska Center for Climate Assessment and

Policy (ACCAP) at the University of Alaska, Fairbanks (UAF), between November 2007 and April 2009. ACCAP is one of several Regional Integrated Science and Assessment (RISA) programs in the United States, funded by the Climate Program Office of the National Oceanic and Atmospheric Administration (NOAA).[2] In operation since 2006, ACCAP's mission is to assess the socioeconomic and bio-physical impacts of climate variability in Alaska, make this information available to local and regional decision makers, and improve the ability of Alaskans to adapt to a changing climate.

In its first three years of operations (2006–2009), ACCAP hosted several projects that engaged Alaska's Indigenous peoples in climate change science outreach and adaptation planning. This chapter interprets three of these events as a way of describing how I have come to understand a deeper sense of my own place as a white, Western-trained social scientist working with Alaska Indigenous peoples on climate change impact assessment and adaptation planning. I also derived ideas and perspectives in this chapter from discussions and commentary during workshops, field trips, and interviews conducted as part of the University of Alaska, Fairbanks, interdisciplinary Human-Fire Interactions project funded by the National Science Foundation Office of Polar Programs.[3]

Interactions: Dialogues, Discussions, and Workshop

Preparing for Climate Change Workshop, Kotzebue, Alaska

In November 2007, ACCAP hosted a two-day climate change adaptation workshop in Kotzebue. This workshop was a response to a request for information and assistance in planning and preparing for continuing climate change impacts in the Northwest Arctic Borough. The workshop was organized in conjunction with Maniilaq Association (the regional Native nonprofit service organization), the Northwest Arctic Borough (NWAB), the Chukchi Campus of the University of Alaska, and the City of Kotzebue. NWAB employees also engaged the NANA Elder's Council (NANA is the regional Native for-profit corporation).

The goals of the workshop were to explore ways that research at the University of Alaska can address the information needs of people in Northwest Alaska; provide community members an opportunity to discuss and develop specific plans to prepare and respond proactively to current and projected future changes; engage community members in current research at UAF, particularly in the Social Vulnerability to Climate Change of Alaskan Coasts.[4] A central focus of this project was to identify specific weather patterns and combinations that most affect economic activity in the region.

ACCAP provided travel funding for representatives from the NANA Regional Elders Council and from tribal and city governments in each village in the region

(Ambler, Buckland, Deering, Kiana, Kivalina, Kobuk, Kotzebue, Noatak, Noorvik, Selawik, and Shungnak). Other participants included representatives from the Alaska Department of Fish and Game, Alaska House of Representatives, Chukchi Campus of UAF, Maniilaq Association, NANA Regional Corporation, National Park Service, NOAA National Weather Service, The Nature Conservancy, the Northwest Arctic Borough, Swiss Public Radio, United States Fish and Wildlife Service, and the University of Alaska. The Kotzebue high school science honors class participated in the discussion and break-out session as fit with their class schedule. The workshop was broadcast live and available on the Internet in simulcast on KOTZ public radio.[5]

During the discussion, the topics of concern included water quality and availability; wild food preservation, availability, and quality; infrastructure, erosion, flooding and village relocation; mental, cultural, and spiritual well-being; trigger points, taking action, and long-term adaptation; emergency preparedness; transportation; and energy generation. Presentations by UAF and National Weather Service (NWS) scientists covered climatological data and trends for the region; model projections for temperature and precipitation in the region, incorporating local knowledge into NWS forecast products, storms, winds, and erosion in the local area; ecological research on changes in tundra vegetation in the region; and model estimates of future infrastructure replacement costs due to climate change. On the second day, break-out groups self-organized into two groups, one with representatives from coastal villages and the other with representatives from inland villages. The emphasis of the discussion was on how best to prepare and respond to environmental changes.

Climate, Language, and Indigenous Perspectives Elders Panel

In August 2008, ACCAP partnered with the Alaska Native Language Center to host an Elders Panel in conjunction with the Climate, Language, and Indigenous Knowledge Conference at UAF. Elders participated from across the state representing Cup'ik from the Yukon-Kuskokwim, Inupiaq from the North Slope and Northwest Arctic, Aleut from St. Paul Island, and Dena'ina, Koyukon, Lower Tanana Athabascan, and Upper Tanana Athabascan. In all, twelve Elders participated. The panel took place over the course of two full afternoons with a concluding picnic. Participants were asked to address the following questions: (1) What are two changes in the natural world most important to you and/or your community, and what are the connections between those changes and how they affect the community? (2) What do you think should be done? What should be studied in your community by scientists? What do you want Western scientists to know about working in your community?

Overall, this Elders' panel underscored the importance of Native language in climate change observation and adaptation (Kovach 2009). This emphasis on Native language was an important component in discussions of environmental change. Emphasizing the ties between language and land, Neal Charlie described language as a key part of a person's identity: "According to our Native way . . . our Native language and the land it's got a very strong connection. That's supposed to be our identity."

Local and Indigenous Knowledge Cross-Regional Video Conferences

In November 2008 and April 2009, ACCAP partnered with two other NOAA RISA programs, the Climate Assessment for the Southwest (CLIMAS) and the Pacific Islands RISA, to host a series of cross-regional video conferences focusing on indigenous impacts and adaptation to drought and water quality stresses resulting from climate change. These video conferences were intended to provide opportunity for cross-regional dialogue, networking, and learning specific to water impacts and adaptation strategies and also to improve the ability of scientists and federal agencies to address the information needs of underserved populations by strengthening communication and prioritizing research and decision-support needs.

Video links were set up in Alaska rural and urban campuses of the University of Alaska and some rural village school sites, at the University of Arizona, Northern Arizona University, and Arizona State University, and at sites at the University of Hawaiʻi, Marshall Islands, and American Samoa. A total of forty-eight people participated in the November meeting and forty-four in April 2009; participants came from Alaska, Arizona, Washington, California, Washington, DC, and the Pacific Islands. Participants included tribal governments and tribal water resource managers, federal agency representatives (EPA, USGS, NOAA), national nonprofit groups (National Congress of American Indians Policy Research Institute and the Union of Concerned Scientists), and private consultants and scientists from the universities of Alaska, Arizona, Northern Arizona, and Hawaiʻi.

Each session opened with two or three presentations about water impacts, drought monitoring, and reporting and building national Native coalitions from university scientists, Indigenous water resource managers, and the National Congress of American Indians Climate Change Community of Practice. Discussion topics focused on sharing water impacts in each region, discussing adaptation strategies, and how best to work with non-Native scientists to address local concerns related to water and climate change.[6] The open discussion that followed presentations was informed by questions identified ahead of time, but was largely driven by the interests, concerns, and vision of the participants.

Obstacles to Collaboration between Western Science and Native Knowledge

> "The temptation to compare scientific and traditional knowledge
> comes from collecting traditional knowledge without the
> contextual elements" (Alaska Native Science Commission).[7]

Contrasts between the intuitive, holistic, experiential, and integrated knowledge of Indigenous knowledge systems and the analytical, reductionist, model- and hypothesis-based Western scientific knowledge system are well documented (Alaska Native Science Commission; Berkes 1993; Cajete 2000; Huntington, Callaghan, et al. 2004; Stephens 1996). Battiste and Henderson (2000) argue that Indigenous knowledge, or ethnoscience, cannot be fully understood from within the Western paradigm or, more generally, Eurocentric thought. However, many contemporary Indigenous peoples are accomplished scientists and skilled at navigating through white, Western institutions and hierarchies of knowledge and power while remaining rooted in the knowledge system and patterns of causal reasoning of Indigenous science (Kovach 2009).

In addition to these epistemological differences, true partnership between Western science and indigenous knowledge is further challenged by differing notions of causality, that is, why things happen (Huntington, Trainor, et al. 2006). Native knowledge systems have different standards for expertise rooted in oral tradition and explicitly include spirituality and emotion in knowledge. Ontologically, humans are understood to be part of the natural world. In discussing adaptation to the rapid changes Alaska's Indigenous peoples are experiencing, Elder Wilson Justin of Chistochina explained, "[The] . . . adaptive discussion you hear often amongst ourselves [involves a] . . . great spiritual component that does not exist outside Indigenous societies . . . because we are laughed at when this happens. . . . It conflicts with the scientists' measurement and philosophy." (Wilson Justin, CLIP Elders Panel)

Alaskan Elders explain that knowledge without wisdom is useless and may be harmful, yet Western scientists are loath to add the term "Wisdom" when referring to Indigenous science (L. Merculieff, personal communication).

Indigenous and Western partnership can be inhibited by the institutional structure of scientific research. Scientific funding cycles often run in one-, three-, or five-year cycles. This can set artificial boundaries on the duration, priorities, and scope of Western research projects and can inhibit the development of long-term, strong, working relationships. The grant funding for a project may be gone, but the need to travel to communities, share results, and discuss local implications and application remains.

Furthermore, rather than approaching Indigenous peoples and their knowledge in partnership, some governmental entities and Western scientists have historically continued a colonizing relationship with local Indigenous people. In some cases, local observations and traditional knowledge passed on by elders are dismissed as "anecdotal" and discredited by scientists and state and federal agencies. In other cases, it is recognized as an important component in understanding climate change in Alaska, but it is either recorded, collected, or otherwise usurped by Western scientists or taken out of context with final research products not returned to the community.

Western scientific practice places high value on written, peer-reviewed documentation of phenomena and events. The written word and especially the peer-review process provide credibility and legitimacy to information. The scientific method requires observations to be recorded (in writing or electronically) and made in a manner that is repeatable and clearly delineated ahead of time (Couzin 2007).

Indigenous cultures, in contrast, place high value on the spoken word and oral tradition. In traditional Alaskan cultures, Native cultural survival was dependent on keen skills of observation—not just sight, but sound, smell, feel, touch, and other senses. Strong observational skills are common in Alaska Indigenous communities today, especially among Elders. Because this worldview does not share the value of the written word, observations are not recorded but rather passed on as stories from the Elders. Oral tradition and its embodied local knowledge is reflexive, implying human agency, responsibility, and a causal chain in the natural world that includes human thought and action (Cruikshank 2001).

Beyond acknowledging the validity of local observation and knowledge, academics and Western scientists must respect the Indigenous "ownership" of information. Contemporary codes of ethics in working in indigenous communities reflect this principle.[8] Some communities even have their own protocols to which scientists must adhere. Armed with the Western scientific method, natural and social scientists alike may enter into a community and "collect data" on local observations (of climate change or anything else). It is important to respect local knowledge and work in partnership with local people rather than viewing local knowledge as data to collect and analyze (Huntington 2000).

In the legal, political, and bureaucratic institutions associated with Western land management, scientific knowledge and expertise carry credibility and legitimacy. However, too often, local knowledge is seen only as expert knowledge when collected by scientists and reported in scientific ways. Reggie Joule expressed his frustration at the Kotzebue workshop,

Any information coming out of this room is [considered] "anecdotal," any information that you bring is "scientific." Yet you are looking to people in this room for answers to your questions. This is an opportunity to see how anecdotal and scientific information quite often will parallel each other. So there is much importance on local knowledge. (Representative Reggie Joule, Kotzebue Workshop)

These are some of the epistemological, ontological, and institutional challenges to indigenous and Western collaboration in documenting, understanding, and crafting proactive responses to environmental change in Alaska.

In addition, obstacles to true collaboration and partnership between climate scientists and Indigenous peoples may be barriers that we don't even see, challenges in cross-cultural communication of which we are completely unaware. For example, as I began to write this chapter and reflect on what I have learned from the workshops, panels, interactions, and partnerships I have had with Alaskan Indigenous peoples in my work with the Alaska Center for Climate Assessment and Policy, I sent drafts to key Elders and collaborators for feedback and comments. For most participants in the Climate, Language and Elders' Conference a highlight of the conference was on the last day when the Elders sang "Happy Birthday" in their respective Native languages, and I noted this in the text of the first draft. Months after reading this draft, Wilson Justin sent me an email to explain his view of the significance of that singing. The ensuing correspondence and phone conversations not only confirmed my intuition that the songs were a significant part of the workshop but also revealed my ignorance as to what function they served in the dialogue and what meaning they actually carried for the Elders present.

As Wilson explained, unbeknown to the Western organizers and observers, in the course of the workshop "the organizers had inadvertently asked the Elders to speak to the sacred." We had asked the Elders to talk about environmental changes that they have observed and how these changes have affected their communities. The religious Elders present could not do this in a multicultural setting (multiple Native cultures as well as white) without offending the Creator, or violating "Clan Protocols or tribal ritual rules." A gift was required to preempt offense. Wilson explained that songs are gifts and that the Happy Birthday song was suggested by one Elder as a way to cross the multicultural setting. It is a Western song that everyone knows and that could be sung in each Native language.

The singing of Happy Birthday was a gift to all from each individual in the group. None of the elders were comfortable in that setting on the topic proposed. One Elder singing the song was not enough. Each

Elder had to agree that this was enough of a gift to cover any "possible breach of Tribal Protocol" within that setting. . . . By singing the song in each language, we were able to proceed on several different levels. One, it was okay to speak to Climate Change in a way that would be noncritical of the will of the Creator and two, we as individuals would not violate our own Clan Protocols in speaking frankly or even critically of the Creator's creation in front of strangers or other clans. (Wilson Justin, personal communication)

Although we had opened each day's panel meeting with a prayer, none of the organizers realized the predicament that they had created for the Elders. Nor did we realize what would be required on so many different levels for the Elders to speak to our questions.

The singing occurred on the second day of the workshop. One Elder volunteered the song in her language. "It could have easily been one person doing one song in one language stopping there again without any place to go," Wilson explained. "We went on, of course, and therein lies the key. We gave ourselves permission to do what was asked in a way we thought would pay homage to our ancestors and then to honor the Creator's creation" (Wilson Justin, personal communication). Thus, as Wilson described, only after the songs, was the discussion able to move forward.

Two of the Elders left the workshop early (before the songs) for what we understood as health reasons. Later, Wilson explained to me that they were uncomfortable with the setting and with what we had asked of them, and they could not reconcile this. The avenue of resolution for them was to remove themselves from the situation.

Thus without our even knowing it, a barrier to communication about climate change was inherent in the panel topic and agenda, even at a workshop where participants were encouraged to speak in their Native language. This barrier was overcome at the initiative and creativity of the Elder participants. I would never have been aware of this barrier or its resolution without the opportunity to write this chapter and the willingness of Wilson Justin to read and comment on early drafts.

Vision of Partnership

There is growing recognition among scientists of the value and legitimacy of local traditional knowledge and the need for both local knowledge and science to create solutions to problems such as climate change (Couzin 2007; Krupnik and Jolly 2002; Riewe and Oakes 2006; Cruikshank 2001; Salick and Ross 2009). The discussions that took place in the workshops and video conferences highlighted the need for Native and non-Native people to work together and share their perspectives. What is required is a vision and a relationship of partnership that goes beyond dichotomies such as Western and Native, basic and applied, scientist and subject of research, or local and scientific knowledge. This means much more than simply incorporating an "Indigenous component" into a conventional research project by interviewing local Native Elders and residents to collect their traditional knowledge about a species, event, process, phenomenon, or location under scientific study. It also means much more than simply soliciting Indigenous input into tools and information resources that have been designed primarily for non-Native users. Instead, such partnerships entail working together to define problems, identify information needs, design research projects, and incorporate research results into climate change adaptation planning.

Oscar Kawagley notes how Western civilization has oppressed Alaska's Indigenous peoples. He describes its imposition as unsolicited, even harmful (Kawagley 1995). Yet in spite of these obstacles, contemporary Native peoples in Alaska continuously bridge these two worlds in their daily lives. Hunting and fishing are traditional activities informed by traditional knowledge and skills yet governed by extremely complex state and federal regulations. The harvest of subsistence foods requires cash for supplies, gas, boats, motors, and ATVs, such that employment within the capitalist economic system is necessary in order to afford the costs involved in hunting, fishing, and gathering. Many of contemporary Alaska's Indigenous peoples have mixed heritage, as recent or distant descendants of non-Native missionaries, trappers, miners, traders, and adventurers. In addition, many Alaska Indigenous peoples straddle a cultural divide daily in their employment in non-Native institutions such as the school system, city government, Alaska Native for-profit corporations, commercial fishing, and federal and state agencies.

The negotiation between these two worlds often requires delicate maneuvering. Topics that are forbidden from discussion in traditional culture must be raised within the non-Native institutional structures such as the Alaska Board of Game in order to advocate for Indigenous access and rights (Catherine Attla, Workshop in Huslia, Alaska, 2004).

Local knowledge cannot be dismissed outright as "anecdotal." Yet, neither can it be recorded verbatim or uncritically as pure fact. As Charlie Campbell explains, partnership between Native observers and Western scientists is important because they "keep each other honest."[9] Local observations often rely on distant memory, which can weaken with time. Memories may falter when recalling the cold spell in January thirty years ago, or even the unseasonably warm spring temperature and early leaf-out three years ago. Without the grounding and legitimacy of local observation, however, Western science can overlook significant and relevant information. For example, state fish biologists may overlook key aspects of a fish run without the larger picture of local observation, experience, traditional knowledge, and contextual information. Similarly, biologists studying bowhead whale populations in the Chukchi Sea needed local observations for accurate whale counts (Huntington 2000).

As feedback for scientists during the CLIP Elders' Panel, Wilson Justin recommended that the university continue convening Elders to talk about their experiences. He said professionals (e.g., university officials and scientists) now recognize the importance of what Elders have to say. They are "starting to listen, and that's a big step forward."

Examples of Partnerships

At the same time, there is a growing willingness among Indigenous peoples, leaders, and organizations to work together with Western scientists. This occurs on local levels with individual scientists and research projects (Gearheard et al. 2010) as well as on the regional, national, and international scale. A groundswell of conferences, workshops, projects, programs, and collaborations were under way at the time of this writing that demonstrate the capacity, commitment, and vision of Indigenous peoples in action toward climate change adaptation and mitigation.

In April 2009, Indigenous peoples from around the planet convened in Anchorage, Alaska, for an International Summit on Indigenous Peoples and Climate Change. They declared to the world a vision of Indigenous leadership linking climate adaptation, greenhouse gas reduction, and Indigenous rights.[10] The Arctic delegation at this meeting emphasized the need for partnership between scientific and indigenous knowledge systems:

> Climate change has been felt most intensely in the Arctic. In the past few decades, the average Arctic temperature has increased twice as much as the global temperature. Last summer, the Arctic Ocean sea ice shrunk to the smallest size ever seen in satellite images, opening previously ice-jammed waterways, such as the Northwest Passage, for navigation. Climate change is having a negative impact on the health of Indigenous Peoples, and leading to increased economic development of the Arctic. To adapt to rapidly changing circumstances, while at the same time preserving important elements of their culture, Indigenous peoples of the Arctic believe they need to find a balance between old and new ways, between scientific and experience-based knowledge. (Galloway McLean et al. 2009, 8)

Other conferences have emphasized activism, Indigenous rights, and climate justice both internationally and on a national scale in the United States. These include the World People's Conference on Climate Change and the Rights of Mother Earth convened in Cochabamba, Bolivia, in April 2010,[11] as well as the Native Peoples Native Homelands Climate Change Workshop II: Indigenous Perspectives and Solutions in Mystic Lake, Minnesota, November 2009.[12]

Several national organizations are dedicated to assisting tribes with climate change adaptation, mitigation, and political lobbying. The National Congress of American Indians (NCAI) has established a Community of Practice dedicated to Climate Change.[13] This forum aims to provide policy-related information as well as organizational and communications support for tribes in climate change adaptation, mitigation, and advocacy. The Institute for Tribal Environmental Professionals hosts a Tribal Climate Change Newsletter and has convened climate change adaptation workshops for tribal professionals; the first one, in May 2010, focused on the Pacific Northwest.[14]

The United States Environmental Protection Agency (EPA)—Tribal Science Council hosted the National Tribal Science Forum in June 2010 with the theme "Mother Earth: Indigenous Knowledge and Science to Promote Positive Change."[15] This meeting showcased research by Indigenous scientists to solve local environmental problems. On the regional scale, for the past several years EPA Alaska tribal coordinator, Michelle Davis, has convened panel discussions and dialogues on Native climate impacts and adaptation at the annual Alaska Forum on the Environment, gathering together EPA environmental coordinators from rural Native villages across the state.[16]

On a smaller regional scale, the sea-ice scientist Hajo Eicken has partnered with the National Weather Service, the Study for Environmental Arctic Change (SEARCH), the National Oceanic and Atmospheric Administration (NOAA), the Arctic Research Consortium of the U.S. (ARCUS), the Alaska Eskimo Walrus Commission, and local communities on the Bering and Chukchi Seas to produce a Sea Ice Outlook for walrus.[17] An extension of the annual Sea Ice Outlook,[18] this regional tool was designed in direct partnership with the communities and provides scientists and walrus hunters with accurate and up-to-date information on sea-ice conditions specific to the animal, which helps hunters navigate changing sea-ice conditions and thereby improves safety.

This is just a sample of the initiatives, projects, and collaborations under way at the time of this writing. The number and types of initiatives, the visibility of Indigenous leadership, and the density of network connections in this realm will continue to grow as scientific and Indigenous leaders forge partnerships and climate change impacts continue to effect Indigenous communities.

A Deeper Sense of Place

How can this vision of a deeper sense of place through partnership improve our ability to adapt to a rapidly changing Arctic? (Chapin et al. 2006). In many respects, climate impacts in Alaska have been most notable in rural Native villages precisely because Alaska Indigenous people have a very "deep sense of place." Identity, consciousness, livelihood, mental and physical heath, and survival all are rooted in the land, water, plants, animals, oceans, rivers, and weather. This has been the case for generations. Climate change affects them directly because they have a direct and sustained connection to land and place, physically in terms of subsistence harvest and nutrition as well as spiritually and culturally. Non-Native geographers, planners, policy makers, and climate scientists can learn from this deep sense of identity connected to place, using it as a touchstone for climate adaptation in various locations and situations.

However, this learning must be achieved through true partnership, not simply by superficial attempts at collaboration or reification or co-optation of traditional knowledge. I have found that this partnership can be achieved only if I can come to terms with my own sense of place, historically, geographically, and personally, in both my personal and professional relationships with Indigenous people and with the land. For me, this has required facing uncomfortable facts and moving beyond misconceptions and social conditioning. True partnership is only possible if we can set aside conscious and unconscious notions of the "noble savage" and eradicate generations of misconception that Indigenous peoples are primitive, ignorant, and technologically or intellectually immature (Berkes and Berkes 2009; Ellingson 2001; Whelan 1999). True partnerships will involve ending the deliberate (and nondeliberate) thought and actions of white dominance and both the reification and off-handed dismissal of Indigenous spirituality. Scientists and decision makers must show Indigenous peoples true respect as fellow human beings on this planet rather than interacting with them through the lens of "other."

For me, this has at least three parts. Each of these practices is evolving and ongoing. I do not expect to arrive at and end point of collaboration, but rather to commit to the process of partnership and continual learning. First, I have had to notice my own connection to place and the land. In my lifetime and throughout my education and career, I have lived in New York, Denmark, Massachusetts, Colorado, Montana, California, Illinois, and Alaska. We cannot truly appreciate the Indigenous identity with land and place, unless we can begin to understand what it means to be committed and deeply rooted to a place and to the land. Second, I have had to come to terms with the ways in which white people, myself included, have benefited from the genocide of Indigenous peoples. This is not easy to do and is not intended to generate guilt or feeling bad about ourselves. The point is to acknowledge the history of colonization and its contemporary legacy in order to generate the capacity to transition into a new form of relationship. Finally, I have had to practice a sense of humor and treating other white people with the same respect, kindness, and generosity that I experience from Indigenous peoples. In these ways, white scientists and decision makers can also achieve a deeper sense of place by setting aside pretense and striving for respectful relationships with Indigenous peoples.

Cultivating leadership for Native communities to take action and providing scientific information and resources for climate change vulnerability assessment and adaptation planning has been a theme of the dialogues and workshops that ACCAP has hosted. True partnership between Native communities and scientists on climate change assessment and adaptation can flourish with participatory engagement and mutual respect.

Notes

This work was supported by NOAA Award #NA06OAR4310112, the Alaska Center for Climate Assessment and Policy, the National Integrated Drought Information System (NIDIS), and IAI CRN 2015 (which is supported by the US NSF Grant GEO-0452325). I am particularly grateful to Wilson Justin, Larry Merculieff, and Uyuriukaraq Ulran for their participation in ACCAP events and for their careful reading and suggestions for improving this text. Many thanks to all of the workshop, Elders' Panel, and video conference participants, including Orville Huntington. Olga Lovik, Colin West, Siri Tuttle, Suzanne Sharp, and Larry Kaplan provided invaluable work in planning, organizing, and writing summaries of the Climate, Language, and Indigenous Perspectives Elders' Panel. Dan Ferguson, Gregg Garfin, and Cheryl Anderson were partners in organizing and implementing the cross-regional climate dialogues. Hazel Smith, Dean Westlake, Charlie Gregg, John Chase, and Katie Qualinguk Cruthers were all essential partners in planning, organizing, and implementing the Kotzebue workshop. Thanks also to all of the others, who continue to help me see a deeper sense of my place in Alaska.

1. State of Alaska, Climate Change in Alaska. http://www.climatechange.alaska.gov.

2. Alaska Center for Climate Assessment and Policy. http://www.uaf.edu/accap/. NOAA Regional Integrated Sciences and Assessments. http://www.climate.noaa.gov/cpo_pa/risa/.

3. NSF Office of Polar Programs Grant No. 0328282.

4. NOAA Grant # NA06OAR4600179– David Atkinson, principal investigator.

5, KOTZ Public Radio. http://www.kotz.org/, FM 89.9 or AM 720.

6. Alaska Center for Climate Assessment and Policy, Cross-Regional Dialogue: Climate Change, Water Impacts and Indigenous People. http://www.uaf.edu/accap/research/cross_region_dialogue.htm.

7. Alaska Native Science Commission. http://www.nativescience.org.

8. National Science Foundation, Principles for the Conduct of Research in the Arctic. http://www.nsf.gov/od/opp/arctic/conduct.jsp.

9. UAF Oral History Program, Climate Change Project Juke Box. http://jukebox.uaf.edu/pjweb/progusecc.htm.

10. International Summit on Indigenous Peoples and Climate Change, 2009. http://www.indigenoussummit.com/servlet/content/home.html.

11. World People's Conference on Climate Change and the Rights of Mother Earth. http://pwccc.wordpress.com/2010/04/24/peoples-agreement/#more-1584.

12. Native Peoples Native Homelands Workshop, 2009. http://portal3.aihec.org/sites/NPNH/Pages/Default.aspx.

13. National Congress of American Indians, Climate Change Community of Practice. http://climatechange.ncaiprc.org.

14. Institute for Tribal Environmental Professional Climate Change Newsletter. http://www4.nau.edu/tribalclimatechange.

15. EPA National Tribal Science Forum, 2010. http://epa.blhtech.com/2010TribalScienceForum/default.aspx.

16. Alaska Forum on the Environment. http://www.akforum.com.

17. ARCUS, Sea Ice Outlook for Walrus. http://www.arcus.org/search/siwo; Alaska Center for Climate Assessment and Policy, Rural Impacts. http://ine.uaf.edu/accap//rural_impacts.html. Alaska Center for Climate Assessment and Policy, Teleconference Archive. http://ine.uaf.edu/accap//telecon_archive.htm.

18. ARCUS, Sea Ice Outlook for Walrus. http://www.arcus.org/search/seaiceoutlook/2010/july

References

ACIA. 2005. *Impacts of a Warming Climate*. Arctic Climate Impact Assessment. Cambridge: Cambridge University Press.

Alaska Native Science Commission. *What Is Native Knowledge?* Anchorage, AK: Alaska Native Knowledge Network.

Battiste, M., and J. S. Y. Henderson. 2000. *Protecting Indigenous Knowledge and Heritage: A Global Challenge*. Saskatoon: Purich.

Berkes, F. 1993. "Traditional Ecological Knowledge in Perspective." In *Traditional Ecological Knowledge: Concepts and Cases,* edited by J. T. Inglis, 1–10. Ottawa, ON: International Program on Traditional Ecological Knowledge and International Development Research Center.

Berkes, F., and M. K. Berkes. 2009. "Ecological Complexity, Fuzzy Logic, and Holism in Indigenous Knowledge. *Futures* 41 (1): 6–12.

Berner, J., and C. Furgal. 2005. "Human Health." In *Impacts of a Warming Climate,* edited by ACIA, 863–906. Arctic Climate Impact Assessment. Cambridge: Cambridge University Press.

Cajete, G. 2000. *Native Science, Natural Laws of Interdependence*. Sante Fe, NM: Clear Light Publishers.

Chapin, F. S., III, A. L. Lovecraft, E. S. Zavaleta, J. Nelson, M. D. Robards, G. P. Kofinas, S. F. Trainor, G. D. Peterson, H. P. Huntington, and R. L. Naylor. 2006. "Policy Strategies to Address Sustainability of Alaskan Boreal Forests in Response to a Directionally Changing Climate." *Proceedings of the National Academy of Sciences* 103 (45): 16637–43.

Couzin, J. 2007. "Opening Doors to Native Knowledge." *Science* 315 (5818): 1518–19.

Cruikshank, J. 2001. "Glaciers and Climate Change: Perspectives from Oral Tradition." *Arctic* 54 (4): 377–93.

Ellingson, T. 2001. *The Myth of the Noble Savage*. Berkeley: University of California Press.

Galloway McLean, K., A. Ramos-Castillo, T. Gross, S. Johnston, M. Vierros, and R. Noa. 2009. *Report of the Indigenous People's Global Summit on Climate Change*. April 20–24, 2009. Anchorage: United Nations University—Traditional Knowledge Initiative, Darwin, Austrialia.

Gearheard, S., M. Pocernich, R. Stewart, J. Sanguya, and H. P. Huntington. 2010. "Linking Inuit Knowledge and Meteorological Station Observations to Understand Changing Wind Patterns at Clyde River, Nunavut." *Climatic Change* 100 (2): 267–94.

Huntington, H. 2000. "Using Traditional Ecological Knowledge in Science: Methods and Applications." *Ecological Applications* 10 (5): 1270–74.

Huntington, H., T. Callaghan, S. Fox, and I. Krupnik. 2004. "Matching Traditional and Scientific Observations to Detect Environmental Change: A Discussion on Arctic Terrestrial Ecosystems." *Ambio,* Special Report Number 13, 18–23.

Huntington, H., and S. Fox. 2005. "The Changing Arctic: Indigenous Perspectives." In *Impacts of a Warming Climate,* edited by ACIA, 61–98. Arctic Climate Impact Assessment. Cambridge: Cambridge University Press.

Huntington, H. P., S. F. Trainor, D. C. Natcher, O. Huntington, L. O. DeWilde, and F. S. I. Chapin. 2006. "The Significance of Context in Community-Based Research: Understanding Discussions about Wildfire in Huslia, Alaska." *Ecology and Society* 11 (1): 40. http://www.ecologyandsociety.org/vol11/iss1/art40/.

Kawagley, O. A. 1995. *A Yupiaq Worldview, A Pathway to Ecology and Spirit*. Prospect Heights, IL: Waveland Press.

Kovach, M. 2009. *Indigenous Methodologies*. Toronto: University of Toronto Press.

Krupnik, I., and D. Jolly. 2002. *The Earth Is Faster Now: Indigenous Observations of Arctic Environmental Change*. Fairbanks, AK: Arctic Research Consortium of the United States.

Kyle, R. E., and T. P. Brabets. 2001. *Water Temperature of Streams in the Cook Inlet Basin, Alaska, and Implications of Climate Change*. Anchorage: U.S. Department of the Interior, U.S. Geological Survey.

Lempinen, E. W. 2006. "In Arctic Alaska, Climate Warming Threatens a Village and Its Culture." *Science* 314 (5799): 609.

Markon, C. J., S. F. Trainor, et al. (2012). *The United States National Climate Assessment—Alaska Technical Regional Report*. U.S. Geological Survey, Circular 1379.

Riewe, R., and J. Oakes. 2006. *Climate Change: Linking Traditional and Scientific Knowledge*. Winnipeg, Manitoba: Aboriginal Issues Press, University of Manitoba.

Riordan, B., D. Verbyla, and A. D. McGuire. 2006. "Shrinking Ponds in Subarctic Alaska Based on 1950–2002 Remotely Sensed Images." *Journal of Geophysical Research :Biogeosciences* 111: G4.

Salick, J., and N. Ross. 2009. "Traditional Peoples and Climate Change." *Global Environmental Change* 19 (2): 137–39.

Stephens, S. 1996. *Culturally Responsive Science Curriculum*. Fairbanks: Alaska Science Consortium, Alaska Rural Systemic Initiative.

Trainor, S. F., F. S. I. Chapin, H. P. Huntington, D. C. Natcher, and G. Kofinas. 2007. "Arctic Climate Impacts: Environmental Injustice in Canada and the United States." *Local Environment, International Journal of Jusitce and Sustainability* 12 (6): 627–43.

Trainor, S. F., A. Godduhn, L. K. Duffy, F. S. I. Chapin, D. C. Natcher, G. Kofinas, and H. P. Huntingon. 2009. "Environmental Injustice in the Canadian Far North: Persistent Organic Pollutants and Arctic Climate Impacts." In *Speaking for Ourselves, Environmental Justice in Canada,* edited by J. Agyeman, R. Haluza-Delay, P. Cole, and P. O'Riley, 144–162. Vancouver: University of British Columbia Press.

Whelan, R. 1999. *Wild in Woods: The Myth of the Noble Eco-Savage.* London: Institute of Economic Affairs.

Reconciling Cultural Resource Management with Indigenous Geographies

The Importance of Connecting Research with People and Place

RICK BUDHWA AND TYLER McCREARY

Although Indigenous peoples have possessed their own ways of knowing and being for millennia, the emergence of studies by researchers trained in the Western tradition that seek to articulate and respect this Indigenous depth of place remains a relatively recent phenomenon. Although there is a long genealogy of colonial research ventures that sought to extend Western epistemic and territorial claims by transliterating Indigenous knowledge into colonial frames (Braun 1997; Milligan and McCreary 2011; Pratt 1992; Smith 1999), emerging Indigenous-academic research is increasingly pursuing an alternate course. Such studies seek to recognize the significance of Indigenous ways of knowing and being, not simply as research data but as frameworks informing research activity (Battiste 2000; Garroutte 2003; Kuokkanen 2007; Wilson 2008). The Indigenization of research methods has been most apparent in Indigenous studies, but recent contributions within geography highlight the important contribution Indigenous ways of knowing and being can make to geographic research (J. T. Johnson and Murton 2007; Koster, Baccar, and Lemelin 2012; Louis 2007; Panelli 2008; Pearce and Louis 2008). In this essay, we seek to extend these discussions through a case study of Indigenous-academic collaboration in cultural resource management (CRM) in northwestern British Columbia, Canada.

Case studies typically revolve around an exploration of a particular community, but in this chapter we flip the gaze and instead investigate the experiences of a particular researcher, Rick Budhwa. In so doing, we demonstrate how research experiences in Indigenous community settings can highlight the shortcomings of governing research paradigms and contribute to the development of alternative approaches that seek to reconcile cultural resource management practices with an Indigenous depth of place. We begin with a discussion of how the prevalent archaeological lens for research on cultural resource management continues to focus on material aspects of culture and displace understanding of Indigenous cultural resources from their relationships to their broader environment. We extend this with a discussion of the importance of being on the land to Indigenous ontologies, and how these ways of being are constituted through the traditional institutions of Indigenous governance. We then examine how the compartmentalization of dominant research paradigms obscures Indigenous ways of being and knowing. Finally, we explore how Indigenous-academic research collaborations, using a "landed" methodology that recognizes the importance spending time on Indigenous territories and listening to the voices of Indigenous peoples, contribute to alternative research paradigms that seek to recognize an Indigenous depth of place.

Interlacing personal narrative and academic argument, this chapter advances through the interplay between the main body of the text and a series of short vignettes drawn from Rick Budhwa's field notes and research reflections (set in italics). These vignettes illustrate the cross-cultural epistemic and ontological negotiation central to decolonizing research methods. Although this essay is the joint publication of both authors, we have chosen to privilege the stories of cultural immersion that occur in community-based research. We both descend from non-Indigenous migrants to northern British Columbia, Rick being born of mixed East- and West-Indian heritage in Kitimat, and Tyler descending from immigrants to Smithers of predominantly Irish heritage. We both continue to live in the north although we now occupy distinct positions with relation to our research work, Rick based in the community and Tyler out of the university. Although neither of us belongs wholly to the field or the cabinet, our collaboration has in part flourished due to our complementary roles. Despite the importance of library shelves and Internet searches in our work, we have increasingly found that it is the knowledge gleaned from personal experiences working in community that most radically revised our understanding. In developing our arguments about the necessity of interlacing academic and Indigenous epistemologies, we have attempted to integrate abstract theoretical and experiential bodies of knowledge. Although the essay remains the dominant mode of academic expression, Watson and Huntington (2008) have suggested the complexities of Indigenous epistemic spaces are best represented through narrative. Thus, we strategically switch between theory and narrative to elucidate the meaning of collaboration in community-based research.

Researching in the Shadow of Colonialism, or Eggheads and Indians

Cultural resource management (CRM) may be defined as the multiple processes through which archaeologists and other professionals manage the impacts of the modern world on cultural resources. Watkins and Beaver (2008, 10) define CRM as the management of "cultural landscapes, archaeological sites, historical records, social institutions, expressive cultures, old buildings, religious beliefs and practices, folk life, artifacts and spiritual places." There are increasing efforts to integrate Indigenous concerns into CRM practices through instituting consultative processes (Budhwa 2005; Klassen, Budhwa, and Reimer 2009; Fuller 2011). Working with Indigenous communities serves to further challenge foundational binaries separating cultural resource management from natural resource management, as within these communities natural resources are often not easily distinguishable from cultural resources (J. T. Johnson and Murton 2007). For the Wet'suwet'en and Gitxsan people in northwest BC, culture and knowledge are not simply about things but refer to an epistemic space constituted through the social and spiritual relations between animals, environments, and humans (L. M. Johnson 2010; Mills 1994). However, in Canada development projects often equate CRM with archaeology (the study of past human behavior through material remains), echoing conditions Reba Fuller (2011) describes in the US context. In practice CRM often overemphasizes the material aspects of culture, particularly with respect to Indigenous peoples, and has yet to develop a robust approach to understanding the importance of the intangible aspects of place. Thus, in British Columbia, governing approaches to CRM continue to fail to register the full depth of Indigenous peoples' sense of place.

Archaeology remains a discipline entangled with the legacies of colonial research that informed its development. The governing practices of archaeology split Indigenous peoples from their complex cultural, political, and economic relationships to their surrounding environment, fixing Indigenous culture to a fragmented geography of villages and campsites, pit houses and caches, fishing holes, and trail markers. Further, as Mary Louise Pratt (1992, 132) describes, Western research "produces archeological subjects by splitting contemporary non-European peoples off from their precolonial, and even their colonial, pasts." Thus, traditional archaeological practice works to relegate Indigeneity to the past, positioning it as an anachronism and denying the dynamism of Indigenous cultures. Recognizing the connections between archaeology and colonial processes of deterritorialization, Joe Watkins (2005, 433) has suggested that archaeology, as a discipline, was "at least partially complicit in the removal of American Indians from their lands." Archaeologists are increasingly working to decolonize their discipline through more collaborative research processes (Budhwa 2005; Nicholas 2006) and an appreciation of how Indigenous knowledge can supplement their work (Budhwa 2002; Martindale and Marsden 2003), yet as a discipline, archaeology remains at a distance from Indigenous communities and their understanding of their cultural heritage. This is exemplified by Rick Budhwa's experience shifting from the academy to the community:

What I was taught in graduate school in the 1990s and actually being in First Nations communities and on the land were two very different things. Although I am grateful for my education, and the direction it propelled me, there remained gaps in my learning. Although I emerged from school with an appreciation for the environment, I lacked a serious and profound connection to the land. But it was only after developing relationships with the First Nations peoples of northwestern British Columbia that I was to become aware of this shortcoming.

After graduating in 2001, I was eager to apply my education. I knew about the Wet'suwet'en from books and media, and in May 2002, it was extremely fortuitous that the Office of the Wet'suwet'en (OW) located in Smithers, BC, had an opening for an archaeologist/anthropologist. The original intention of the OW was to guide the Wet'suwet'en through the British Columbia treaty process. However, by the time I had arrived, the OW's mandate became much larger and inclusive of many other sociocultural aspects of Wet'suwet'en governance and land management. Governed by the Wet'suwet'en hereditary chiefs residing throughout their traditional territories, the OW had developed into a central office for the exercise of Wet'suwet'en governance. Interacting with First Nations and public governments and institutions, including the provincial and federal government, development agencies, and research and educational institutions, the OW developed a significant profile. In fact, working together with the neighboring Gitxsan in the Delgamuukw and Gisdaywa case, the Wet'suwet'en achieved recognition by the Supreme Court of Canada of the evidentiary weight to First Nations' oral traditions. Suffice it to say, I was keenly aware of the OW, and leapt at the opportunity.

From the beginning of my work with the OW, I didn't have any apprehension about engaging their world—I never thought once about maintaining any level of distance, I just did it. I was learning about Wet'suwet'en culture immediately, and this learning process was like no other. I was seeing the world through a different lens that was radically enhancing everything. Being raised by a grandparent, I always respected my elders. But it's one thing to be raised by one grandparent and another thing to be raised by many. That's what it felt like, being surrounded by dozens of grandparents. There was an immediate connection that way. I listened. I heard their stories. And showing that respect got me a long way. These elders continually reminded me of the power of the spoken word.

It reminded me of how I saw the landscape differently after learning land formation processes when I took my first geomorphology course during my undergraduate studies in the mid-1990s. Where geomorphology brought to life the dynamic nature of the geophysical landscape, listening to people's stories exposed me to the living cultural landscape. Relating to people's connections to the landscape, I started viewing my surrounding environment differently. I began noticing the completeness, the holistic nature of our resource base—all the values and resources that exist on the landscape and how they're connected. It took a while to establish trust, but once that was there, I was immersed in a different world. I didn't plan any of it. None of it was conscious. It was just happened through spending time with the Wet'suwet'en people on the territories.

Through this experience, I started connecting my research to the land and seeing it as one component of the big picture. From the perspective of a First Nations community, what is valued might have no bearing on what environmental scientists suggest. However, within my work, understanding the First Nations cultural landscape became primary, overriding the values that science, industry, and government prioritize. Needless to say, my views were (and continue to be) somewhat different from those of my colleagues who didn't experience that level of immersion with First Nations' culture. I was valuing science less than they were, and instead found myself increasingly pushing boundaries and incorporating other perspectives. I was really focusing on social science and prioritizing First Nations' community values. This is where my sense of belonging, purpose, and place as a scientist and community member began to define itself.

Being on the Land, or Discovering What You Don't Learn in the Classroom

Indigenous geographies are fundamentally informed by holistic— subjective and material—relationships to territory. As Jay T. Johnson and Brian Murton (2007) note, Indigenous geographies do not reflect the foundational culture/nature dualisms of Enlightenment thought that inform the development of Western geography; instead Indigenous communities integrate their understandings of their culture and natural environment. Indigenous geographies are deeply interconnected with generations of experience on the land. The stories, songs, and symbols of these histories continue to circulate within Indigenous communities. Indigenous landscapes are composed of relationships with physical sites but also a set of cultural essences, intangible structures of belief, that tend to be difficult to bind to a particular location (Pearce and Louis 2008). The matrix of relationships within this physical and spiritual landscape defines Indigenous ways of being.

For Gitxsan and Wet'suwet'en peoples, the relationship to territory is one of reciprocal stewardship between the people and "the land and the life and spiritual energies it contains" (Daly 2005, 271). Being on the land is vital to maintain these reciprocal relationships with the land itself. According to Sterritt et al. (1998, 12), "The process of claiming territory is described as 'walking the land' or 'surveying' it and includes naming mountains, rivers, lakes, and other areas. These names are highly descriptive and reflect a detailed knowledge of the landscape." Being on the land, understanding the rhythms of the land along with the histories and meanings of its occupation, are fundamental for demonstrating a claim to territory through the proper ceremonies. Indigenous relationships to territory are governed by dynamic, interconnected processes in the social, natural, and spiritual world (Henderson 2000, 2006).

These relationships to the land are fundamental to the maintenance of Indigenous collective identity. The Assembly of First Nations (1993, 39) began its submission on the environment to the Royal Commission on Aboriginal Peoples by stating, "The environment is fundamentally important to First Nations Peoples. It is the breadth of our spirituality, knowledge, languages and culture." Gitxsan hereditary chief, Delgamuukw (Ken Muldoe) (1992, 7) explained, "The ownership of a territory is a marriage of the Chief and the land. Each Chief has an ancestor who encountered and acknowledged the life of the land. From such encounters came power. The land, the plants, the animals and the people all have spirit—they all must be shown respect. That is the basis of our law."

The land is the basis of Gitxsan and Wet'suwet'en culture, and their cultural resources remain directly and inextricably bound to their land and its natural resources. Their law and culture, beliefs and values, and the ability to maintain identity as a people remain strongly connected to territory.

> For nearly three years (from March 2002 to December 2004), I worked for the Wet'suwet'en hereditary chiefs. It was a change from the approach to research I learned in university. We all had desks, offices and schedules—in keeping with scientific Western society—but my manager was the Lands and Resources Department manager and also a hereditary chief. Sometimes those two hats conflicted. Beyond office work, I was sometimes mandated, on random sunny days, to go out onto the territories and just be. No agenda. No words, really. Just being on the land.

The first time this happened, my manager told us we were all going out; we just needed to be on the territories. The "territories" were referred to often. That's how we referred to the land base. I interpreted his request as, "We're going into the field." So, I got ready for the field. I went to the office, got maps, got a GPS, got tools for the field, got my caulk boots, my vest, my compass, everything—I was ready for the field.

When I came down to the twelve-passenger van, all the chiefs and elders that were joining us that day were in their normal, everyday street clothes. Some had cowboy boots, but no one looked like me. I thought to myself, "This is not very conducive to good fieldwork," but I was confident in my field abilities. I arrogantly assumed I was even prepared to "care for" some of these folks in the field, if need be. How could someone sixty years old in cowboy boots be as ready for the elements as a thirty-year-old in caulk boots?

Most of the ride out to the territory was spent laughing at me. The chiefs particularly liked the spikes on the bottom of my boots, and were curious if I was planning on spending time on the glacier. I was even asked if my field vest doubled as a life preserver. The teasing and humor, while at my expense, indicated the ways I was being integrated into the community.

Once we got out there, the chief who governed that particular territory welcomed us with a short speech. He reminded us about the importance of respecting our land. After his words, people started walking around. I wasn't really told to do anything. Some people looked like they knew where they were going; others seemed to be leisurely strolling.

That was the first day I actually felt and learned what it was like to just be out on the land, not with a specific purpose, but going there just to exist and let connections happen. That was really eye-opening and important for how I learned to view the territories. That was the day I understood the difference between getting ready for the field and being on the territories.

Belonging, or the Archaeologist Goes Native

In northwest British Columbia, the local Wet'suwet'en and Gitxsan peoples have occupied their traditional territories for thousands of years and continue to maintain their relationship to their territories through their traditional house system of governance. As Richard Overstall (2005, 31) describes it, their system of territoriality is fundamentally defined by "the power created by fusing the spirit of a reincarnating human line with the spirit of a specific area of land—a partnership in which both the human and the non-human parties have reciprocal obligations and privileges." Each house is a matrilineal kinship group that shares a common ancestry, with distinct claims and relationships to its own particular house territories and responsibility for a number of reincarnating chiefly names (P. D. Mills 2008; Roth 2008). When a house member dies, his or her name is passed on to another member of the house. The Wet'suwet'en concept of law centers "on acknowledgement of the rights invested in ever-reincarnating lineages" rather than individual rights (A. Mills 1994, 24).

Within the feast, the main business of the host house is conducted in the transfer of titles and reaffirmation of a house's relationship to its territories. It is at the feast that chiefly names are transferred down a house lineage after the death of a hereditary chief. Other houses act as observers, witnessing that business is conducted in accordance with the laws. Gitxsan hereditary chief, Ax Gwin Desxw (Glen Williams quoted in P. D. Mills 2008, 109–10) explained,

> What the chief is doing is that he is demonstrating publicly in that feast to the other chiefs that he has invited, that he knows the laws that he has to follow for that particular feast, and he is demonstrating publicly that he has land, that he has fishing holes, that he has power, that he has wealth and that he owns the land; and these are my other members of my immediate house. He is publicly telling all the people in that feast hall, that this is who I am, I am chief, I am a high chief, and this is my authority.

In the feast, a house renews social bonds with other houses while reasserting definitional power relationships through the display of "the power of life in all the creatures and the land itself" (P. D. Mills 2008, 120). Edward Chamberlin (2000, 127) recounts how a Gitxsan hereditary chief, astonished by claims of forestry officials to Crown jurisdiction over Gitxsan traditional lands, condensed his discomfort into a question: "'If this is your land,' he asked, 'where are your stories?'" The stories, songs, and crests of a house work to establish that house's connection to their territories. Performances in the feast reaffirm a house's connection to the spirit of the land, and through this affirmation its title to those lands.

In this way, the feast is a central institution for the social and political maintenance of the relationships between Gitxsan and Wet'suwet'en houses and their territories (Daly 2005). Antonia Mills (1994, 38) describes the feast as "a forum in which Witsuwit'en law is both enacted and upheld." The feast determines how territory is owned and used, and provides structure to the practice of Wet'suwet'en and Gitxsan governance. This extends to interactions with researchers.

In May 2006, I was adopted into the Cas'Yex (Grizzly House) of the Gitdumden (Bear Clan) of the Wet'suwet'en. This has been one of the great honors in my life thus far. I had always known what the feast system meant to First Nations peoples, specifically its centrality in their epistemology. However, being involved to this degree exposed me to another level of intimacy with Wet'suwet'en culture.

The feast that was held had two purposes: payback and adoption. In the payback portion, chiefs and clan members collected money and paid back other clans for previously borrowed resources. In the adoption portion, it was announced that Roy Morris, House Chief Woos of Cas'Yex, was adopting me into his house, and that from that point onward, I was to be considered a clan member, just like everyone else.

I will never forget shopping for the "resources" that I was to give away to anyone who witnessed this event. This is one of the aspects that many non-Native people don't understand, that a person's wealth is measured not by how much they accumulate, but rather how much they give away. My chief informed me of what I had to buy (items such as teacups, towels, blankets, drinking glasses, as well as other useful household items). As I shopped for these items, I remember thinking how interesting it was to see how the feast system remained intact, but the resources that were involved had changed over time.

During the feast at the appropriate time, I "gave away" all of the items I brought to those in attendance (the chiefs, then distinguished members of the clans, and finally any other witnesses who were in attendance). I shook each person's hand, expressed my gratitude for their acceptance of me and their attendance as a witness. Each person, in turn, impressed some words of wisdom upon me. It was a profound experience that has added yet another layer of depth to my perspective of our landscape and the resources within it.

Since my adoption, I am regularly teased about being more "Indian" than the Wet'suwet'en, since my mother is of East Indian descent and my father is from the West Indies, and now I am adopted. Many times, in jest, chiefs and clan members refer to me as "the real Indian." While this teasing highlights the increasing level of community acceptance of me, my inclusion into the community has heightened my sense of responsibility to ensure that the Wet'suwet'en are meaningfully involved in the resource management process.

From Compartmentalization toward an Indigenized Interdisciplinarity

CRM is governed predominantly by a universal approach that often is antithetical to a broader recognition of the depth of Indigenous cultural geographies. The particular temporal and geographic frames conventionally used to define Indigenous cultural heritage resources do not reflect Indigenous systems of knowing and being in the world. Instead they impose Western managerial frames grounded in a set of Eurocentric presumptions about progress in accordance with a presumed "linear movement of progress from an original, wild state to a developed, civilized and domesticated state" (Howitt and Suchet-Pearson 2006, 324).

Legislative definitions of cultural heritage in British Columbia's *Heritage Conservation Act* (1996) that protect those sites or artifacts in existence before 1846 reflect colonial, not Indigenous, timelines. The British and Americans signed the *Oregon Treaty* in 1846, delineating the boundary of a British territorial claim that extended to the west coast of North America. This year marks the assertion of Crown sovereignty over the territory that would become British Columbia. In the next century, the government sought to reconstruct Indigenous space through application of a colonial land policy that denied Aboriginal title and sought to restrict Indigenous peoples to reserves (Tennant 1990; Harris 2002). The Gitxsan and Wet'suwet'en peoples in the region, however, never consented to ceding sovereignty to the British in 1846 or the Dominion of Canada in subsequent years. While the government refused to make treaties with Indigenous peoples for the land and simply claimed jurisdiction over their territories, the Gitxsan and Wet'suwet'en maintained their relationships to their territories and continued to resist government impositions (Galois 1993; McDonald and Joseph 2000; P. D. Mills 2008). As a result of the continuity of their traditions, the necessity of predating the assertion of Crown sovereignty holds little relevance within Gitxsan and Wet'suwet'en frameworks for determining the importance of their cultural resources, and they do not recognize 1846 as a relevant date to delineate their heritage resources.

The constrained and compartmentalized spatiality of dominant CRM practices often renders Indigenous geographies unintelligible, and further entrenches the gap between how Indigenous communities and CRM practitioners understand the meaning of cultural heritage resources. CRM works through a Cartesian cartography in which space can be segmented into a linear coordinate system. Within this paradigm, cultural sites become discrete and exclusive, and interconnections between sites and the larger cultural landscape are silenced (L. M. Johnson 2010; Pearce and Louis 2008). Further, the reduction of cultural resources to material artifacts and features aggravates the segmentation of cultural spaces in CRM practice in BC. Prevailing CRM practices fail to account for the significance of intangibles such as sense of place in maintaining group traditions and identity, thereby neglecting the bodies of knowledge available through traditional knowledge. In neglecting the depth of Indigenous sense of place, conventional CRM practices often even misapprehend the cultural significance of material artifacts, features, and human remains. This is further aggravated by the often token and sometimes entirely nonexistent involvement of Indigenous communities in the management of their archaeological and other cultural heritage resources.

Developing multidisciplinary and community-based approaches to collaboration requires a major paradigm shift. Undoubtedly, there will be challenges to achieving these changes. Although the courts institutionalize a Eurocentric tradition of jurisprudence, they have recognized the salience of Indigenous knowledge and the need to reconcile Aboriginal rights and title with development (Persky 1998; Slattery 2006). By defending their territories and cultural resources through legal activism and direct action, Indigenous peoples have created new spaces of negotiation (Blomley 1996; Morris and Fondahl 2002). Furthermore, the academy has increasingly recognized the value of Indigenous knowledge and the need to develop holistic frameworks that transcend conventional disciplinary boundaries (Turner, Ignace, and Ignace 2000). Although limitations in cross-cultural understanding and community capacity still hinder the development of intercultural exchange, these constraints can be transcended by incorporating community capacity and cross-cultural education into CRM projects (J. T. Johnson, Louis, and Pramono 2006). Interdisciplinary models of community-based research mark the beginning of a paradigm shift, developing an integrated research program that recognizes the depth of Indigenous cultural attachments to place as well as the complexity and diversity of Indigenous cultures.

> One of the worst things that can happen in a First Nation community is that their ancestors become unearthed.
>
> Working with First Nations since 1993, I've encountered several situations where either industry or the government have inadvertently unearthed human remains. While non-Native perspectives may appreciate that it's unsettling for the community, unless they've lived in that community and understand the Indigenous worldview, they have no idea the profound, long-lasting impacts something like that can have on the community.
>
> In October of 2006, I received a phone call from Hagwilget Village Council, which represents and administers services to the mixed

Gitxsan and Wet'suwet'en membership of their community. They told me that a developer had come to re-anchor some power poles and didn't consult with anyone. As a result, they came and dug a hole on the reserve in an area known to the community as a burial area. Not only that, it was in the immediate area where it is believed a great Wet'suwet'en prophet was buried generations ago. Any ten-year-old child in the community could have told them that this was not an area to dig holes.

Excavators unearthed the remains of an unknown number of individuals. Once that happened, they packed up their equipment and left. The First Nation community was left to deal with those remains.

The First Nation had no budget, no resources, no technical expertise, and no plan for something like this. Given the sensitive nature of the issue, it had to be dealt with immediately. The unearthed remains were put in the church and the hole was covered up. A tarp was put over the hole, and earth that had been removed was put over the tarp. That's where the situation sat for four years.

Since 2006, there's been significant unrest in the community— spiritual issues, an elevated number of suicides, elevated poverty and negative energy—and it's all been attributed to this event. There's no closure to it. The negotiations with the industry interests have been excruciatingly slow. No resources have been provided to the First Nation to manage the situation.

Hagwilget Village Council, however, has been proactive, working to develop tools that will express their concerns in a way that planners and officials with the utility will understand. We have produced a cultural impact assessment of the impact of accidentally unearthing human remains on the entire culture. In August of 2010, an interim burial ceremony was held in the Village of Hagwilget, where the unearthed human remains were temporarily buried in the church cemetery. Many community members and hereditary chiefs were in attendance, as was I. It was a highly emotional event which provided some temporary peace for community members. In 2011, a comprehensive cultural resource management initiative was performed, including an archaeological excavation. The purpose of this project was to recover and reunite the remains of these people, and to bring closure to those individuals who were involved in the initial disturbance, and to the community as a whole. At a later date, an all Clans feast will be held (which will require great resources) and much time to plan in a culturally appropriate manner.

Reconciling CRM with the Depth of Indigenous Sense of Place

Recognizing the vital subjective importance of place remains a central task to reconciling CRM with Indigenous cultural geographies. Cultural resource management needs to recognize space not simply as a container but also as a constitutive element in human experience and social relations. Place exists in between the material and subjective, and serves an important role in the construction of identity as a subjective and embodied experience. The loss of this distinct sense of place can have significant impact on individuals and communities with such connections. J. E. Windsor and J. A. McVey (2005) describe how large-scale hydroelectric projects have contributed to the loss of place and identity for Indigenous peoples. Using the case of the Cheslatta T'en, whose reserves were flooded by the construction of the Kinney Dam, the authors expose how the government prioritized the private hydroelectric demands of the Aluminum Company of Canada (Alcan) and the possibilities for development and jobs over the traditional sustainable livelihoods of the Cheslatta T'en. The flooding dispossessed the Cheslatta of their traditional lands and annihilated culturally important sites, including churches and cemeteries, resulting in marked increases of socioeconomic, mental health, and addictions problems. People committed suicide in the aftermath of their dispossession, but the hurt transmitted down the generations. "By 1990, alcohol use amongst the Cheslatta had reached epidemic proportions and welfare dependency was 95%" (Windsor and McVey 2005, 157). Describing the impact of alienation from the land from an Indigenous perspective, Clarkson, Morrisette, and Regallet (1992, 5) write, "When we begin to separate ourselves from that which sustains us, we immediately open up the possibility of losing understanding of our responsibility and our kinship to the earth." In failing to respect and protect material and intangible relationships to place, the current CRM process is inherently flawed, both conceptually and in practice.

In order to protect the land and its vital connections to Indigenous culture and identity, research needs to recognize the integral connection between Indigenous culture and the land, and refuse the separation of cultural and natural resources. Any development that transforms the environment in the territory also affects Indigenous cultural resources. Furthermore, research must recognize the continuity and vitality of Indigenous heritage resources, and reject the colonial framing of Indigenous peoples as an anachronism within the time-space of the Canadian state through the legislated imposition of specific dates delineating heritage resources. Maintaining connections to the land reflects the centrality of the land to traditional forms of Indigenous education (Marker 2006). Cultural heritage sites also serve as evidence of Indigenous historical use and occupancy of their territories, backing claims in Canadian courts and verifying distinctive Indigenous oral histories and laws.

It is necessary to recognize the integrity of Indigenous traditional territories as an interconnected whole. Researchers need to emphasize the interconnection of multiple facets of Indigenous geographies as encompassing the spiritual, emotional, historic, practical, legal, educational, cultural, and economic realms. An integral component of all of these connections is the sense of place embedded in all these forms of a connectivity that defines and distinguishes Indigenous relationships to their territories.

Recognizing the importance of both tangible and intangible relationships to place within CRM contributes to registering the ways in which the land is a cultural resource for Indigenous communities. Archaeological sites are but a small subset of the important cultural resources that Indigenous peoples derive from their lands. CRM practitioners must attempt to gauge the impacts of proposed developments on Indigenous sense of place. CRM practitioners have too frequently avoided place as a concept, thus evading the psychological, cultural, and environmental components in favor of more empirical, quantifiable research. But this fails to account for the substantial impacts development may bring to Indigenous ways of being in the world.

In 2006, I was asked by the provincial government's lands agency to participate in a sustainable resource management planning process. By this time, I had developed a reputation. In addition to anthropological work with industry, government, and academia, people knew that I had worked within a First Nation organization in the past and had been adopted into the Wet'suwet'en Bear Clan.

The government was negotiating the management of the Gitanyow traditional territory. Forestry licensees wanted to develop much of that territory, while conversely, the Gitanyow wanted to conserve and preserve much of that territory for cultural reasons. I was tasked with assessing the situation to find some common ground moving forward. I interviewed both sides to understand their perspectives and produced an assessment stating that the Gitanyow people needed to articulate their cultural interests in the form of a policy so everyone could make informed decisions. That's how the Gitanyow Cultural Heritage Resources Management Policy started.

Developing the policy took almost two years. Working as an independent contractor for the Office of the Gitanyow Hereditary Chiefs on the policy, I had to develop a relationship of trust with the Gitanyow. We didn't rush that relationship. They were very encouraged by my previous work with other First Nations, particularly the Wet'suwet'en. Over time I was trusted more and more. For example, I was given some "Indian Hellebore" or "Melgwasxw" as a gift by a hereditary chief to keep bad energy and spirits away from me and my family. This was indeed a symbol of trust, and with it came an increased sense of responsibility on my part.

With that trust, I was able to work with a team of consultants to get their cultural heritage concerns meaningfully represented in a policy format. All of the members of this policy team had earned the trust of the Gitanyow. We lived in nearby communities and had worked with local First Nations for years. We were part of the community.

The team worked in a collaborative relationship with the Gitanyow hereditary chiefs. They shared their cultural information and concerns with us, and we worked to articulate their concerns in a format legible to industry and government officials. Working to bridge Western and Indigenous perspectives, we produced a document that represents the Gitanyow interests for cultural resource management. While expressing Gitanyow concerns in a format familiar to Western resource managers, the policy also powerfully articulates the necessity of recognizing that natural resources are cultural resources, and cultural experts need to be involved in resource management to account for the importance of tangible and intangible relationships to place.

Since it was unveiled in its complete form in 2009, several First Nations have adopted components of the management policy and fit it to their specific contexts. While the document provides clarity and certainty for industry and government as to what the Gitanyow value, their formal acceptance of this document is still being negotiated. But the process constructed a tangible policy that increases Gitanyow influence over the management of their resources.

The Western resource management process, which compartmentalizes the Indigenous worldview into components such as cultural heritage, fisheries, wildlife, and socioeconomic measures, has forced Indigenous peoples and some consulting archaeologists to address epistemological issues (Budhwa 2005; Howitt 2001).

Foundational concepts to resource management, including the notion of management itself, are embedded within Western frameworks that separate humans from the environment and assume the inevitability of progress and development (Howitt and Suchet-Pearson 2006). However, archaeologists are working increasingly with anthropologists, geographers, and other social scientists to develop new interdisciplinary perspectives that recognize the interconnections between culture and nature and register the continuity of heritage into the present. Indigenous communities' participation in research has been key to the construction of new cross-cultural research practices that attempt to place Western research in dialogue with Indigenous knowledge systems. This productive exchange is evident in the development of new approaches to cultural resource management. Through Indigenous-academic collaborations, research has developed an increasingly holistic approach. This clearly demonstrates an evolution from interpretations of the past based predominantly on material remains to ones that value multiple lines of inquiry and evidence. However, until the resource management system genuinely attempts to understand Indigenous epistemologies and ontologies, management processes and policies will not be appropriate for or acceptable to the Indigenous peoples who are affected. Without this awareness, the overall CRM process will continue to be flawed, and Indigenous peoples will continue to respond to and resist its shortcomings.

Although there is a tendency to look toward the development of new institutions as the solution to difficult relations between Indigenous and non-Indigenous peoples, our experiences of cultural immersion and cross-cultural education highlight that changing the dynamic begins by building better relationships and recognizing the cultural institutions that already exist in Indigenous communities. Researchers and officials grounded in Western institutions need to develop better baseline cross-cultural understanding. Moving meetings outside office buildings in major cities such as Vancouver or Victoria is a significant gesture, as cross-cultural understanding often begins with simply spending time in the community and on the land. Being on the land with elders highlights the importance of listening rather than constantly working with a set agenda. Furthermore, being on the land and visiting the territory with Indigenous knowledge holders exposes outsiders to the relationships that inform Indigenous epistemologies and ontologies. Similarly, recognizing the importance of traditional cultural institutions, such as the feasts, by attending and offering financial support can significantly improve relations. Researchers must be grounded and experienced in the geographic region, not just the academic discipline, to fully understand the culture, the people, and their landscape. There is no substitute for experience on the territories. Such experience forms the foundation for meaningful personal relationships between Indigenous and non-Indigenous peoples. Researchers attempting to work with an Indigenous people or within an Indigenous people's traditionally claimed territory must be responsive to the unique relationship and responsibilities to place of those people.

There is no universal template for a solution, but rather a need to develop diverse approaches that respect the unique cultural traditions and cultural protocols of different Indigenous communities. Within various Indigenous communities and nations, communities may desire different forms of representation, and cultural management processes need to be attentive to the different levels of administrative, traditional, and treaty governance that communities may favor. Although studies often include token Indigenous participation, it is necessary to understand how Indigenous communities are organized to identify the appropriate knowledge holders.

The colonial history of underdevelopment and dispossession has also left many communities without adequate financial, technical, and cultural capacity. Gaps between the educational attainment of First Nations community members and the general Canadian population remain significant (Clement 2009). It is necessary to integrate capacity building into CRM processes, developing skills and institutional competence in the community through research projects. Researchers need to work to empower communities with critical knowledge of Western knowledge systems so they can make informed choices about CRM processes (J. T. Johnson, Louis, and Pramono 2006).

Interdisciplinary and community-based work in CRM presents the opportunity to develop new paradigms that recognize the depth of Indigenous cultural attachments to place and the complexity and diversity of Indigenous cultures. Although such approaches would certainly be considered daunting by the resource management industry, the qualitative and contextual sensitivities of interpretive social science methodologies are paramount to the accuracy and integrity of cultural resource management. Continuing to redefine CRM can broaden the work of consulting archaeologists in collaboration with other social scientists and Indigenous community members to recognize the importance of the relationships at the center of Indigenous cultural identity.

Acknowledgments

We dedicate this chapter to the memory of Roy Morris (Chief Woos), who held a wealth of knowledge on Wet'suwet'en traditions and worked through his life to ensure the transmission of this knowledge to future generations of not only Wet'suwet'en people but also their Canadian neighbors. We also thank all of the other First Nations people and communities with whom we work every day—we consider them all contributors to this essay. Research for this essay was funded in part by a Canada Graduate Scholarship from the Social Sciences and Humanities Research Council. Thanks also go to the editors and the anonymous reviewers for their invaluable feedback on earlier drafts of this essay.

References

Assembly of First Nations. 1993. *Reclaiming Our Nationhood: Strengthening Our Heritage.* Prepared for the Royal Commission on Aboriginal Peoples. Ottawa.

Battiste, M., ed. 2000. *Reclaiming Indigenous Voice and Vision.* Vancouver: University of British Columbia Press.

Blomley, N. 1996. "Shut the Province Down: First Nations Blockades in British Columbia, 1984–1995." *BC Studies,* no. 111, 5–35.

Braun, B. 1997. "Buried Epistemologies: The Politics of Nature in (Post)colonial British Columbia." *Annals of the Association of American Geographers* 87 (1): 3–31.

Budhwa, R. 2002. *Correlations between Catastrophic Paleoenvironmental Events and Native Oral Traditions of the Pacific Northwest.* Burnaby, BC: Simon Fraser University.

———. 2005. "An Alternate Model for First Nations Involvement in Resource Management Archaeology." *Canadian Journal of Archaeology* 29 (1): 20–45.

Chamberlin, J. E. 2000. "From Hand to Mouth: The Postcolonial Politics of Oral and Written Traditions." In *Reclaiming Indigenous Voice and Vision,* edited by M. Battiste, 124–41. Vancouver: University of British Columbia Press.

Clarkson, L., V. Morrissette, and G. Regallet. 1992. *Our Responsibility to the Seventh Generation: Indigenous Peoples and Sustainable Development.* Winnipeg: International Institute for Sustainable Development.

Clement, J. 2009. "University Attainment of the Registered Indian Population, 1981–2006." In *Aboriginal Education,* edited by J. P. White, J. Peters, D. Beavon, and N. Spence, 69–106. Toronto: Thompson Education Publishers.

Daly, R. 2005. *Our Box Was Full: An Ethnography for the Delgamuukw Plaintiffs.* Vancouver: University of British Columbia Press.

Delgam Uukw (K. Muldoe). 1992. "Delgam Uukw Speaks." In *The Spirit in the Land: Statements of the Gitksan and Wet'suwet'en Hereditary Chiefs in the Supreme Court of British Columbia, 1987–1990,* edited by Gisday Wa Delgam Uukw, 7–9. Gabriola, BC: Reflections.

Fuller, R. 2011. "Consultation in Cultural Resource Management: An Indigenous Perspective." In *A Companion to Cultural Resource Management,* edited by T. F. King, 373–84. Oxford: Wiley-Blackwell.

Galois, R. 1993. "The History of the Upper Skeena Region, 1850 to 1927." *Native Studies Review* 9 (2): 113–83.

Garroutte, E. M. 2003. *Real Indians: Identity and the Survival of Native America.* Berkeley: University of California Press.

Harris, Cole. 2002. *Making Native Space: Colonialism, Resistance, and Reserves in British Columbia.* Vancouver: University of British Columbia Press.

Henderson, J. Y. 2000. "Ayukpachi: Empowering Aboriginal Thought." In *Reclaiming Indigenous Voice and Vision,* edited by M. Battiste, 248–78. Vancouver: University of British Columbia Press.

———. 2006. *First Nations Jurisprudence and Aboriginal Rights: Defining the Just Society*. Saskatoon: Native Law Centre.

Howitt, Richard. 2001. *Rethinking Resource Management: Justice, Sustainability, and Indigenous Peoples*. London: Routledge.

Howitt, Richard, and Sandra Suchet-Pearson. 2006. "Rethinking the Building Block: Ontological Pluralism and the Idea of 'Management.'" *Geografiska Annaler—Series B: Human Geography* 88 (3): 323–35.

Johnson, J. T., R. P. Louis, and A. H. Pramono. 2006. "Facing the Future: Encouraging Critical Cartographic Literacies in Indigenous Communities." *ACME* 4 (1): 80–98.

Johnson, J. T., and B. Murton. 2007. "Re/placing Native Science: Indigenous Voices in Contemporary Constructions of Nature." *Geographical Research* 45 (2): 121–29.

Johnson, L. M. 2010. *Trail of Story, Traveller's Path: Reflections on Ethnoecology and Landscape*. Edmonton, AB: Athabasca University Press.

Klassen, M. A., R. Budhwa, and R. Reimer. 2009. "First Nations, Forestry, and the Transformation of Archaeological Practice in British Columbia, Canada." *Heritage Management* 2 (2): 199–238.

Koster, R., K. Baccar, R. H. Lemelin. 2012. "Moving from Research on, to Research with and for Indigenous Communities: A Critical Reflection on Community-Based Participatory Research." *Canadian Geographer* 56 (2): 195–210.

Kuokkanen, R. 2007. *Reshaping the University: Responsibility, Indigenous Epistemes and the Logic of the Gift*. Vancouver: University of British Columbia Press.

Louis, R. P. 2007. "Can You Hear Us Now? Voices from the Margin: Using Indigenous Methodologies in Geographic Research." *Geographical Research* 45 (2): 130–39.

Marker, M. 2006. "After the Makah Whale Hunt: Indigenous Knowledge and Limits to Multicultural Discourse." *Urban Education* 41 (5): 482–505.

Martindale, A. R. C., and S. Marsden. 2003. "Defining the Middle Period (3500 BP to 1500 BP) in Tsimshian History through a Comparison of Archaeological and Oral Records." *BC Studies*, no. 138/9, 13–50.

McDonald, J. A., and J. Joseph. 2000. "Key Events in the Gitksan Encounter with the Colonial World." In *Potlatch at Gitsegukla: William Beynon's 1945 Field Notebooks*, edited by M. Anderson and M. Halpin, 193–214. Vancouver: University of British Columbia Press.

Milligan, R., and T. McCreary. 2011. "Inscription, Innocence, and Invisibility: Early Contributions to the Discursive Formation of North in Samuel Hearne's *A Journey to the Northern Ocean*." In *Rethinking the Great White North: Race, Nature and the Historical Geographies of Whiteness in Canada*, edited by A. Baldwin, L. Cameron, and A. Kobayashi, 147–68. Vancouver: University of British Columbia Press.

Mills, A. 1994. *Eagle Down Is Our Law: Witsuwit'en Law, Feasts, and Land Claims*. Vancouver: University of British Columbia Press.

Mills, P. D. 2008. *For Future Generations: Reconciling Gitxsan and Canadian Law*. Saskatoon: Purich Publishing.

Morris, P., and G. Fondahl. 2002. "Negotiating the Production of Space in Tl'azt'en Territory, Northern British Columbia." *Canadian Geographer* 46 (2): 108–25.

Nicholas, G. P. 2006. "Decolonizing the Archaeological Landscape." *American Indian Quarterly* 30 (3/4): 350–80.

Overstall, R. 2005. "Encountering the Spirit in the Land: 'Property' in a Kinship-Based Legal Order." In *Despotic Dominion*, edited by J. McLaren, A. R. Buck, and N. E. Wright, 22-49. Vancouver: University of British Columbia Press.

Panelli, R. 2008. "Social Geographies: Encounters with Indigenous and More-than-White/Anglo Geographies." *Progress in Human Geography* 32 (6): 801–11.

Pearce, M., and R. P. Louis. 2008. "Mapping Indigenous Depth of Place." *American Indian Culture and Research Journal* 32 (3): 107–26.

Persky, S., ed. 1998. *Delgamuukw: The Supreme Court of Canada Decision on Aboriginal Title.* Vancouver: David Suzuki Foundation and Greystone Books.

Pratt, M. L. 1992. *Imperial Eyes: Studies in Travel Writing and Transculturation.* London: Routledge.

Roth, C. F. 2008. *Becoming Tsimshian: The Social Life of Names.* Seattle: University of Washington Press.

Slattery, B. 2006. "The Metamorphosis of Aboriginal Title." *Canadian Bar Review* 85 (2): 255–86.

Smith, L. T. 1999. *Decolonizing Methodologies: Research and Indigenous Peoples.* London: Zed Books.

Sterritt, N. J., S. Marsden, R. Galois, P. R. Grant, and R. Overstall. 1998. *Tribal Boundaries in the Nass Watershed.* Vancouver: University of British Columbia Press.

Tennant, P. 1990. *Aboriginal Peoples and Politics: The Indian Land Question in British Columbia, 1849–1989.* Vancouver: University of British Columbia Press.

Turner, N., M. B. Ignace, and R. Ignace. 2000. "Traditional Ecological Knowledge and Wisdom of Aboriginal Peoples in British Columbia." *Ecological Applications* 10 (5): 1275–87.

Watkins, J. 2005. "Through Wary Eyes: Indigenous Perspectives on Archaeology." *Annual Review of Anthropology* 34:429–49.

Watkins, J., and J. Beaver. 2008. "What Do We Mean by 'Heritage'? Whose Heritage Do We Manage, and What Rights Have We to Do So?" *Heritage Management* 1 (1): 9–36.

Watson, A., and O. H. Huntington. 2008. "They're Here—I Feel Them: The Epistemic Spaces of Indigenous and Western Knowledges." *Social and Cultural Geography* 9 (3): 257–81.

Wilson, S. 2008. *Research Is Ceremony.* Halifax: Fernwood Publishing.

Windsor, J. E., and J. A. McVey. 2005. "Annihilation of Both Place and Sense of Place." *Geographical Journal* 171 (2): 146–65.

TELLING STORIES IN THE CLASSROOM

Awakening to Belonging

ANNE GODLEWSKA

This essay is about the sense of place rather than the ontology of place. All creatures share ontology of place, as place is inseparable from being (Malpas 1999, 31–32), but as sensory, experiential, historical, social, and attitudinal differences create distinctions of being in the world, we do not necessarily have the same sense of place (Basso 1996; Feld and Basso 1996; Casey 1997; Johnson and Murton 2007). Although senses of place differ between individuals and cultures, we are capable of understanding each other's perceptions and sharing a sense of place if we are willing to listen and to open ourselves to the experiences of others (Gruenewald 2003; Ingold 1993; Johnson 2010).

In this essay I will tell you a story that I first told to seventy students who enrolled in my Aboriginal geographies course. I sensed the importance of this story then but did not appreciate its full significance. As a non-Aboriginal person teaching such a course, I needed to position myself. I wanted to bridge the gap between myself as a child of immigrants and the First Peoples of the territory that has come to be known as Canada. The students had to know where I came from and why I was teaching this course.

My experience teaching this class prompted my research into what, if any, knowledge first-year university students in Canada have of First Nations, Métis, and Inuit people and their issues. I began to realize that a barrier more invidious than ignorance lies between understanding Aboriginal people and these young people, although ignorance is the mortar of this barrier. In 2010, with a survey and objective test based in part on a survey developed by the Coalition for the Advancement of Aboriginal Studies and further developed with the advice and direction of First Nations, Métis, and Inuit educational leaders, I tested the knowledge of first-year and fourth-year university students and students graduating to become school teachers. On this test, composed of thirty-four to thirty-eight carefully worded questions addressing issues of profound importance for Aboriginal people in Canada, students performed poorly: the average score was 29 percent for first-year students, 35 percent for fourth-year students and 37 percent for graduating teachers. Students retained most knowledge about what they had been taught in elementary school (the last time Aboriginal content had been presented to most of them), and were least knowledgeable about the political, legal, and social circumstances shaping the lives of First Nations, Métis, and Inuit people today. Most significantly, although the majority of the students expressed dismay at their lack of knowledge, some blaming their teachers for their ignorance, others explained that Aboriginal people hardly existed, were not important, or were beneath contempt. The survey taught me that opening to others requires more than knowledge. It demands acknowledgment of commonality and a sense that most human battles are universally recognizable, even when waged against one another. I employed my story, ostensibly about a sense of place, to suggest shared sensibilities despite difference.

Stories are powerful teachers because they are accessible, often deceptively profound, oblique; they demand complicity and transport us. Storytelling is natural to us. As Joseph Gold and others have argued persuasively, we are the storied species: we live by and through stories, and stories structure our existence and give it meaning (Gold 2002; King 1993, 2003; Cruikshank 2005). Children gather attentively around a storyteller. Friends meet and exchange stories. Scientists engage listeners with stories from the field. Religious leaders inspire fortitude with stories of suffering and salvation. We continually retell the stories of our own lives and those of others, incorporating recent events and experience, subtly changing who we are. Stories are quotidian but also profound. Told to children, they ignite imagination, re-creating their worlds. The stories friends tell illustrate how differently and similarly we perceive the world. Religious stories shape the lives of billions; biographical stories explore the full range of human emotion, creativity, resourcefulness, and despair. Storytelling is powerful because it shows us ourselves from surprising angles, engages our complicity, and creates a bond of sympathy between teller and audience that invokes receptivity to a variety of messages (Rankin 2002). Stories touch us, broaden our perceptions, transport us to places that live within our imagination, places where relationships are not our own, yet reflect our own.

The story I told my class was about a place of great importance to me, a property of about 160 acres near the town of Barry's Bay, southeast of Algonquin Park in Central Ontario. The Polish immigrants to this area know it as Kaszuby, so named after the Pomeranian people of northeast Poland who migrated to that part of Ontario during the nineteenth century. The Kaszubs may be familiar to some of you from the opening scenes of Volker Schlöndorff's film of Günter Grass's *The Tin Drum*. Pomerania is a lowland area of lakes, forests, and small towns on the Baltic Sea coast, with poor soils nevertheless cultivated for cereals, sugar beets, and potatoes. On the fault line between Germany and Poland, the language spoken is most like Polish with overtones of German. My family is not Kaszub but Polish/ Lithuanian. My father called the property in Ontario "Godlewo," after his family's name (since the eleventh century), but also after the town Godlewo (or Garliava in Lithuanian) in what is now Lithuania.

Godlewo means much more than a property to our family; it is a place, or land in the Aboriginal sense: a network of relations including people, plants, animals, insects, the earth, light, and air. My parents did not live entirely off the land, but they gathered berries and mushrooms and grew food crops during the summer, imbibing a sense of rhythm with the land. The name Godlewo reveals what that land meant to them, as names so often do (Lounsbury 1960; Day 1977; Black Rogers and Rogers 1980; Hartley 1981; Booker, Hudson, and Rankin, 1992; Gooding 1994; Preston 2000; and Derounian-Stodola and Levernier 1993; Carter 2005). From the eighteenth century until World War I my father's family was important in the community of and around Godlewo, Poland (or Garliava, Lithuania). His ancestors were founders in 1809 of the Catholic church, Garliavos Bažnycia, also a synagogue and Lutheran church. My great-, great-, great-grandfather's bones lie encased, visible behind the dark glass of the altar near the entrance to the Catholic church. Franciszek Godlewski owned an estate where his descendants lived, managing the lands and negotiating with Lithuanians, Germans, and Jews to survive Russian dominance of that area. It has since been converted into botanical gardens for the city of Garliava.

I need to pause here and talk about the meaning of land in that other place and time. My father's family were landed gentry, meaning that, endowed with social status they lived off the land and worked to improve it. From my great-great-grandfather's time to my grandfather's time this was more difficult than for their predecessors. Poland was under occupation or under threat of occupation, often from three or more sides (Zamoyski [1987] 1994; Davies 1981). During my grandfather's time, civil society disintegrated: land was expropriated; ethnic groups were pitted against each other and, for some, being different justified the violation of agreements, contracts, and basic human rights (J. Godlewski 1978). My grandfather, an idealist, lost more than one farm through his trust, generosity, and openness. As land meant much more to him than property, honorable land transactions were paramount. His decision to farm in the shadow of both the German and Russian borders was to declare dedication, commitment, and a passion for the land in at least two senses: land as environment and land as homeland. Working the land with respect to the environment, making it productive and beautiful, led to a prosperous and joyful life that nurtured relationships with the soil itself, with extended family, domesticated and nondomesticated animals, neighboring landowners, peasants, and tradesmen. He was known well beyond his local region for the management of his properties and his relations with neighbors. He maintained the forests, planted orchards, grew beets, potatoes, rye, and wheat, installed beehives and fishponds, built an alcohol factory that provided fuel and revenue, allotted land for neighboring villages in lieu of gleaning rights, and employed a significant number of laborers and skilled craftsmen, encouraging them to come from afar and settling them on his land. Land in the other sense, homeland, is a more difficult concept, bound up as it is in the now largely abhorrent idea of nationalism. Yet my grandfather's memoirs make clear that cultivating the land in this sense was an extension of the first: an attempt to bring the peace and prosperity he created on the scale of a few thousand hectares to the larger society that, in the end, afforded the only security for his family and farm. That is why, in spite of his dislike of politics, he served in the army, undertook risky missions all along the Eastern front, served in local agricultural improvement organizations, in local government at the municipal and county levels, and ultimately became a national senator. It is why he held steadfast to the idea of a Polish commonwealth in which all nationalities would have status and rights, and why he argued for managed land reform: so that everyone would have the basis for building wealth and a stake in a peaceful society. It is a great leap of imagination for me, someone who has lived unthreatened by war, conflict, or violence of any sort, to come to terms with his life: repeatedly shattered by having to defend his country through the First World War (1914–19), the Russian Revolution (1917), the Polish Ukrainian War (1917–21), the Polish Russian War (1917–21), the Stock Market Crash (1929), the Great Depression (1930–39), and finally and decisively the Second World War (1939–45). I realize now, more than fifty years after his death, how deeply his experience of land and relationships influenced my father's life and the lives of his grandchildren.

On September 1, 1939, at the outbreak of war, with artillery booming in the distance my grandfather packed up his family, taking little more than a change of clothes and, making a circuit of nearby farms, gathered all the family members and friends he could into a small convoy heading northeast toward Vilnius (later Lithuania) from their farm in what is now Byelorussia, between the pincer movement of approaching Nazi and Soviet forces. I grew up listening to discussions of whether it was preferable to be captured by Nazis or Soviets, which, of course, depended on who you were: Jews had to avoid the Nazis at all costs, and landowners the Soviets, but other Byelorussians, Lithuanians, Ukrainians, and Poles of the time had varying opinions, which often created a maelstrom of society. After many close calls and what must have been high adventure for my eighteen-year-old father, they reached Vilnius, not far from their ancestral property, just in front of the Russian army. They stayed hidden in the apartments of friends and relatives while the Russians first invaded, then withdrew, leaving army bases, pausing before their final occupation of the territory. My family remained more or less hidden for five long months, working to improve health, gather sufficient resources, and waiting for the opportunity to escape by car to Latvia, by plane from Riga to Stockholm, to Brussels, and finally by train to Paris. In France, the family split up. My grandmother went south to Biarritz to care for Polish children lost to their families in the war (Godlewska 1994); my grandfather worked with the Polish forces in Paris and Marseilles gathering Polish servicemen to send to Britain; and my father pursued his studies until he chauffeured the American ambassador William Christian Bullitt from Paris as Nazi forces occupied the city. Sometime after May 1940, all members of the family arrived in Great Britain, but it took a while for them to find each other.

For many central Europeans, the aftermath of war was an unsettled period. The older generation lived out their days in Western Europe, hoping to find a way home: my grandfather died in London in 1968 at the age of seventy-seven, and my grandmother in her eighties in Madrid in 1974. But, in 1952, with Poland under continued Soviet domination, my father resolved to find a better life for his wife (another displaced person: born in Mexico of French and English parentage, then living in England) and family. After obtaining a degree in agriculture at Cambridge and working at the National Institute of Agricultural Engineering in Bedfordshire, he left for Canada to find work. My parents came to Canada during a period of considerable economic growth In Toronto. My father found employment with Massey Ferguson (then Massey Harris) and housing, with some difficulty, as rental signs excluded DPs ("displaced persons," as they were then called). Toronto was still raw and provincial compared with any European metropolis (M.-C. Godlewski 2010, 49).

Massey Ferguson was one of the few truly international Canadian businesses in the 1950s (Denison 1948; Fraser 1972; Cook 1981; Neufeld 1969). After establishing, building, and managing their test track, my father rose through the ranks as an engineer to management and finally to a corporate position. Like his father, he paid more attention to creating and building than to negotiating his salary or accumulating wealth. Prior to its takeover in 1979 by Conrad Black and Victor Rice, Massey Ferguson was an expanding company, facilitating the mechanization of agriculture worldwide and very much involved in the Green Revolution. My father traveled abroad for as long as six months at a time. The family moved with the company from Toronto to Iowa and back. After a period of experimentation with his own company, Recreatives (New York), and two years running Shasta Corporation (a subsidiary of W. R. Grace in California), my father returned to Massey Ferguson in a corporate position, based in London, that involved him in more international travel.

My grandfather built strong ties to land and community, but my father, to his sorrow, spent his working life at the cutting edge of agriculture but not on the land.

In his experience, companies and corporations provided unreliable and transient allegiances to which loyalty was ultimately quixotic. When he retired in 1979 at the age of fifty-eight, he wanted nothing more than to return home and attempt to heal the traumatic loss of his first home. But in the early 1980s there was no home: Poland was not accessible to the children of landowners exiled during the war. He bought the land near Algonquin Park to rebuild something of what he had lost as a young man and, perhaps, to show his family what it meant to be him and give them a chance to live that life too. But by then, his children were adults, living in Calgary, Wisconsin, Montreal, and then Toronto.

His choice of region was not haphazard. He gravitated to a community of exiled Poles. Given the difficult conditions of life under Prussian (1772), Austrian (1793), and especially Russian (1795) occupation, Poles had, since the nineteenth century, been leaving what had been Poland for France, the United Kingdom, Sweden, the United States, Brazil, and elsewhere in South America and Canada (Preuss 1846–57, Robinson and Beard 1908–9; Vernadsky and Pushkarev 1972). The first major group who arrived in Canada in 1858 were Kaszubs (or Kashubians). Under the 1853 Public Land Acts they were granted land along the Opeongo road in central Ontario, where they founded the settlements of Wilno, Barry's Bay, and Round Lake (Zurakowska 1991; Makowski 1987). The Kaszubs came from the poorest regions of Pomerania, Bytow, and Koscierzyna, which were under Prussian domination, and where the land was least good for farming. They were looking not only for fertile land, but the freedom to practice their language, faith, and culture. Much of the land along the Opeongo line was not suitable for farming, as Irish immigrants had discovered in 1857, so many of the Irish and Kaszubs who stayed went into the lumber industry supplying timber to Great Britain, where significant stands of native trees had long since been felled. They were followed by generations of Poles in waves that corresponded to peaks in oppression and hardship back home as the Prussians and Russians sought to secure occupied Poland by forcing the population to adopt their languages, cultures, and religions. Migrations followed during the nineteenth and twentieth centuries (1890–1914, 1920s, 1930s, 1939–45 and after the fall of the Berlin Wall in 1989). The Poles who left Poland during the Second World War were often educated business or professional people who came to Kaszuby, as they called it, to settle or stay for the summer among Polish-language speakers in a place and landscape that reminded them of their lost homeland. In this landscape they memorialized their lives between two landscapes: the Polish Canadian scout camp, the Cathedral in the Pines, St. Hedwig's, St. Mary's, and St. Casimir's churches, trees, properties, and barns carved with Polish art, names, and poetry, a memorial to Father Rafal Grzondziel and a Warsaw uprising memorial, among other things.

My mother, although not Polish, understood displacement and loss and my father's need to settle on land that he could work. They explored the area and, after getting severely lost during the height of the black fly season and returning from the bush unrecognizable, settled on the piece of land they called Godlewo. There they built a house. It was a beautiful house featuring elements of every home they had lived in and loved. It had vaulted ceilings and a study overlooking the living room, atrium and central gathering place, a cozy secluded dining room, a library that was cool in summer and warm in winter, a palatial kitchen, decks on two sides, a huge garage in which you could wash your car, and five spacious bedrooms with large windows overlooking the land, designed to draw children and friends home. The house nestled in a grove of statuesque red pines at the back, with a well-worked vegetable plot and hard-won open garden at the front. My parents dug a large pond. which they lined with a Dupont membrane from relatively nearby Kingston. A war survivor, my father equipped the house with multiple heating systems in case it was ever necessary to go off grid: electric, oil, wood, and heat pump. The house sounds swank, but it was not a holiday home, nor the plaything of a rich family. My parents sank all their resources into the land and house and then lived there as frugally and environmentally as possible. The house was clad with cedar planking, to fit into the landscape, and they planted thousands of trees, constantly experimenting with what could grow and prosper in the soil and the harsh climate of the region.

The landscape of the 160-acre property was surprisingly varied. The area had suffered a devastating fire some eighty years before they moved in, resulting in treeless "savannas" surrounded by relatively young growth of shrubs and deciduous trees, a small jack pine stand carpeted with a remarkable display of lichen in the fall, and mixed woods of tall red pine that had survived the fire, interspersed with new-growth birch. The winding kilometer-long road into the property and the hydro cut generated their own micro-topographies. Tree planting created distinctive groves of red pine and spruce. A stream passed through the northeast corner of the property and, from a great hill, one might, but for the dense tree growth, survey the countryside in the dead of winter. During their mating season tree frogs could be heard in the evening, and two vernal ponds resounded with the clamor of frogs. The land was rich in food plants: wood strawberries, dense blueberry bushes courtesy of the fire, wild raspberries; animals: beavers, otters, ground hogs, fox, deer, bats, small rodents, including flying squirrels, the odd feral cat and occasional bear, and a plethora of insects. The many habitats encouraged a wide variety of bird species, including an eastern screech owl,[1] a common barn owl perhaps that woke me one night with its eerily human scream next to my window. Of all the local birds our favorites were the common nighthawks and ravens. The nighthawks with their late evening "bzzzt" call were there when my parents first arrived and then vanished, not just from their property but sadly from a vast continental territory (Cadman 2007; Dunn 2002). The ravens, such intelligent birds, called to each other over our heads and ran a flying school in the nearby savanna for their young. My parents watched, admired, recorded, and fed the birds that would come to them. I watched my parents with delight: my father who could not hear, thanks to service in the artillery during World War II, and my mother who had cataracts, and was, until surgery, going blind, would serve as each other's ears and eyes when identifying birds.

They worked this land, not to produce for a market but to live a rewarding life surrounded by an environment they loved. By removing weak and overcrowded trees, they let others grow stronger; by leaving trees to fall and rot they established diverse habitats, rich smells, and a lovely crop of mushrooms. My father hired a local Kaszub forester, his wife, and their draft horse, and together they logged a section of the forest in the traditional way to avoid scarring the land with the great skidders that leave ruts three and four feet deep. They grew flowers for their home, asparagus for May, cucumbers for Polish-style pickling, tomatoes for August, potatoes for all winter, sugar snaps for me, beans for a wide circle of friends, and twice a day they patrolled the furrows for potato beetles, which they removed by hand. They cut winding paths to allow us all to wander through the different habitats while disturbing them as little as possible.

My father did not forget Poland. But his homeland was now under Soviet rule, and his family had lost a working farm, an apartment in Warsaw, an extensive tract of forest since nationalized by the Soviet-dominated Polish government, and other property besides. Poland is not a wealthy country, and the particular poverty of my grandfather's region is the legacy of extensive periods of war and oppression. Those previously in positions of social influence were deemed morally suspect and without rights, or, if they had left under coercion, were considered to have abandoned their properties. It did not matter that had they stayed they would have been murdered along with other of Poland's leaders by the Soviet NKVD in Katyn Forest in April–May of 1940, a mass murder so nefarious that Stalinist and post-Stalinist Russia denied it for fifty years. But international law, human rights, and the European courts did not agree that people like my grandparents and others, including the Jews and their descendants, had abandoned their land or property. Such disputes are complex because they often fall into the cracks between nations: cases might have to be made simultaneously against Germany, Poland, Byelorussia, and the Russian Federation. Only since the establishment of the permanent European Court of Human Rights in Strasbourg in 1998, with judicial authority over all States of the Council of Europe, had my father's by then two-decade-long effort to pursue the matter legally begun to show any signs of hope. But the case remained difficult: his father's properties are now in Byelorussia, the only state in Europe that does not accede to the Council of Europe nor recognize the European Convention on Human Rights; both Poland and Byelorussia have resold the land to others who now also have interests; or the state simply refuses to recognize past rights. Poland has accused Byelorussia of persecuting the 400,000 Poles on its territory as a result of the border change following World War II (BBC News 2005). Furthermore, these cases must be fought by complainants possessed of a diminishing understanding of the law (and the society behind the law) governing the court actions, using lawyers distant from them and their interests. Disputes take decades to be resolved as governments stall and equivocate, waiting for the last immediately affected generation to die out.

Meanwhile, back in North America, I visited my parents as often as I could, sometimes spending as long as a month with them. I came from wherever I was working; from Worcester, Massachusetts, from Paris, London, and from Kingston, Ontario. My brothers and their children came from Toronto, Montreal, Calgary, Vancouver, Edinburgh, and much further afield. Through three generations of German shepherds, I walked all the paths and watched as the micro-landscapes of the property changed, foxes, beavers, groundhogs, and otters grew up and moved on, migratory birds came and went, as nighthawks hunted over the fields at dark and then vanished altogether. Godlewo became my zone of refuge, the place where I healed after bruising experiences, the place where, with my family, I re-centered, restored the strength to battle on with life's challenges. There were a few alarming moments: storms that took down trees, a lightning strike that almost burned down the house, snows so deep and fluffy that a fall with snow shoes resulted in a prolonged struggle to stand up, winters so cold that vehicles simply stopped. Gradually my parents became acquainted with the neighboring townsfolk; my mother's wicked sense of humor and my father's ingenuity won them friends.

In 2006, with much pain and regret, they put the property up for sale. Time had been working not only on the landscapes through which they walked but on their bodies. They needed proximity to family and medical services. As with many rural residents, family members lived in distant cities and could not move without giving up the benefits of hard-won education and careers. Although beautiful, the house and property required an unusual amount of work to remain so. With winter temperatures well below -30 C and summer electrical storms, and all manner of critters only too eager to move in, the house could not be left empty. It would not be easy to sell well: there was nothing like it within 100 kilometers. For a variety of reasons, in October 2006 the property sold for below two-thirds of its market value. I felt that the price and conditions amounted to theft, though my father patiently explained that their declining health and need to move was a negotiation weakness with a capital value.

Although in the sciences and to some extent the social sciences, we tend to regard emotion as extraneous to the matter at hand, it is at the heart of what we do, from science, to investment, to government, and for most of us it colors, if not governs, our social relations. Emotion, understood, can teach us a great deal: we ignore it at our peril. So, at this stage in the story I invite my students to imagine my feelings. Grief: that this property, so much a part of my life, part of my relations with my parents, my siblings, and their children, with the land, with our dogs, with every living being I encountered there, part of my peace of mind, was gone. Anger: because the land's true value had not been recognized; essentially it was taken from my family. Determination: that that no matter who moved onto the property henceforth, it would still be mine/ours, always. It lives in me still, even if I cannot live in it.

At about the time my parents put Godlewo on the market, I discovered that much of Eastern Ontario is subject to a land claim dispute with the descendants of Algonquin peoples who inhabited, and many who still inhabit, the region. The complexity of land ownership and use rights in the former eastern territories of Poland pales in comparison to the morass created by centuries of expropriation-driven treaties that recognized neither Aboriginal land values nor Aboriginal social structures and communities, nor in many instances legal status on which land rights were based. The subversive nature of treaties, very particular to colonial territories, added to a surfeit of other legal, semilegal and illegal land expropriation and assimilative strategies employed by both private interests and governments (Ray 1996, chap. 14; Ripmeester 1995; Asch 1997; Dickason 1997; Usher, Tough and Galois 1992; Huitema 2000). In particular, the 1853 Public Land Act that resulted in colonization roads, like the Opeongo Road settled in part by Kaszubs, opened Indian country to a flood of settlers, the destruction wrought by lumber companies, the imposition of a taxation system that disadvantaged those not part of a cash economy, the linking of all claims to either agricultural development or commercial lumbering, or reserve settlement and therefore land expropriation. The Algonquin, Nipissing, Mississauga, and Haudenosaunee peoples in Eastern Ontario were also subject to invidious divide-and-rule strategies employed by governments in dealing with their claims and interests. I believe, but perhaps I mostly hope, that, had my grandfather seen and understood the long history of colonial dispossession of Aboriginal people in Canada, he would have deplored it. Though he came from a long tradition of settled private landownership, he was concerned not just with land law but with justice, as he granted the Byelorussian peasantry ownership rights to some of his land in replacement of the much disputed but traditional gleaning rights. The Algonquin of Eastern Ontario did not occupy land the way settlers do. They did not map, subdivide, farm, forest, or mine it. But they did use it, considered it theirs, and for almost three centuries, from the end of the eighteenth century to the present day, have fought to retain control over their land with documented peti-tions to the government (Huitema 2000, chaps. 3, 4; Boyden 2010). Under the Royal Proclamation of 1763 and by Canada's repatriated constitution, Canada recognizes those rights. But as my family and many others are witnessing in Europe, between the recognition of a right and restitution of land rights lies a battlefield littered with legislation, measures, and practices designed to protect governments and the ben-eficiaries of dispossession. The Canadian Godlewo is not part of the 36,000 square kilometers of the Algonquin land claim that stretches from the southeast of North Bay to Hawkesbury, as the claim involves only the expropriation of land by the Commissioner of Crown Lands until 1862 and any future development on Crown land (see map in Huitema 2000, 75). Although dispossession is not the aim of the land claim, having a say in the development of the remaining undeveloped land is.

If we recent immigrants thought we could find peace in the assertion that we cannot be held accountable for the sins of people who were not even our forefathers, then it is well to remember that we lay claim to our land, urban, suburban, and rural, by virtue of those injustices, and that the injustices are perpetuated within the institutions we maintain with our taxes, from our schools that ignore Aboriginal realities to our governments that uphold the Indian Act in the face of criticism from international human rights organizations. There is no escaping the fact that the moral right by which we ever owned the Canadian Godlewo is as problematic as the moral right of the Byelorussian government to expropriate and retain my grandfather's farm.

I lived on the Canadian Godlewo part-time for twenty-seven years, not even a generation. Yet the bond my family and I shared with that land was profound. There we shared a deeper sense of place. How must people who have lived and traveled through these lands for thousands of years feel about losing their land? And not even for two-thirds of its value! Because land in this sense is about more than property: it is about place, at-home-ness, living in ways that make sense to you, being yourself in a place that is somehow as much in you as you are in it, belonging.

My family was lamenting a loss that would not have been possible but for the much greater loss from which, one way or another, they had benefited. Meanwhile, back in Poland and Europe, our lawsuits wend their way through labyrinthine court systems, from which, most probably, they will never emerge. This is the immigrant experience: we profit from old injustices in the new country to repair more recent injustices in the old, and sometimes we are more concerned about those distant injustices than the near ones, often unable to see injustices right here in North America.

Because my family were educated Europeans, I spent the first forty-five years of my life with my eyes turned to Europe and its intellectual institutions. But now,

I tell the students, I am spending my remaining years looking to Canada, to the foremost issue in this country, the question of Aboriginal justice and how to build a Canadian identity not founded on fundamental injustice. I share with them my growing awareness of the linked nature of place, identity, the past, and belonging, and how such awareness can reveal the complexity of Aboriginal identities, place attachment, and belonging. This has been a genuine exploration, because I have not always known how to do it. Although they may come from somewhere else and be going somewhere else again, I invite the students to join me on this uncertain but important voyage.

When I tell this story to my first-year university geography course, the room of 450 students is largely silent. Many approach me after class to say how touched they are by what I have said. Certainly, the vast majority are more interested in and receptive to this story than to my lecture on land claims, Aboriginal rights, the Indian Act, and the history of dispossession that is so much part of Canada. They have learned in high school that Canada is a just society. How can what I say be true or important if hitherto it has received so little attention? But this story, which locates many of them in the history of the Americas, begins to make them think about how the past shapes the present and how it might not be irrelevant to them or simple after all. I do not imagine that I can change minds with one lecture. In fact, I don't imagine that I can change minds. But I do think that I can help students begin to question what they see and hear, and I believe that in such questioning lies our hope for a better future.

Notes

I thank my family and my students who have taught me so much.

1. B-song. See http://www.owlpages.com/sounds.php.

References

Asch, Michael. 1997. "Aboriginal and Treaty Rights in Canada: Essays on Law, Equality, and Respect for Difference." Vancouver: University of British Columbia Press.

Basso, Keith H. 1996. *Wisdom Sits in Places: Landscape and Language among the Western Apache.* Albuquerque: University of New Mexico Press.

BBC News. 2005. Belarus-Poland dispute escalates. Thursday, 28 July. http://news.bbc.co.uk/2/hi/europe/4724013.stm.

Black Rogers, Mary, and Edward S. Rogers. 1980. "Adoption of Patrilineal Surname System by Bilateral Northern Ojibwa: Mapping the Learning of an Alien System." *Papers of the 11th Algonquian Conference*, 198–230. Ottawa: Carleton University.

Booker, Karen, Charles M. Hudson, and Robert L. Rankin. 1992. "Place-name Identification and Multilingualism in the Sixteenth-Century Southeast." *Ethnohistory* 39 (4): 399–451.

Boyden, Joseph. 2010. "Why We Try to Protect Our Land: Lessons from Barriere Lake. *Globe and Mail,* Monday, December 13.

Cadman, Michael D. 2007. *Atlas of the Breeding Birds of Ontario, 2001–2005* Toronto: Ontario Nature.

Carter, Lyn. 2005. "Naming to Own: Place-names as Indicators of Human Interaction with the Environment." *Alternative: An International Journal of Indigenous Peoples* 1 (1): 6–25.

Casey, Edward S. 1993 *Getting Back into Place: Toward a Renewed Understanding of the Place-World.* Bloomington: Indiana University Press.

———. 1997. *The Fate of Place: A Philosophical History* Berkeley: University of California Press.

Cerna Christina M. 1994. "Universality of Human Rights and Cultural Diversity: Implementation of Human Rights in Different Socio-Cultural Contexts." *Human Rights Quarterly* 16 (4): 740–52.

Cook, Peter. 1981. *Massey at the Brink. The Story of Canada's Greatest Multinational and Its Struggle to Survive.* Don Mills, ON: Collins.

Cruickshank, Julie. 2005 *Do Glaciers Listen? Local Knowledge, Colonial Encounters and Social Imagination.* Vancouver: University of British Columbia Press; and Seattle: University of Washington Press.

Davies, Norman. 1981. *God's Playground: A History of Poland.* Oxford: Clarendon Press.

Day, Gordon M. 1977. "Indian Place-Names as Ethnohistoric Data." *Papers of the 8th Algonquian Conference,* 26–31. Ottawa: Carleton University.

Denison, Merrill. 1948. *Harvest Triumphant: The Story of Massey-Harris: A Footnote to Canadian History.* Toronto: McClelland and Stewart.

Derounian-Stodola, Kathryn Zabelle, and James Arthur Levernier. 1993 *The Indian Captivity Narrative, 1550–1900.* Toronto: Maxwell Macmillan Canada.

Dickason, Olive P. 1997. *Canada's First Nations: A History of Founding Peoples from the Earliest Times.* 2nd ed. Toronto: Oxford University Press.

Dunn, Erica H. 2002. "Using Decline In Bird Populations To Identify Needs for Conservation Action." *Conservation Biology* 16 (6): 1632–37.

Feld, Steven, and Keith H. Basso. 1996. *Senses of Place.* Santa Fe, NM: School of American Research Press; Seattle: University of Washington Press.

Fraser, Colin. 1972. *Harry Ferguson: Inventor and Pioneer.* London: John Murray.

Godlewska, Fabjanna. 1994. *Memoirs of Fabjanna Godlewska, nee Countess Hutten Czapska.* Edited by Marie-Christine Godlewska and Karol J. M. Godlewski. N.p.

Godlewski, Józef. 1978. *Na Przełomie Epok.* London: Polska Fundacja Kulturalna. Translated from Polish as *Between Two Epochs* by Marietta Brzeska and edited by Marie-Christine Godlewski, Anne Godlewska, and Karol Jozef Maria Godlewski, Toronto, 1993.

Godlewski, Marie-Christine. 2010. *Stories from My Life.* Toronto: Heritage Memoirs.

Gold, Joseph. 2002. *The Story Species: Our Life-Literature Connection.* Allston, MA: Fitzhenry and Whiteside.

Gooding, Susan Stauger. 1994. "Place, Race, and Names: Identities in the United States v. Oregon, Confederated Tribes of the Colville Reservation, Plaintiff-Intervenor." *Law and Society Review* 28 (5): 1181–1229.

Gruenewald, David A. 2003. "Foundations of Place: A Multidisciplinary Framework for Place-Conscious Education." *American Educational Research Journal* 40 (3): 619–54.

Hartley, Alan H. 1981. "Preliminary Observations on Ojibwa Place-Names." *Papers of the 12th Algonquian Conference*, 31–38. Ottawa: Carleton University.

Huitema, Marijke E. 2000. "'Land of which the savages stood in no particular need': Dispossessing the Algonquins of Southeastern Ontario of Their Lands, 1760–1930." Master's thesis. Queen's University, Kingston, Ontario.

Ingold, Tim. 1993. "The Temporality of the Landscape." Special Issue: Conceptions of Time and Ancient Society. *World Archaeology* 25 (2): 152–74.

Johnson, Jay. 2010. "Place-Based Learning and Knowing: Critical Pedagogies Grounded in Indigeneity. *GeoJournal* DOI 10.1007/s10708-010-9379-1.

Johnson, Jay T., and Brian Murton. 2007. "Re/placing Native Science: Indigenous Voices in Contemporary Constructions of Nature.: *Geographical Research* 45 (2): 121–29.

King, Thomas. 1993. *One Good Story, That One*. Toronto: Harper Perennial.

———. 2003. *The Truth about Stories: A Native Narrative*. Toronto: House of Anansi Press.

Lounsbury, Floyd G. 1960. *Iroquois Place-Names in the Champlain Valley*. Albany: State Education Department. Report Number 9.

Makowski, William. 1987. *The Polish People in Canada: A Visual History*. Montreal: Tundra Books.

Malpas, Jeff. 1999. *Place and Experience: A Philosophical Topography*. Cambridge: Cambridge University Press.

Neufeld, E. P. 1969, *A Global Corporation: A History of the International Development of Massey Ferguson Limited*. Toronto: University of Toronto Press.

Preston, Susan M. 2000. "Exploring the Eastern Cree Landscape: Oral Tradition as Cognitive Map." *Papers of the 31st Algonquian Conference*, 310–32. Ottawa: Carleton University

Preuss, J. D. E. 1846–1857. *Oeuvres de Frédéric le grand*. Vol. 6, 6–7. Berlin: Rodolphe Decker.

Rankin, Jenny. 2002 "What Is Narrative? Ricoeur, Bahktin, and Process Approaches." *Concrescence: The Australasian Journal of Process Thought* 3:1–12.

Ray, Arthur J. 1996. "I Have Lived Here since the World Began." In *An Illustrated History of Canada's Native History*. Toronto: Lester Publishing, Key Porter Books.

Ripmeester, Michael R. 1995. "Vision Quests into Sight Lines: Negotiating the Place of the Mississaugas in South-Eastern Ontario, 1700–1876." PhD thesis. Queen's University, Kingston, Ontario.

Robinson, James Harvey, and Charles A. Beard. 1908-9. *Readings in European History*. Vol. 2. Boston: Ginn.

Schlöndorff, Volker, dir. 1979. *The Tin Drum (Die Blechtrommel)*. Argos Films.

Usher, Peter, Frank I. Tough, and R. M. Galois. 1992. "Reclaiming the Land: Aboriginal Title, Treaty Rights, and Land Claims in Canada." *Applied Geography* 12 (2): 109–32.

Vernadsky, George, and Sergei Germanovich Pushkarev. 1972. *A Source Book for Russian History*. Vol. 2. New Haven: Yale University Press,.

Zamoyski, Adam. (1987) 1994. *The Polish Way: A Thousand-Year History of the Poles and Their Culture.* New York: Hippocrene Books.

Zurakowska, Anna. 1991. *The Proud Inheritance.* Ontario's Kaszuby. Ottawa: Polish Heritage Institute—Kaszuby.

Contributors

Editors

JAY T. JOHNSON is an Associate Professor of Geography and Indigenous Studies at the University of Kansas and of Delaware and Cherokee descent. His research interests concern the broad area of Indigenous peoples' cultural survival with specific regard to the areas of resource management, political activism at the national and international levels, and the philosophies and politics of place that underpin the drive for cultural survival. Much of his work is comparative in nature but has focused predominantly on North America, New Zealand, and the Pacific.

SOREN C. LARSEN is an Associate Professor of Geography at the University of Missouri with research and teaching interests in the cultural geography of Indigenous, rural, and resource-dependent communities. His first ethnographic research project was undertaken in collaboration with the Cheslatta-Carrier First Nation in north-central British Columbia. Larsen's research has been published in such outlets as the *Annals of the Association of American Geographers, The Professional Geographer, Geografiska Annaler,* and *The Journal of Rural Studies.*

Contributors

RICK BUDHWA is a leading figure in cultural resource management in British Columbia and principal of Crossroads Cultural Resource Management Ltd. For the past twenty years, he has been involved in issues pertaining to Indigenous cultural resources. He works with government, industry, and First Nations to create cultural resource management policies and protocols considered acceptable to multiple stakeholders. His research includes oral traditions and their relationships to science, government policy and legislation, Indigenous perceptions and interpretations of past and present, catastrophic paleoenvironmental events, geoarchaeology, and indigenous archaeology. Rick is also a Professor at Northwest Community College, where he teaches anthropology, archaeology, and First Nations studies.

LAKLAK BURARRWANGA is a Datiwuy Elder, Caretaker for Gumatj, and eldest sister. As such she has both the right and the cultural obligation to share certain aspects of her knowledge and experiences with others. She has many decades' experience sharing this knowledge with children through years teaching in the community and at Bawaka and through writing and translating books for the Yirrkala Community School. She has also communicated this knowledge through weaving, painting, and printmaking and is a member of the National Museum of Women in Art. In 2006 she helped establish her family-owned tourism business Bawaka Cultural Experiences (BCE) and through this business, as well as being a member of the Yothu Yindi Garma Foundation, she has taken advantage of being able to share her knowledge with tourists, including government staff in cross-cultural programs. This further developed her expertise at cross-cultural communication and made her aware of the knowledge that non-Indigenous people want and need to understand.

KALI FERMANTEZ is an Assistant Professor at the Jonathan Napela Center for Hawaiian and Pacific Islands Studies at Brigham Young University Hawaiʻi. A Native Hawaiian, he grew up in nearby Hauʻula and received his undergraduate degree from BYU-Hawaiʻi and his PhD in Geography from the University of Hawaiʻi at Mānoa in 2007. Returning to Laie enables Dr. Fermantez to continue teaching and conducting research at home in the indigenous context. His research focuses on the ways place, culture, and identity are meaningfully linked in the contemporary Pacific. He is particularly interested in the way cultural revitalization can empower island peoples as they work toward social justice in the postcolonial context.

ANNE GODLEWSKA is a Professor of Geography at Queen's University and Past President of the Canadian Association of Geographers. Her work is concerned with transcultural communication, the geographic imagination, and the mechanisms and consequences of imperialism. Among her publications are *Geography Unbound* (1999), *The Napoleonic Survey of Egypt* (1989) and the co-edited book *Geography and Empire* (1994). She has also authored a web-based atlas: http://geog.queensu.ca/napoleonatlas/. She is currently engaged in research on teaching and on the problem of ignorance of Aboriginal peoples and issues in Canada.

DOUGLAS (RDK) HERMAN is Senior Geographer for the Smithsonian National Museum of the American Indian and adjunct Associate Professor at Towson University, Maryland. An early architect of NMAI's Indigenous Geography project, he went on to create Pacific Worlds, a web-based indigenous-geography education project for Hawaiʻi and the American Pacific. Both projects focus on Indigenous cultural knowledge and environmental understandings. He has published several articles and given numerous scholarly presentations regarding the representation of Indigenous cultures and the importance of Indigenous knowledge. He earned his doctorate in geography from the University of Hawaiʻi in 1995.

PAUL HODGE is a critical development geographer in the Discipline of Geography and Environmental Studies at The University of Newcastle, Australia. His primary areas of research are development aid relations in Oceania, practice-based learning theory especially in Indigenous contexts, and more recently strengths-based approaches focusing on organizational relationships with Aboriginal and Torres Strait Islander communities. Paul has co-published work in *Studies in Higher Education* and the *Journal of Geography in Higher Education* (with Sarah Wright) on practice-based learning, and in *Third World Quarterly* on governmentality in Fiji.

KATE LLOYD is a development geographer focusing on transitional economies within the Asia-Pacific Region and crossings and connections within Australia's Northern Borderlands. Her research focuses on tourism as a lens to investigate state and societal responses to globalization and change. She has been involved in a number of projects in Laos, Papua New Guinea, and most recently Northern Australia, which examine the relationships between community, industry, and government in developing sustainable tourism outcomes. Her current research focuses on crossings and connections in Australia's northern borderlands, where, with her colleagues Dr. Sandie Suchet-Pearson and Dr. Sarah Wright, she has highlighted the importance of quotidian experiences of the border through an investigation of quarantine practices, tourism as development, and storytelling. Together they are working with Indigenous communities and government departments in North East Arnhem Land to explore opportunities that tourism can offer in seeking self-determination.

TYLER McCREARY is a doctoral candidate in the Department of Geography at York University. His research interests include the geographies of indigeneity, development, conservation, and education. His current research explores the geographies of contemporary relationships between settlers and Aboriginal peoples in north-western British Columbia, Canada.

DEBORAH McGREGOR is an Anishinaabe from Whitefish River First Nation, Birch Island, Ontario. She is currently the director for the Centre for Aboriginal Initiatives and the Aboriginal Studies at the University of Toronto. Her research background and interests are varied, but generally concern Indigenous governance and relationships with the natural world. She has focused particularly on Traditional Knowledge (TK) and its application in various contexts, including environmental governance, sustainable development, water conservation, cultural sustainability, ethics, and consultation in her research and teaching. Primary themes found throughout her work include determining how to improve relations between Aboriginal and non-Aboriginal parties, and how to ensure the appropriate consideration of Aboriginal peoples' knowledge, values, and rights in environmental and resource management in Canada.

BRIAN MURTON is a New Zealander of part-Māori descent (*Te Popoto* and *Te Honihoni* of *Ngāpuhi* and *Te Ihutai*, *Ngāti Kuri* and *Waiariki* of *Te Rarawa* of northern New Zealand with *whanaunga* (relatives, family) among *Te-Aitanga*-a-*Māhaki* of the Gisborne area). He has his BA and MA from the University of Canterbury, and his PhD (1970) from the University of Minnesota. After teaching for a year at York University in 1969 he joined the geography department at the University of Hawai'i, where during the 1990s and early 2000s he mentored a number of students of various Indigenous backgrounds. He is now Professor Emeritus following his retirement in 2005. His early research was primarily on agrarian historical geography, including the role of food scarcity and famine, in southern India. In the mid-1990s he was called back to Aotearoa/New Zealand to become involved in research to support claims to the Waitangi Tribunal, as well as with a project on landscape change in northern Aotearoa.

LAURIE RICHMOND is an Assistant Professor in the Department of Environmental Science and Management at Humboldt State University. Her research focuses on developing collaborative relationships with natural resource-dependent communities to examine how they navigate both political and ecological changes in their resource systems. She has spent over five years working with and living in the Alaska Native village of Old Harbor, Alaska, to explore how the community has experienced changes in the ecology and management of the Pacific halibut fishery. She has also worked with Indigenous communities in New Mexico, Hawai'i, and California on natural resource issues. Though she relies on diverse methodologies, her research nearly always incorporates a strong ethnographic component in order to highlight the importance of sense of place, stories, and even humor to questions of environmental planning and management.

MARGARET SOMERVILLE is Professor of Education and Director of the Centre for Educational Research at the University of Western Sydney. She has a long history of empirical research in place-based education and decolonizing methodologies using creative and alternative approaches. A significant aspect of this is experimenting with different forms of writing as represented in *Singing the Coast* in collaboration with Gumbaynggirr co-author Tony Perkins. Her latest book, arising from her long-term collaboration with Indigenous artists in the Murray-Darling Basin, *Water in a Dry Land: Learning through Art and Story*, is published in Routledge's Innovative Ethnography Series in 2013.

SANDIE SUCHET-PEARSON is a Senior Lecturer in Human Geography at Macquarie University. Her research and teaching experiences since the late 1990s have been in the area of Indigenous rights and environmental management. She has worked on Cape York Peninsula on community development in the context of a major mining operation and examined the strategies used by Indigenous peoples and local communities to assert their rights in wildlife management in Canada and southern Africa. Her current work focuses on Indigenous self-determination in the context of cultural tourism in North East Arnhem Land, northern Australia.

SARAH F. TRAINOR is Associate Research Professor at the International Arctic Research Center with joint appointment in the Water and Environmental Research Center at the University of Alaska, Fairbanks. She is Director of the NOAA-funded Alaska Center for Climate Assessment and Policy (ACCAP; www.accap.uaf.edu), Director of the Alaska Fire Science Consortium (AFSC; http://akfireconsortium. uaf.edu; funded by the Joint Fire Sciences Program) and stakeholder liaison for the University of Alaska Scenarios Network for Alaska and Arctic Planning (www.snap. uaf.edu). She holds an MA (1996) and PhD (2002) in Energy and Resources from the University of California, Berkeley, and a BA in Philosophy and Environmental Studies from Mount Holyoke College (1992).

SARAH WRIGHT is the convenor of the Development Studies degree and lecturer in geography and development studies at the University of Newcastle. She has worked in and with the community sector since 1992 both within Australia and internationally (the Philippines, Cuba, the United States, and Mexico). She has also worked with Indigenous communities on enterprise development for seven years, in particular within a long-standing and award-winning collaboration with Yolŋu women from Northeast Arnhem Land.

Index

Page numbers in italics refer to illustrations